Contents

Notes on Authors

Robert A. Paton

Robert Paton is a former Director of both undergraduate and post-graduate programmes at the University of Glasgow Business School. As an MBA and Marketing Director for the School he has developed extensive industrial and commercial links. These have led to numerous consultancy and training contracts, as well as research and publications, in the fields of management development and change. He has recently worked with, or been a key contributor on programmes associated with, ScottishPower, Associated Newspapers (ANL), Scottish Enterprise, SHARE and Glaxo Wellcome.

His most recent book, co-authored with David Boddy, *Management: An Introduction*, has been well received and is now on many, both domestic and international, recommended reading lists. He has recently rejoined 'mainstream' academia, taking a much earned rest from programme and School directorships to concentrate on research and consultancy. He is currently working on an evaluation of competency and business focused management development programmes, as well as investigating the role that gender differences play in the management of change. He can be contacted at r.paton@mgt.gla.ac.uk.

James McCalman

Dr James McCalman is Reader in Organizational Behaviour at Brunel University, London. A former Director with a major health care company, Dr McCalman has been involved in managing change programmes within organizations at several levels from strategy formulation to the introduction of shop floor teamworking.

He is the author of four books, several book chapters and over 30 journal articles related to organizational behaviour and change in organizations. Dr McCalman has been involved in teaching and consultancy in the UK, the United States, most of Western Europe and South East Asia in the areas of organization development, change management and teamwork. He has worked for several blue chip organizations including

British Petroleum, China Light and Power, Compaq Computers, Guinness, Motorola, National Semiconductor, NEC and the Bahrain government.

Dr McCalman's current research interests involve the politics of organizational change and the use of politicking by male and female managers. He can be contacted at j.mccalman@talk21.com

Acknowledgements

The ability to get on well with people is a distinct benefit in both teaching and writing about the management of change. We therefore, once again, need to thank a host of friends, colleagues and acquaintances.

In particular, we wish to express our gratitude to Kirsteen Daly and Angela McAulay for their assistance in transforming the second edition from a mass of disks into a text with associated tables and figures. Special thanks to Janie Ferguson, the management and business librarian at the University of Glasgow, for her tolerance and diligent endeavours.

From a professional point of view we would like to thank the following individuals and organizations for their assistance:

Argyll and Clyde Health Board, in particular Rosemary I. Jamieson
Benefits Agency, in particular Linda Dempster, Business Development Manager
British Airports Authority (Scotland), in particular Liz Drummond, Head of Business Strategy
British Gas (Scotland) PLC, in particular James Kelly, Purchasing Manager
Caledonian Airmotive Ltd, in particular David J. Crews
Ethicon Ltd, in particular Rosaleen McNeill
Froud Consine Ltd and Babcock Industries PLC, in particular Brian A. Wilson of Babcock Industries
Glenlight Shipping Ltd, in particular Alex Fawcett, former Managing Director (presently a partner with FASH Associates)
McGriggor Donald Solicitors, in particular Carole Thomson, Director of Administration
National Health Service, in particular Sean McCollum
Scottish Homes, in particular Aileen McFadden
SmithKline Beecham, Irvine, in particular John Hunter
Southern General Hospital Trust
Terley, R. Ltd (Texstyle World), in particular John Gilchrist
United Kingdom Atomic Energy Authority, in particular Stephen Rutledge.

We would also like to express our graditude to Sara Marian Todd for providing the basis of Chapter 10 'The Learning Organization' from her own research works.

Robert Paton
James McCalman

PART 1

The Impact and Definition of Change

Introducing Change Management

Change may be regarded as one of the few constants of recorded history. Often society's 'winners', both historical and contemporary, can be characterized by their common ability to effectively manage and exploit change situations. Individuals, societies, nations and enterprises who have at some time been at the forefront of commercial and/or technological expansion have achieved domination, or at least 'competitive' advantage, by being innovative in thought and/or action. They have been both enterprising and entrepreneurial.

Management and change are synonymous; it is impossible to undertake a journey, for in many respects that is what change is, without first addressing the purpose of the trip, the route you wish to travel and with whom. Managing change is about handling the complexities of travel. It is about evaluating, planning and implementing operational, tactical and strategic 'journeys' – about always ensuring that the journey is worthwhile and the destination is relevant.

Our purpose in writing this book is to try to begin to resolve some of the questions that managers ask when faced with the concept and reality of change. We have deliberately set this book out in a framework which offers models for tackling the different change scenarios facing organizations. However, we have also set out to provide examples of how and where the models are used. What we wanted from this book, for ourselves and for the reader, were four things:

1 valid and defined models for the effective management of change
2 proactive approaches to change that relate to internal and external business performance
3 practical, step-by-step means of handling change
4 illustrations of the use and validity of the models through current, real-life case studies.

If we are successful, the reader will leave this book with the sense that the management of change is a complex, dynamic and challenging process rather than a set of recipes. In most examples of successful change management, those responsible have developed clear and shared visions of where they are going and have linked these to implementation strategies designed to produce the desired results. We believe that change management is never a *choice* between technological, organizational or people-oriented solutions, but involves combinations for best fit – integrated strategies designed to produce results. In this sense, the management of change adopts the contingency approach to organizations: it all depends. However, recognition of what it depends *on* is the subject of this book.

Change in an historical context

Genghis Khan (1162–1227), the inspirational leader of the Mongol tribes, not only managed to unify a disparate people, but succeeded in conquering most of China, Asia, Iran and Russia by revolutionizing, from the perspective of the conquered, the 'art' of war. His highly mobile troops, operating with a significant degree of autonomy, directed by a leader aware of the need to adopt flexible and progressive tactics and strategies, swept the regimented, staid and ponderous opposition aside – a practical lesson in identifying and exploiting a competitive advantage.

Shortly after the great Khan's exploits, the Far East was visited by what appeared, on the surface and in the context of the time, to be a far less aggressive 'tourist'. The Venetian traveller Marco Polo (1254–1324) 'explored' the region in the late thirteenth century, developing trade and cultural awareness and returned to the West with the 'recipe' for gunpowder.

For those interested in change there are two points worth noting. Firstly, the originators of gunpowder, the Chinese, saw the substance as primarily a 'harmless', if entertaining, concoction capable of releasing impressive forces if managed properly. However, developments in the West dwelt upon the destructive properties of the substance. The West, especially during the last quarter of the nineteenth century and the early twentieth century, repackaged gunpowder and exported it back to the East, in particular China, with a great deal of 'commercial' success. Secondly, for over three centuries the literary product of Marco Polo's endeavours, *The Travels of Marco Polo*, was the seminal work on the Far East. Although widely read this work did not stimulate significant action. Europeans failed to 'exploit' the region's resources for many years. A 'trigger' for change, the journey and its potential value, was not recognized by the 'managers' of the day.

History shows us that there is more to success than simply recognizing a 'trigger' for change. Successful exploitation of a change situation requires:

- knowledge of the circumstances surrounding a situation
- understanding of the interactions
- awareness of the potential impact of associated variables.

In early September 1513 the King of Scotland, James IV, closed his summer campaigning season against the English with the battle of Flodden. After initial manoeuvrings, James organized his foot soldiers, armed with six metre pikes (long spears), into well-organized, tightly compacted, units or phalanxes. To the charging cavalry, or advancing foot soldiers, such phalanxes would appear as impenetrable forests of spears resembling a hedgehog or porcupine. The Swiss employed the phalanx in the battle of Nancy in 1477 and triumphed over superior numbers; they went on to further refine the tactic through the Italian wars of the late fifteenth century. James intended to emulate their triumphs, but unfortunately for himself, and indeed Scotland, he failed to execute his battle plan. The intended tactics were sound, but when enacted on rough and uneven marshland, while advancing downhill, the Scots' phalanxes disintegrated and exposed the pikemen to the advancing English. In change situations a *little knowledge* can be a dangerous thing and *limited understanding* catastrophic.

The nineteenth century 'gunboat' diplomacy, typified by the attitude and actions of Lord Palmerston, but endemic throughout the British establishment, was effectively employed in the service of the 'British Empire'. A new technology, a powerful, far reaching and devastating weapon, the gunboat, extended the global grip of the British Empire. Britain, France, Germany and Italy were beginning to flex their newly acquired industrial might. Industry needed trade to survive, trade required development and protection, and industry provided not only the trade goods but also the means of 'selling' them, namely, the gunboat and associated mechanized weaponry.

The Industrial Revolution, which developed in Europe between 1750 and 1880, accelerated the rate of change to an extent never previously thought possible. Other economies followed and the rate of change has never declined; indeed, many would claim it has now accelerated out of control. The spear and sword gave way to the gun; the scribe to the printing press; manpower to the steam engine of James Watt; the horse and cart to the combustion engine; the typewriter to the word-processor; and so the list goes on.

READER ACTIVITY

Pause and consider the changes you, your organization, family, town or country have faced over recent years. Note the changes. What triggered them? Were they anticipated? Were they well managed? Who benefited? Did you learn from them?

One can try to predict the future. However, predictions produce at best a blurred picture of what might be, not a blueprint of future events or circumstances. The effective and progressive management of change can assist in shaping a future which may better serve the enterprise's survival prospects.

The importance of change

Change will not disappear or dissipate. Technology, civilizations and creative thought will maintain their ever accelerating drive onwards. Managers, and the enterprises they serve, be they public or private, service or manufacturing, will continue to be judged upon their ability to effectively and efficiently manage change. Unfortunately for the managers of the early twenty-first century, their ability to handle complex change situations will be judged over ever decreasing time scales.

The pace of change has increased dramatically; mankind wandered the planet on foot for centuries before the invention of the wheel and its subsequent 'technological convergence' with the ox and horse. In one 'short' century a man has walked on the moon; satellites orbit the Earth; the combustion engine has dominated transport and some would say society; robots are a reality and state of the art manufacturing facilities resemble scenes from science fiction; your neighbour or competitor, technologically speaking, could be on the other side of the planet; and bio-technology is the science of the future. The world may not be spinning faster but mankind certainly is!

Businesses and managers are now faced with highly dynamic and ever more complex operating environments. Technologies and products, along with the industries they support and serve, are converging. Is the media company in broadcasting, or telecommunications, or data processing, or indeed all of them? Is the supermarket chain in general retail, or is it a provider of financial services? Is the television merely a receiving device for broadcast messages or is it part of an integrated multi-media communications package? Is the airline a provider of transport or the seller of wines, spirits and fancy goods, or the agent for car hire and accommodation?

As industries and products converge, along with the markets they serve, there is a growing realization that a holistic approach to the marketing of goods and services is required, thus simplifying the purchasing decision. Strategic alliances, designed to maximize the 'added value' throughout a supply chain, while seeking to minimize costs of supply, are fast becoming the competitive weapon of the future. Control and exploitation of the supply chain make good commercial sense in fiercely competitive global markets. The packaging of what were once discrete products (or services) into what are effectively 'consumer solutions' will continue for the foreseeable future.

Car producers no longer simply manufacture vehicles, they now distribute them through sophisticated dealer networks offering attractive servicing arrangements, and provide a range of financing options, many of which are linked to a variety of insurance packages. Utility enterprises now offer far more than their original core service. ScottishPower have acquired utilities in other countries and have recently moved into water, gas and telecommunications, to become a 'unified' utilities company offering 'one-stop shopping' to domestic and commercial customers.

The above, combined with the general ability to replicate both 'hard' and 'soft' innovations within ever diminishing time scales, places the creative and effective management of change well towards the top of the core competencies required by any public or private enterprise. Indeed, throughout Europe, regulatory change, in the form of EC Directives on working practices, quality, the Euro, and international trade and competitive tendering, further complicates an already complex commercial environment. In this environment, simply staying marginally ahead of the game is no longer enough to ensure survival.

Woody Allen tells a story of a race of aliens who peacefully colonize Earth, on a cohabitation basis with the original populace. They are not technologically advanced, nor do they have substantially improved physical characteristics. However, they have an uncanny ability to be first for everything! First to launch new products; first to modify an old technology; first to secure the deal; first, and therefore the 'winners', in the commercial stakes.

READER ACTIVITY

Identify two or three colleagues, friends or relations who are, or have been, in management/business positions. Ask them, without prompting, what they find challenging about their job. What do they find most frustrating? Attempt to find out what strategies and/or skills they employ to manage challenging and frustrating situations.

How can we manage change in such a fast moving environment, without losing control of the organization and existing core competencies? There are, as one would expect, no easy answers and certainly no blueprints detailing best practice. Designing, evaluating and implementing successful change strategies largely depend upon the quality of the management team, in particular the team's ability to design organizations in such a way as to facilitate the change process in a responsive and progressive manner.

The imperative of change

Any organization that ignores change does so at its own peril. One might suggest that for many the peril would come sooner rather than later. To survive and prosper organizations must adopt strategies that realistically reflect their ability to manage multiple future scenarios. Drucker, for example, argues that: 'Increasingly, a winning strategy will require information about events and conditions outside the institution . . . Only with this information can a business . . . prepare for new changes and challenges arising from sudden shifts in the world economy and in the nature and content of knowledge itself' (1997: 20–4).

If we take an external perspective for a moment, the average modern organization has to come to terms with a number of issues, which will create a need for internal change. At the point of writing we can identify six major external changes that organizations are currently addressing or will have to come to terms with in the new millennium:

1   A larger global marketplace made smaller by enhanced technologies and competition from abroad. The liberalization of Eastern European states, the creation of a single European currency, e-trading, the establishment of new trading blocs such as the 'tiger' economies of the Far East, and reductions in transportation, information and communication costs, mean that the world is a different place from what it was. How does your organization plan to respond to such competitive pressures?
2   A worldwide recognition of the environment as an influencing variable and government attempts to draw back from environmental calamity. There are legal, cultural and socio-economic implications in realizing that resource use and allocation have finite limits and that global solutions to ozone depletion, toxic waste dumping, raw material depletion, and other environmental concerns will force change on organizations, sooner rather than later. How does the individual organization respond to the bigger picture?
3   Health consciousness as a permanent trend amongst all age groups throughout the world. The growing awareness and concern with the content of food and beverage products has created a movement away from synthetic towards natural products. Concerns have been expressed about salmonella in eggs and poultry, listeria in chilled foods, BSE or 'mad cow disease' and CJD in humans, genetically engineered foodstuffs, and the cloning of animals. How does the individual organization deal with the demands of a more health-conscious population?
4   Changes in lifestyle trends are affecting the way in which people view work, purchases, leisure time and society. A more morally questioning, affluent, educated and involved population is challenging the way in which we will do business and socialize. How will you and your organization live your lives?
5   The changing workplace creates a need for non-traditional employees. Many organizations have downsized too far and created management and labour skill shortages as a result. In order to make up the shortfall,

organizations are currently resorting to a core/periphery workforce, teleworking, multi-skilled workers and outsourcing. A greater proportion of the population who have not been traditional employees (e.g. women with school aged children) will need to be attracted into the labour force. Equal opportunity in pay and non-pecuniary rewards will be issues in the future. How will the individual organization cope with these pressures?

6 The knowledge asset of the company, its people, is becoming increasingly crucial to its competitive wellbeing. Technological and communication advances are leading to reduced entry costs across world markets. This enables organizations to become multinational without leaving their own borders. However, marketing via the Internet, communication via e-mail and other technology applications are all still reliant on the way you organize your human resources. Your only sustainable competitive weapon is your people. How do you intend managing them in the next millennium? The same way as you did in the last?

The fact that we could have picked half a dozen other issues for discussion indicates the imperative for change in organizations. What is important, however, is recognition that change occurs continuously, has numerous causes, and needs to be addressed all the time. Lawler (1986) sums this up quite effectively by noting that:

> Overall, planned change is not impossible, but it is often difficult. The key point is that change is an ongoing process, and it is incorrect to think that a visionary end state can be reached in a highly programmed way.

The difficulty is that most organizations view the concept of change as a highly programmed process which takes as its starting point the problem that needs to be rectified, breaks it down into constituent parts, analyses possible alternatives, selects the preferred solution, and applies this relentlessly – problem recognition, diagnosis and resolution. Simple, straightforward and relatively painless. But what if the change problem is part of a bigger picture? For example how do recognition, diagnosis and resolution address the problem of global warming? 'It's not our problem, we'll leave it for the politicians to sort out': a simple and effective response, until the point in time when the political solution begins to have an organizational impact.

We are not suggesting here that all organizations need to come up with an answer that solves the problem of ozone depletion. This is a problem that nations have difficulties trying to address. However, what we are trying to point out is that, as an issue, it creates an imperative for change in organizations. There are two ways of responding to that imperative. The individual organization can wait for legislation to hit the statute book and react to the legislation, or it can anticipate and institute proactive change. Most organizations won't. That's because they are geared and managed to run on traditional, analytical lines of decision making – if it ain't broke, why fix it? What we would like to suggest here is that before it even gets to the point where a slight stress fracture appears, organizations should be addressing the potential implications of change scenarios, and dealing with them accordingly.

The impact of change

What makes an organization want to change? There are a number of specific, even obvious factors which will necessitate movement from the status quo. The most obvious of these relate to changes in the external environment which trigger reaction. An example of this in the last couple of years is the move by car manufacturers and petroleum organizations towards the provision of more environmentally friendly forms of 'produce'. Pettigrew's (1985) analysis of change at ICI attempted to identify what precipitates change. He pointed out that there were no clear beginnings and ends to strategic change. Environmental disturbances were seen as the main precipitating factor, but he also believed that these were not the sole causes of or explanations of change.

To attribute change entirely to the environment would be a denial of extreme magnitude. This would imply that organizations were merely 'bobbing about' on a turbulent sea of change, unable to influence or exercise direction. This is clearly not the case. Pettigrew (1985) went on to argue that changes within an organization take place in response both to business and economic events and to processes of management perception, choice and action. Managers in this sense see events taking place that, to them, signal the need for change. They also perceive the internal context of change as it relates to structure, culture, systems of power and control. This gives them further clues about whether it is worth trying to introduce change. But what causes change? What factors need to be considered when we look for the causal effects which run from A to B in an organization?

We would like you to think of changes that have occurred in your organization over the last year. How often were these changes the reaction to events that occurred outside your organization? For example, can you cite examples linked to your company's response to:

- changes in technology used
- changes in customer expectations or tastes
- changes as a result of competition
- changes as a result of government legislation
- changes as a result of alterations in the economy, at home or abroad
- changes in communications media

- changes in society's value systems
- changes in the supply chain
- changes in the distribution chain?

Internal changes can be seen as responses or reactions to the outside world which are regarded as external triggers. There are also a large number of factors which lead to what are termed internal triggers for change. Organization redesigns to fit a new product line or new marketing strategy are typical examples, as are changes in job responsibilities to fit new organizational structures.

The final cause of change in organizations is where the organization tries to be ahead of change by being proactive. For example, where the organization tries to anticipate problems in the marketplace or negate the impact of worldwide recession on its own business, proactive change is taking place (Buchanan and Huczynski, 1997: 461).

Change and transition management

If the concept of change can be examined from an internal, external or proactive set of viewpoints, then the response of managers has to be equally as widespread. Buchanan and McCalman (1989) suggest that this requires a framework of 'perpetual transition management'. Following from Lawler's (1986) concept of the lack of a visionary end state, what appears to be required is the ability within managers to deal with constant change. This transition management model, although specifically related to large-scale organizational change, has some interesting insights into what triggers change in organizations, and how they respond. It suggests that four interlocking management processes must take place both to implement and sustain major organizational changes. These processes operate at different levels, and may involve different actors in the organizational hierarchy. The four layers are:

- *Trigger layer* Concerning the identification of needs and openings for major change deliberately formulated in the form of opportunities rather than threats or crises.
- *Vision layer* Establishing the future development of the organization by articulating a vision and communicating this effectively in terms of where the organization is heading.
- *Conversion layer* Setting out to mobilize support in the organization for the new vision as the most appropriate method for dealing with the triggers of change.
- *Maintenance and renewal layer* Identifying ways in which changes are sustained and enhanced through alterations in attitudes, values and behaviours, and regression back to tradition is avoided.

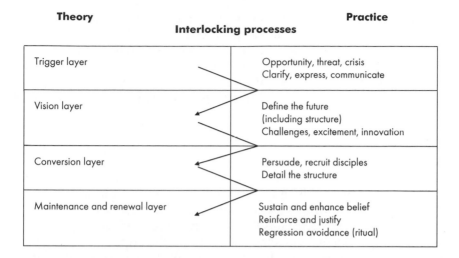

Figure I.1 *Buchanan and McCalman's model of perpetual transition management (Buchanan and McCalman, 1989: 198)*

Transition management suggests that organizations have to plan for, divert resources to, and implement four sets of interlocking processes. These are designed to implement, to sustain, and to build on change and its achievements in an attempt to address the issues associated with change over time. The argument here is that these layers – trigger, vision, conversion, and maintenance and renewal – are necessary processes that occur in change management. The respective emphasis and priority attached to each of them will alter over time, but recognition of their existence goes a long way in determining the management action needed.

The model of perpetual transition management starts out with a number of questions. How do we explain successful change? How do we explain attempts at change in organizations that were doomed from the start? How do we explain change that is initially successful but wanes or fizzles out halfway through? Effective large-scale change demands a series of management actions linked to the four interlocking layers or processes (see Figure I.1).

In terms of the trigger layer, it is necessary to understand what is causing a need for change in the organization. These triggers need to be expressed in a clear way and communicated throughout the organization. For example, poor trigger identification and communication processes are best seen when the first that employees know of the difficulties facing the organization is when they are called in to discuss redundancy terms. People are generally willing and able to deal with change but many managers do not understand this. They are afraid that change is associated with some form of failure and feel they need to hide the changes. People will accept change when they know it is necessary and accept the explanation for the need for change.

It is necessary for these triggers to be expressed and communicated throughout the organization in clear and identifiable terms. For example, the trigger in many organizations is often a crisis, but it does not necessarily have to be a threat. People will respond to the challenge of a crisis but may react negatively to a threat. Expressing any potential crisis as an opportunity for change may assist the process itself. In this sense, the language in which the triggering mechanism is transmitted to the internal organization has to be clearly expressed as opportunity, and communicated widely. The chances of successfully implementing change are significantly improved when everyone concerned has a shared understanding of what may happen and why.

If the trigger for change has been clearly recognized and expressed, it is also a requirement for management within the organization to define the future. This does not call for crystal ball gazing but for the establishment of a vision layer. The requirement here is for definition and expression of where the organization intends to go. Just as shared understanding and awareness of the triggers for change help smooth the process, so do shared awareness and understanding of the new vision and the desired organizational goals. Management must visualize the future in terms of three criteria. The first is that change is seen to provide an effective response to the events triggering change. Second, there is identification of the desired future condition of the organization in terms of its design, its products and its goals. Finally, it must provide challenges and stimulation. Change is assisted by a climate of enthusiasm and participation; resistance is a result of fear, prejudice, anxiety and ignorance.

The third layer of perpetual transition management is related to gaining recruits for the change. By this it is meant that those who have to work through the change process need to be converted to the ideas and concepts and own them. Defining a future that no one can 'buy into' will slow or hinder the change itself. Everyone involved in making change work has to feel part of it and accept the reasoning for the vision and how this is to be realized. It is at this point that the vision has to be detailed and aspects such as the future structure and patterns of work explained. There is a need at this point to recruit disciples to the vision. This is time-consuming, as it requires detailed explanation. Failure to do so results in negotiation, renegotiation or decay. This is related to the 'You've introduced this without consulting us first' syndrome. Managers at this stage need to get involved in two main activities. First, there is the planning team, the main core change unit. The most appropriate mechanisms here will depend on the organization and its consultation systems. Second, it is also necessary to talk to people about the change at every opportunity, formal or informal. This establishes a shared understanding of the change programme through debate.

The last question that perpetual transition management attempts to resolve is related to the decay associated with the management of mid-term change. Maintenance and renewal attempt to address the 'moving goalpost' features of change. There are four main examples of this. First, the events that triggered change in the first place fade in the memory or lose their relevance over time. Second, articulation of the vision becomes less expressive when the originators move on. Third, replacements feel less committed to the ideas and have to be taken through the reasons for, and responses to, the triggers. Fourth, the change that took place settles down and becomes the norm in the organization. To avoid this sort of decay process there is a requirement for organizations to allocate resources to maintaining and renewing the original visions in an evolutionary framework. In this sense, management takes part in a process that is described as one of permanent transition. It is this point that can be regarded as the crucial concept. Getting managers to recognize that change is a constant feature in modern organizations, and one which they have to deal with, goes a long way towards addressing some of the factors which lead to resistance to change.

Outline of the book

The book is divided into four parts. Part 1, which includes this chapter, discusses the impact and definition of change. Part 2 looks at intervention strategies designed to cope with systems-related change. Part 3 examines organization development models of change dealing with the behaviour of people. Finally, Part 4 offers a number of practical cases designed to further explore the validity of the models outlined in this book.

In Chapter 1, the need to address the nature of change is introduced. All organizations, from both an external and an internal perspective, operate within dynamic environments. Prior to entering a change situation the manager must classify the nature of the change facing their organization. It is the 'nature' which will determine one's initial approaches to the management process. Chapter 1 also identifies key issues that must be addressed in any transition process and discusses the importance of the problem owner to the change event. The problem owner(s) can be the manager, or managing group, deemed to be responsible for the change process. They may operate and control the process of change through change agents, who are key players in the change environment.

In Chapter 2, 'Change and the Manager', we look at the managerial competencies associated with effectively managing change. The importance of remaining in 'control' of ongoing dynamic change situations is reviewed. Management must manage change, no matter its source or impact, in a planned and controlled manner.

The means of identifying change agents and defining the change environment are fully discussed and illustrated in Chapter 3. A systems-based analytical approach, involving the use of diagramming techniques, is suggested as being one of the optimal ways to define a change environment. The diagramming tools covered within this chapter may be employed to define an environment no matter the classification of the change. Each diagram introduced is illustrated with a practical example of its application. The value of the diagrammatic approach to change definition cannot be understated. It offers a communications vehicle, analytical processes, planning and control aids, and a means of defining complex organizational environments.

In Part 2 of the book we deal with systems intervention strategies. In Chapter 4 the systems-based approach to change is discussed. The intervention strategy model (ISM) is introduced and its steps are examined. This model is designed to tackle change from the 'hard', technical end of the change spectrum, although, as we will see, it may be employed to deal with 'softer', people-related issues. The origins and justification of the model are discussed and this is followed by a sequential review of the model's component parts. Application issues, along with 'dos and don'ts', round off this chapter. Chapter 5 is dedicated to the exploration of practical cases that illustrate each stage of the model. The key implementation issues and management processes are illustrated by a number of cases, which are topical from both a change and a business perspective.

Another method of dealing with project-based change is introduced in Chapter 6 when we examine total project management (TPM). To a greater or lesser extent all managers are project managers. This chapter describes the TPM process and outlines its rationale. Very often it is poor people management, not the degree of technical competence, which leads to less than effective project implementation.

In Part 3 we examine the need for an organization development model for change. In many Western organizations, the concept of management is so restrictive that control and decision making operate as a hindering device on performance. The belief is that management and workforce are separate entities that sometimes come together to manufacture products or deliver services, but often act as polar opposites in some form of industrial struggle for superiority. Chapter 7 puts forward the proposition that it doesn't have to be like this. By examining some of the basic concepts of design and development, organizations can begin to combine the needs of the individual worker with those of business to find a mission that results in effective performance. This effective perform-ance is reflected in results which are categorized in terms of numbers – profits, sales revenue etc. – but also in terms of the quality of working life. However, to achieve this, managers have to suspend some of their inherent assumptions about work organization, the nature of work and how they attain commitment from the workforce. The basis of design is couched in the organization and its mission. As Matsushita (1984) comments, there has to be more to life than profit:

> Every company, no matter how small, ought to have clear cut goals apart from the pursuit of profit, purposes that justify its existence among us. To me, such goals are an avocation, a secular mission to the world. If the chief executive officer has this sense of mission, he can tell his employees what it is that the company seeks to accomplish, and explain its *raison d'être* and ideals. And if his employees understand that they are not working for bread alone, they will be motivated to work harder together toward the realization of their common goals.

To be able to manage change effectively, organizations need to be able to go through a process of identifying possible faults, looking at alternatives to the current situation, weighing up the pros and cons of these alternatives, reaching decisions on the future state of the organization, and implementing the necessary changes. This belies the pain and suffering that is often caused by the instigation of change. The resentment that is often felt during the management of change is not resentment to change *per se* but to the processes by which it is managed. Where people are involved, the potential for pain and the likelihood of resistance are increased tenfold. Peters and Waterman (1982), in their inimitable fashion, sum this up quite succinctly:

> The central problem with the rationalist view of organizing people is that people are not very rational. To fit Taylor's model, or today's organizational charts, man is simply designed wrong (or, of course, vice versa, according to our argument here).

In Chapter 8, we examine the organization development model (ODM) for managing change. In this, we look at how organization development can assist the move from a situation that is regarded as undesirable to a new state that, hopefully, is more effective. The key to the ODM is looking at what change is required, what level the change takes place at, who is likely to be involved, and the processes by which change is instigated. Chapter 8 outlines the techniques of organization development and the steps that the change agent is likely to be involved in.

The concept of a change agent is similar to that of the problem owner, identified in Part 2 of the book. We change the name, not to protect the innocent, but to imply significance to the role. In Chapter 9, we examine the role of the objective outsider. The organization development model suggests the need for an individual from outwith the area of change who displays a number of unique characteristics. Chief amongst these are their ability to remain impartial or neutral and their ability to facilitate the process of change. Chapter 10 looks at recent developments in the field of OD by examining the learning organization movement.

In Part 4 of the book, Chapters 11 and 12, we move on to deal with in-depth practical issues illustrating the application of both the intervention strategy and the organizational development approaches. Finally, we provide the reader with an Epilogue which outlines the 10 key factors associated with the effective management of change.

1 The Nature of Change

A manager or an individual, whether at work, home or play, when faced with a change situation must firstly, no matter how informally, analyse the nature of the change. Only by considering the nature of the change can we determine its likely magnitude and potential impact. Successful determination of the nature of the change, at an early stage of the change cycle, should indicate the most appropriate means of managing the situation.

A full definition of the change environment is required prior to the final selection of a change management methodology. Defining a change environment is the subject of Chapter 3. There are many factors and considerations that must be taken into account prior to selecting a solution methodology. The aim of this chapter is to provide a means of evaluating the nature of an impending change situation so as to facilitate the marshalling of management expertise in readiness for the transition process. This will be accomplished by examining six key factors associated with successful change classification. They will be considered under the following headings:

1   *The role and selection of the problem owner*   The right person for the job in terms of their managerial skills, involvement and commitment to the problem or project.
2   *Locating change on the change spectrum*   Determining the nature of the change with regard to both its physical and its organizational impact. Is it, for example, a purely technical or a more complex people-related change?
3   *The TROPICS test*   A quick, yet effective, means of addressing the following key factors affecting the classification of a change situation: time scales, resources, objectives, perceptions, interest, control and source. By considering the change in relation to the above factors the manager responsible may determine, through an enhanced knowledge of the nature of the change, the optimal route forward.
4   *Force field analysis: a positioning tool*   A diagramming technique that assists in answering questions such as: what forces are at play and what is their likely magnitude? Who is for the change and who is against? Can a proactive stance be adopted? The aim is to determine

the nature and magnitude of the forces acting upon the change environment.

5 *Success guarantors: commitment, involvement and a shared perception* Successful change management requires an understanding of the likely impact of the change on those systems most affected by it, and thereafter the development of a means of establishing a shared perception of the problem amongst all concerned. The commitment and involvement of those charged with managing the change and those affected by it are crucial to achieving effective transition management.

6 *Managing the triggers* Change, as we discussed in the previous chapter, can be triggered by either internal or external events. The problem owner, or change agent, must understand both the nature of the trigger and how best to handle its management. The nature of the 'trigger' will influence the reaction of the organization and its staff, along with the associated supply chains, to the impending change, as well as assist in determining the appropriate course of action to follow.

The role and selection of the problem owner

How does one become a problem owner? There are essentially two routes. The first is the most straightforward and will positively influence the manager's evaluation of the change situation. Effective managers monitor their environment. By doing so, they may identify change situations developing on the horizon and as identifiers of the change they at least initially become the change owners. Such ownership may lead to a more positive evaluation of its nature in relation to the degree of 'threat' associated with its arrival. Early identification and ownership tend to increase the probability of a change being seen in an opportunistic manner and therefore possibly being considered to be less threatening.

It must be noted that ownership of the change by a single change agent as outlined above does not ensure that all those ultimately affected by the change will identify with the owner's positive evaluation. Later chapters investigate the important role which organizational culture plays in the management of change. In organizations, where an effort has been successfully made to secure a culture that exhibits both enterprising and democratic characteristics, one may expect to find an almost automatic sharing of the problem owner's initial view of the change.

The other route to problem ownership is the traditional one of delegation. The need for change is identified elsewhere and senior management appoints the problem owner. 'Ownership' does not belong to the individual, or group, charged with the management of the change and they simply become change 'minders' rather than change agents. Such situations are unlikely to produce positive opportunistic evaluations of the nature of the change, as it is difficult to be proactive and positive when you have been 'left holding the baby'. This can lead to rather messy situations developing!

For delegation to be effective in a change context, or for that matter in management in general, it must be accompanied by both an educational process and a selling exercise designed to pass over the ownership, responsibility and capability for the task at hand. Again, organizational culture plays a crucial role in determining the success of devolved ownership. When one feels part of a team working towards common goals, delegated problems will be viewed as common to all. On the other hand, if alienation and confrontation exist then achieving devolved ownership may be a long process.

Problem ownership affects our perception of a change situation. Positive feelings of ownership will result in a more opportunistic evaluation, whereas delegated ownership, which has been managed poorly, will highlight the threats and disrupt existing positions. The problem owner plays a pivotal role in the successful management of change. Given the obvious advantages of securing a proactive stance towards the change situation, it is essential to identify the most effective problem owner. They must possess both the skills to manage the transition process and the determination to see the change through. In short they must be the change *agents*.

All too often the problem owner is selected due to their proven management skills in the general field of project management. It must be noted that this does not guarantee that they possess ownership of the problem at hand and are therefore motivated towards achieving the change objectives. An additional difficulty may arise if their 'skill' is of a technical or process nature. Successful change management requires far more than the understanding of network analysis, risk management and budgetary control. Alternatively, the selection decision may be based on who is least busy: resource constraints rather than logic determine the problem owner. The problem owner must be directly involved in the change process and must see clear linkages between their future success and the effective implementation of the change.

A positive problem ownership is clearly an important factor associated with successful change management. Ownership need not be directly linked to management ability and position, and it may on occasion be advisable to invest resources in developing the necessary management skills and providing additional support to the most appropriate individual or group. One volunteer is worth a hundred conscripts!

Often the problem owners identify themselves since they have initiated the change process. No matter their position within the hierarchy it is, in an ideal world, the initiator who should own the process. In circumstances where those at the core of the change do not have the necessary skills, authority or resources to manage the change process, management must facilitate the change in such a way as to ensure their continued commitment and involvement. Initiators, although not directly involved in the actual management of the change, are generally still the problem owners and as such make committed and useful change advocates. When the pivotal role of problem ownership has to be delegated and/or assigned, then every care must be taken to select according to a detailed examination of the systems affected and the nature of the change. Such a key role should not be assigned solely to an individual or a group from outside the affected system.

The manager responsible for the change has to this point been termed the 'problem owner'. Similar terms in common usage would include 'change agent', 'project manager' and 'transition manager'. The terminology is relatively unimportant; their role is not. The previous paragraphs have hinted at the fact that the original problem owner may, for a number of reasons, not be the actual manager appointed to handle the change process. The remainder of this chapter, unless otherwise stated, will refer to the manager of the change process as the problem owner. When, as is generally the case, the owner acts as part of a management team, the individuals concerned and the team as a whole will be termed 'change agents'.

Locating change on the change spectrum

The nature of change influences our reaction to it. When a change is of a purely technical nature, such as a machine or component upgrade, then the expectation would be that existing systems-based knowledge would be applied in a mechanistic manner to implement the change. Change that requires the problem owner to apply their existing knowledge base in a systematic manner to problems requiring technical solutions, with minimal inputs from other quarters, may be regarded as the management of change in a static and isolated environment. The management process is simplified, as the impact is limited to a clearly identifiable and the semi-autonomous component of a technical system. Systems-based technical problems that call upon the application of knowledge of a highly structured and mechanistic nature do not create major managerial difficulties. Solution methodologies are based firmly in the systems school of managerial decision making and analysis:

Definition:	(a) objective clarification
	(b) data capture and performance indicators
	(c) systems diagnostics
	(d) systems analysis
Design:	(e) determination of solution options
	(f) solution evaluation
Implementation:	(g) solution implementation
	(h) appraisal and monitoring.

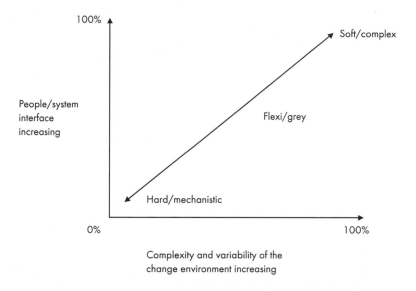

Figure 1.1   *The change spectrum*

The basic building blocks of definition, design and implementation are applied to the problem by like minded technocrats who measure success against quantifiable and well-defined performance indicators. A technical change requires a systematic analysis and a mechanistic solution. That is not to say the solution will be easily arrived at, as the degree of intellectual input and technical expertise is likely to be significant, but rather that the methodology employed will be well tried and tested.

Obviously, not all technical change situations are of the pure, totally systems-oriented variety described above. The mechanistic solution methodologies of the systems school of management can be applied to a wide range of problems and provide optimal solutions to system interventions. A truly technical problem would be placed at the extreme 'hard' end of the change spectrum as shown in Figure 1.1.

Purely technical change, 100 per cent 'hard' or mechanistic change, exists towards the left-hand side of the spectrum. It will be characterized by a reasonably static change environment, clear quantifiable objectives and constraints, immediate implications, short time scales and minimal man–machine interfaces: in short, a purely scientific or engineering problem. Such problems are reasonably uncommon as some form of human interface, even if it is only an operative who lubricates and checks a machine periodically, can generally be found if one digs deep enough.

At the extreme 'soft' end of the spectrum, one finds change situations that have a 100 per cent people orientation. Objectives and time scales will be unclear; the affected environment will be highly dynamic and difficult to specify, with exceptionally subjective performance measures. Typical of the kind of problems found towards the 'soft' end of the spectrum would be ones in which personal relationships and emotional responses are predominant. As in the case of purely technical change, 100 per cent people change is also uncommon, as most individuals and groups interface with systems of a physical nature.

Solution methodologies applied to the softer end of the spectrum must reflect the highly volatile and dynamic nature of the change environment; they will originate in the organizational development school of thought. The systematic and mechanistic solution methodologies associated with scientific management will not provide answers to predominantly soft change situations. In fact they are more likely to create greater instability if applied.

By far the majority of change situations which managers are called upon to address fall within the 'flexi' region of the spectrum. A tendency towards either end of the spectrum indicates the appropriate solution methodologies that should be adopted. Part 2 of this book deals with systems-based approaches designed to deal with situations which tend towards the harder end of the change spectrum, and Part 3 tackles change from an organizational development perspective in which 'softer', people focused situations and approaches are examined.

As often is the case in management, a contingency model or theory is required to cover all the *ad hoc* situations that may arise. Within the final sections of this book a contingency approach to change management will be argued. No single school of thought holds the answer to change management. One must not be afraid to adopt a systematic methodology when faced with people-oriented, messy situations. It must of course be flexible enough to incorporate organizational development techniques and concepts as and when appropriate. If necessary one can abandon all pretexts of systems methodology in the face of an increasingly dynamic environment. Similarly, the management of organizational change can be enhanced through the adoption of systems-based solution techniques when more static environmental circumstances are encountered.

Table 1.1 highlights the attributes associated with change situations from both ends of the spectrum. It should help clarify the position regarding the classification of change.

A brief review of the factors associated with a pending change, conducted as seen fit by the problem owner, would be sufficient to classify the change position on the spectrum. Exact positioning is not required. The more complex the change the greater the probability that the problem owner will have insufficient knowledge to conduct the investigation on an individual basis. Force field analysis, which is discussed later in this chapter, may assist in determining the appropriate change management team. Such analysis may have to be augmented by the application of the diagrammatic techniques outlined in Chapter 3.

Table 1.1   'Hard' and 'soft' problem attributes

Hard/mechanistic problems	Soft/complex problems
Objectives, constraints and performance indicators are predominantly quantifiable	At best subjective, interrelated and semi-quantifiable objectives etc. will be available
A tendency towards static environmental forces	A volatile and complex environment will prevail
Time scales known with reasonable certainty	Fuzzy time scales will predominate
The environment of the change will be well bounded with minimal external interactions	The environment of the change will be unbounded and characterized by many internal and external interactions
The problem or change will be capable of clear and concise definition	It will be difficult to define problem characteristics
It may be defined in systems/technological terms	It will be defined in interpersonal and social terms
Resources required to achieve a solution will be reasonably well known	Resource requirements will be uncertain
Potential solutions will be limited and knowledge of them obtainable	There will be a wide range of solutions, all of which may appear relevant and interconnected
Structured approaches will produce results	No clear solution methodology will be visible
Consensus on the best way forward will be easily reached	Consensus on the way forward and a shared perception of the problem will not exist

The TROPICS Test

The TROPICS test can be applied as an early warning device to access both the impact and the magnitude of the impending change. It is capable of determining the most appropriate solution methodology for entering the change management process: this may have to be altered as the problem unfolds, by examining certain key factors associated with the transition process. It requires a minimal expenditure of management time and resources as it does not need detailed quantifiable information as input.

The factors that should be considered by both the problem owner and any associated management team are as follows:

- Time scales
- Resources
- Objectives
- Perceptions
- Interest
- Control
- Source.

By considering TROPICS the manager, or the appropriately identified management team, will get a feel for the nature of the change and thus be able to establish the optimal route forward. Table 1.2 illustrates the use of TROPICS.

Table 1.2   *The TROPICS test*

TROPICS factor			Solution methodology (tendency towards)
Time scales	Clearly defined: short to medium term A	Ill defined: medium to long term B	A = hard B = soft
Resources	Clearly defined and reasonably fixed A	Unclear and variable B	A = hard B = soft
Objectives	Objective and quantifiable A	Subjective and visionary B	A = hard B = soft
Perceptions	Shared by those affected A	Creates conflict of interest B	A = hard B = soft
Interest	Limited and well defined A	Widespread and ill defined B	A = hard B = soft
Control	Within the managing group A	Shared outwith the group B	A = hard B = soft
Source	Originates internally A	Originates externally B	A = hard B = soft

'Hard' refers to a systems-based, mechanistic solution methodology.
'Soft' refers to an organizational development, complex solution methodology.

Management faced with straight As or Bs are shown a clear path to a solution methodology of which they can be reasonably certain. TROPICS can only provide a starting point and a tentative indication of the generic type of methodology to follow. Difficulties arise when the output is garbled in some way, with the user facing a combination of As and Bs. The examples below provide combinations of outputs and suggest possible user interpretations:

Case (a): time scale A, with all other factors B

This scenario would indicate an emergency situation, a time of crisis. Organizational development approaches are called for but the time scale indicates a need for an 'immediate' solution. A hard hitting deterministic solution is needed to overcome the short-term difficulties, followed by a longer period of education and cultural change to gain acceptance of the new state.

Case (b): source B, with all other factors A

This could represent an external technical change to a system, possibly as a result of a manufacturer's technical update. A systems approach to implement the change along with a limited education programme for operatives and maintenance may be required.

Case (c): control B, with all other factors A

This may represent an internally driven change that requires external permission to proceed. A satellite plant may wish to diversify into product design rather than act as an assembly plant. A system-based methodology may provide the answers to the internal systems changes but it is unlikely to convince the parent organization of the need to change.

TROPICS offers the manager an efficient and effective means of entering the change situation. Inputs need not be based on hard factual evidence; all that is needed is an educated assessment of the change's likely impact and general characteristics. It is important to get a feel for the change as early as possible, as the Mini Case 1.1 illustrates.

Frequent use of this model with managers from a wide range of enterprises – Philips, IBM, JVC, National Semiconductor, British Airports Authority and Scottish Homes – suggests that although a change situation may be defined as tending towards the 'soft' end of the spectrum it need not mean that an organizationally based solution methodology is best. Very often the key factors are time and money. If time scales are tight and resources are limited then, even though all other indicators point to the complexity of the situation, a more mechanistic solution methodology will be selected. In such a situation it is best to employ a methodology which is at least capable of addressing the more complex issues while pursuing a direct path to the goal.

Force field analysis: a positioning tool

As we have seen in the previous sections it is important that the nature of the change facing the organization, department and/or problem owner is defined according to its position on the change spectrum. Force field analysis is a positioning tool that assists the management of change by examining and evaluating, in a basic yet useful manner, the forces for and against the change. Such analysis, as seen in Mini Case 1.1, can then be integrated with the spectrum positioning tool and/or the TROPICS test. It is also of use when considering the position of the problem owner and/or management team with reference to the power sources, both internal to and external to the change, which may influence their ability to effectively manage the situation.

The organizational or individual view of a change situation will be strongly influenced by the source of the change and their position relative to it. Ownership of the problem or project is the key element in establishing our reaction to change. When an individual or a group has initiated certain actions, which in turn have to be managed, then they are more likely to display positive attitudes towards the situation and view

Mini Case 1.1   Scottish Homes

Scottish Homes, a national housing agency, faced major changes in the 1990s. For example, the Citizen's Charter held public bodies accountable for the raising of standards and the wise distribution of funds; compulsory competitive tendering for public bodies threatened in-house service functions; and the government had instigated the transfer of its housing stock to tenant managed housing associations. All this created a challenging operating environment for the Agency. In the face of such massive change the Board of the Agency, in 1995, instigated a strategic review.

A senior manager with the agency employed the TROPICS test, in association with a force field analysis, as a means of establishing a feeling for the problem. Changes were being imposed, but the organization was attempting to internalize them and determine a way forward.

TROPICS analysis

Time scales:	ill defined and at best medium term	soft
Resources:	unclear and variable	soft
Objectives:	as yet unclear: need to be qualified	soft
Perceptions:	believed to be common	soft
Interest:	shared amongst staff and stakeholders	hard
Control:	with the executive and government, but must 'e localized to effect changes	soft
Source:	internalized within the Agency	hard

Force field analysis

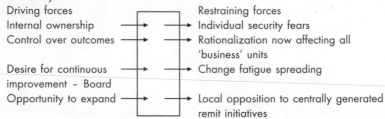

Driving forces	Restraining forces
Internal ownership	Individual security fears
Control over outcomes	Rationalization now affecting all 'business' units
Desire for continuous improvement – Board	Change fatigue spreading
Opportunity to expand	Local opposition to centrally generated remit initiatives

For the manager concerned the above clearly showed that any organization response to the externally driven, but now internally owned (at least at head office) impending changes fell into the 'grey' area of the change spectrum. The organizational implications of such dramatic change were that it affected the original core business, the promotion, development and management of rented housing stock (the stock had to go); in turn the business units created to service the core business were under threat from a lost 'market' and the need to compete with external enterprises to secure business. However, if the problem was treated purely as one requiring a repositioning of the organization, then there was a danger that owing to the unclear situation regarding resources and time scales, and the competitive threat, the opportunity would be lost and the Agency would be forced into a purely reactive role.

The Agency recognized that it had to undertake a form of corporate renewal in an attempt to ensure that the organizational design and strategy matched the new environment. It also recognized the need to drive this change through as a matter of urgency and set about identifying change agents, prime movers, to instigate change within their spheres of control. Scottish Homes now saw itself not only as being a support service to housing initiatives, but also as being involved in local economic regeneration, finance and legal services etc.

Table 1.3 *Features and attitudes associated with the source of a change*

Internally generated change	Externally generated change
Proactive stance	Reactive response
Positive feelings	Negative feelings
Greater driving forces	Greater restraining forces
Viewed from an opportunistic position	Viewed from a problem solving position
Greater certainty	Greater uncertainty
Greater control	Reduced control
Less disruption	Greater disruption
Closed boundaries and fixed time scales	Vague boundaries and variable time scales

the whole transition process as an opportunity to be exploited.

When the feeling of ownership is combined with the knowledge that one controls, or at least has influence over, the surrounding environment then the driving forces for the change will be significant. However, one must be aware (the TROPICS test can be of assistance here) of the degree of control within the managing group. Control shared with others, especially those above in the hierarchy, when they exhibit greater restraining forces will lead to conflict and potential blockages.

Table 1.3 illustrates the attitudinal responses and key features that can be attributed to the source of a change.

Externally generated change produces the greatest degree of negative feedback from those affected. External change need not solely relate to change generated outwith the organization. A department, section or individual will regard external change as being any development forced upon them from outwith their own environment.

Proactive attitudes and actions permit the management of a situation in an opportunistic and progressive manner. A proactive management team identifies and exploits opportunities associated with a transition between two states well in advance of the environment impinging on them.

A generic representation of a force field diagram is illustrated by Figure 1.2. Please note that the format of the diagram is of little interest. The value of such a diagram is in its power to force the problem owner into considering the position of other power sources with regard to the change at hand.

By producing a force field diagram for each individual, group or function affected by the change, the problem owner can analyse the relative magnitude of the conflicting forces, as well as develop an understanding of the underlying arguments, fears and influencing factors. The systems diagramming tools introduced in Chapter 3 will assist the identification of interested parties.

Generally speaking, change that has been generated by the 'system' most affected is likely to produce driving forces that outweigh any restraining forces, the opposite being true for externally generated change.

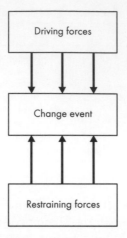

Figure 1.2   *A force field diagram*

Success guarantors: commitment, involvement and a shared perception

Possibly one of the most fundamental steps in achieving the successful implementation of change is that of obtaining a shared perception amongst those affected, concerning their viewpoint regarding the issues and implications associated with the change. If the problem owner can reach a point at which all those parties with a vested interest in change view it in such a way as to see common objectives and mutual benefits, then a great deal of progress will have been made.

One major obstacle to the formation of at least a partially shared perspective is the 'common-sense' approach to both change management in particular and decision making in general. All too often individuals and groups attempt to sell their own particular brand of 'common sense' as if they are the only possible providers of wisdom and truth. Unfortunately, each individual or grouping affected by a changing environment is bound to possess its own particular brand. All that can result from such an approach is a mini brand war, with no clear winners and a confused market.

There are a number of influential factors which will come together in such a way as to mould the way in which individuals, groups and organizations view particular change situations. The main factors are as follows and may be applied to all concerned and/or affected by the impending change:

- *Organizational culture*   Is it open or closed, enterprising or mechanistic, democratic or autocratic, progressive or entrenched, conducive to group work and common goals or oppressive?

- *Source of change* Is it internal to the affected groups and/or individuals, or externally generated and less easily controlled?
- *Social background* Is it one that inhibits collaboration with other groups and/or individuals, or welcomes the opportunity to develop as one moves towards mutually beneficial goals?
- *Education history* Exposure to topical management ideas and practices combined with both a good general education and proven managerial ability may lead to proactive stances. However, inward looking internally focused development reinforcing traditional practices and customs may work against prior educational understanding and external ideas.
- *Employment history* Has historical experience coloured the way in which change will be viewed? Will the 'them and us' mentality interfere with the attainment of a shared perception?
- *Style of management* The style of management exhibited by those directly involved in the change situation will obviously influence those whose cooperation and assistance they require. They may mirror the global organizational style of management, or possibly be at odds with it, but to be successful they must achieve general commitment and involvement within their terms of reference.
- *Problem ownership* The importance of the problem owner, and where appropriate the management group, has been emphasized throughout this chapter. The involvement and commitment of the problem owner is essential, as is the managerial suitability of the problem owner to the task at hand.
- *Experience* The track records identified with the individuals, groups and organization affected by the change, judged in terms of their past ability to cope with change, will influence the expectations of all concerned. If experience of a particular situation is lacking then, culture and style permitting, external sources of expertise must be approached and engaged.

A crucial factor associated with the successful implementation of change is the ability of the problem owner to overcome any personal prejudices regarding the change. However, they also need to ensure that the views and indeed prejudices exhibited by all other affected parties are taken on board. These need to be understood, countered or incorporated where appropriate.

To summarize, the problem owner must:

- Recognize that not all the suggestions offered and views expressed can be totally wrong, just as the problem owners are unlikely to be totally correct at all times.
- Ensure that they are seen to be actively encouraging collaboration. Change management of all but the simplest projects is a multi-

disciplinary group activity; everyone must be pulling in the same direction.
- Be seen to have as much support and authority as possible. Senior management must be clearly identified with the project.

A change management consultant, while making a company presentation, provided the following quote, which he attributed to Bertrand Russell, to emphasize the dangers of adopting a common-sense approach:

> When an intelligent man expresses a view which seems to us obviously absurd, we should not attempt to prove that it is somehow not true but we should try to understand how it ever came to seem true.

By following this advice the problem owner can begin the process of modifying perspectives through both education and understanding, moving along with those involved towards a shared perception of the situation and the ultimate solution of the problem.

Managing the triggers

Those involved in the management of change need to ensure that they have established, within reason, the exact nature of the change they face. They must not lose sight of the fact that change must be viewed as an event capable of causing multiple dislocations to the organization's culture, structure, systems and outputs. Leavitt's (1965) model in Figure 1.3 highlights the impact of organizational change and illustrates this point.

Leavitt views organizations as comprising four interacting variables. A change that affects any one variable will, to a greater or lesser extent, interact with the others to create knock-on effects. Change the task or the purpose of the organization, and the competencies (people), technology (processes which accomplish the task) and structures (communication, power, reporting systems) must also adapt and change.

Change may be directed at any 'entry point' and have a resulting, possibly predictable, knock-on effect elsewhere. Understanding the complexity of this organizational network is the first step in anticipating the likely response to any applied trigger. Once pulled the change 'trigger' will set off a chain reaction of interrelated events, which may quickly, if not managed, create discord and inefficiency. A shock wave will reverberate, as Leavitt identified, throughout the organization. What are these triggers and can they be managed? Triggers may be classed as

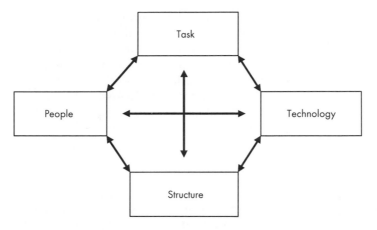

Figure 1.3   *The Leavitt model*

being either internally or externally generated. In addition, they may be further subdivided into whether or not a proactive or reactive stance is likely to be adopted to them – who pulled the trigger?

Some possible triggers could be:

- *Government legislation*   The case of the BSE scare facing the British meat industry in the late 1990s illustrates this point. In managing the crisis the government acted by strengthening existing health-related legislation and by introducing new systems of registration and monitoring. Another, more global illustration is that a single European currency will result in new trading procedures and an updating of financial practices.
- *Advances in process or product technology* The converging of technologies within the communications and electronics industries is both creating new markets and revolutionizing existing ones. Some examples include: interactive home entertainment centres, which may double as communication ports, are now a reality; home banking and shopping; intelligent home appliances and motoring aids; and the integration of telecommunications, broadcasting, software and computing enterprises. Services as well as products will be affected. Michael Porter predicts the demise of the university as we know it today; he sees an electronic future capable of networking the learners with centres of knowledge.
- *Changing consumer requirements, expectations or taste*   The British meat scare not only affected the producers and distributors. Consumers developed tastes for alternatives to beef and accordingly modified their purchase patterns. The environmentally friendly 1990s led to consumer demands for more resource friendly products and packaging. The electric car, always technologically viable, is now fast

becoming a commercial reality. There is a growing expectation that new for old products should attempt to minimize their usage of the Earth's limited resources. Consumers are now demanding more integrated and immediate delivery of services: for example, banks and financial institutions are entering partnerships with supermarket chains to deliver integrated financial packages.

- *Competitor or supply chain activities* Organizations are developing strategic alliances with both representatives of their own supply chain and providers of related services and products. This is done in an effort to meet more cost effectively the requirements of a sophisticated and technologically adept marketplace. They are essentially challenging the past and creating new and exciting ways of doing business: they are changing. The advent of the Channel Tunnel not only introduced a new mode of cross-Channel transport; it also affected the ferry companies, haulage companies, road and rail networks and travel agencies.

- *General economic or social pressures* In the global economy and marketplace, societies are becoming less isolated and more interdependent. Economic downturns in the United States; or political upheavals in Russia; or mounting German unemployment; or French rural decline; or the prospect of a truly integrated Europe; these act not only on their immediate locality. They can create a ripple effect throughout an increasingly sensitive global society. These points are further developed in a very interesting case concerning 3M and the implications of an integrated Europe developed by Ackenhusen et al. (1996a; 1996b).

- *Unpredictable environmental catastrophes* Unpredictable, or at least unavoidable, catastrophes have been and always will be a source of disruption and despair. If they cannot be avoided then they must be effectively managed when they occur. California has elaborate disaster plans that will, hopefully, help it cope when the 'big one' comes. The repercussions of Chernobyl are still being felt, not only at the source, but also across Europe. In Bhopal, India, negligence at a chemical plant resulted in disaster that left many blind.

- *Acquisition or merger* For example: the mutual life and building societies in Britain are locked in an ever more complex spiral of acquisition and strategic mergers and alliances; BMW are rejuvenating the production and design processes of the Rover car group; and when Peugeot acquired Chrysler UK in the 1980s the effective management of change was one of the keys to their success.

The way in which a 'trigger' impacts upon a situation will, to a certain extent, depend upon its source, as well as its nature. Internally generated change is likely to be managed far more proactively, creatively and effectively, owing to clear ownership and prior knowledge and understanding. This point will be returned to at a later stage.

READER ACTIVITY

Throughout our lives we experience change. List below three significant 'triggers', and alongside identify their source and rank your feeling of 'control' over them.

Trigger	*Source* *(internal/external)*	*Ranking* *(5 high level of control;* *1 bystander status!)*
1		
2		
3		

No matter the source or nature of the trigger, it will initiate the change process. Buchanan and McCalman (1989) illustrate this through their model of perpetual transition, previously detailed in Figure I.1. The model offers a basis for managing change. From initial identification of the trigger the organization must clarify the situation, then express it in understandable terms and finally communicate its nature, impact and rationale. Next, it must formulate its response to the change, focusing as far as possible on creating an innovative and opportunistic environment within which ideas and actions will be generated. Having decided on where and how to proceed the organization must convert the stake-holders; a shared perception of the change must be reached. Finally, the impetus for change must be maintained.

Being alert to the potential triggers is the first step an enterprise can take on the road to effectively managing change. Early identification and classification permit the creative, or at least proactive, management of subsequent events. According to Kanter (1983) effective organizations, or at least the masters of change within them, are adept at handling 'the triggers of change', namely:

- departures from tradition
- the crisis of a galvanizing event
- strategic choice
- prime movers
- action vehicles.

Kanter's triggers activate the senses of the change master. They are ready to exploit changes to the operating environment; they are also aware of the prime movers within the organization, and are capable of exploiting and enhancing their initiatives; crisis situations are harnessed and used as a means of securing rapid response without incurring organized resistance; the value of a well-selected vehicle for change, for example, quality improvement or customer awareness programmes, is not overlooked. However, Kilman (1995) questions the ongoing value of excessive use of action vehicles and suggests that workforces merely become apathetic towards them as their sustained use turns them into little more than fads. Practitioners often echo this view.

Prior to considering the need for, and the means of, defining the nature and environment of a change event, it is worthwhile pausing to consider the benefits of creating and managing your own crisis. Often organizations have to change fast. For example, an unwanted takeover bid may require immediate and dramatic responses. By anticipating and managing the situation in such a way as to create the environment of a *crisis* the organization may induce a willingness amongst the stakeholders to act as one in defence of the enterprise. The crisis may act as a galvanizing event and lead to rapidly agreed responses.

READER ACTIVITY

Organizations are, with good reason, reluctant to discuss the creation and management of crisis situations. Practitioners will admit to minor falsifications: the prearranged panic which coincides with the visit of a superior, with the hope of securing additional funds; or the deliberate stimulation of a crisis environment to encourage staff to give that little bit more.

Have you ever manipulated the true facts to get what you want? Consult your acquaintances: what have they been up to?

As always, the key to good management lies in the ability to read environmental signals, categorize them and take appropriate action. Don't wait for the trigger to be pulled: the best you will then be able to do is avoid the bullet. Look for the initial move, act fast and be the first to draw!

The lesson

It is always advisable to ensure that you know what you are talking about, especially at those points in life when your utterances may shape your future career and lifestyle. The best way to ensure this is by doing your 'homework'. The successful management of a change event commences as soon as the decision is made to tackle the problem, or to react to an opportunity or a threat, through the simple task of doing your 'homework'. By identifying the nature of a change the manager, or change agent, begins the process of determining the most probable solution methodology.

Given that managers operate in increasingly complex and dynamic environments, both within and outwith the organization, time is one vital commodity that they never seem to have in abundance. If we spend too long on the 'homework' then we might just miss that once in a lifetime 'party'. A balance must be struck. In an ideal world it would be nice to know all that can be known about an impending event, but reality dictates otherwise. The best we can hope for is to identify and research the key issues, or variables; make our decisions, based on informed but incomplete information; trust to judgement and experience; and pray! We need tools that allow us to review, appraise and respond to situations quickly and appropriately. The intervention strategy model, introduced in Chapter 4, could be one such tool.

2 Change and the Manager

Organizations and their managers must recognize that change, in itself, is not necessarily a problem. The problem often lies in an inability to effectively manage change: not only can the adopted process be wrong, but also the conceptual framework may lack vision and understanding. Why is this the case? Possibly, and many practising mangers would concur, the problem may be traced to the managers' growing inability to appropriately develop and reinforce their role and purpose within complex, dynamic and challenging organizations. Change is now a way of life; organizations, and more importantly their managers, must recognize the need to adopt strategic approaches when facing transformation situations (Burnes, 1996).

Competency and change

Throughout the 1980s and 1990s organizations, both national and international, strived to develop sustainable advantage in both volatile and competitive operating environments. Those that have survived, and/or developed, have often found that the creative and market-driven management of their human resources can produce the much needed competitive 'cushion'. This is not surprising: people manage change, and well-managed people manage change more effectively. Buchanan and Huczynski (1997) identified the key managerial competence of the 1990s as being the ability to handle change, which in turn creates an increasing demand for the development of associated competencies.

Managing change is a multi-disciplinary activity. Those responsible, whatever their designation, must possess or have access to a wide range of skills, resources, support and knowledge. For example:

- Communications skills are essential and must be applied both within and outwith the managing team.
- Maintaining motivation and providing leadership to all concerned is necessary.
- The ability to facilitate and orchestrate group and individual activities is crucial.

- Negotiation and influencing skills are invaluable.
- It is essential that both planning and control procedures are employed.
- The ability to manage on all planes, upward, downward and within the peer group, must be acquired.
- Knowledge of, and the facility to influence, the rationale for change is essential.

The list of competencies or attributes could be further subdivided, or indeed extended, as there is no such thing as a standard change event. Personal managerial attributes and skills will be returned to at a later stage.

Change and the human resource

Organizations over the past decade have been moving towards flatter, leaner and more responsive structures. This has undoubtedly made many of them more efficient in terms of their resource utilization, and more effective in terms of their responsiveness to market demands. Technology has played a major role in ensuring that a coherent business approach and managerial performance can be maintained from a reduced resource base. The key to success in such moves has been the mobilization of the human resource (Peters and Waterman, 1982; Kanter, 1983; 1989; Pettigrew and Whipp, 1993). The revolution in organization design has been achieved by creating responsive working environments which emphasize the need to cooperate across and within functions; focus on service and quality; and search for holistic and integrated responses to trigger events; while encouraging participation, ownership and shared accountability (Spector, 1989; Handy, 1990).

IBM, Compaq, Motorola and Steelcase (the world's biggest manufacturer of office furniture) have, amongst many others, adopted team-based solutions to the management of their manufacturing facilities. Responsibilities increase as the team matures and gains confidence. Teams are being asked to participate in the process of innovation and change; employers are seeking, and ensuring that they get, enhanced performance through greater involvement and empowerment (Piczak and Hauser, 1996; Anderson and West, 1996). British Aerospace and the British Broadcasting Corporation, along with Diageo, Fiat and Volvo, have all positively embraced the movement towards autonomous business units. The airlines, possibly with British Airways in the vanguard, have revolutionized their business in terms of the degree of emphasis that they place upon customer service and awareness. Many organizations – Power-Systems, Telecom Sciences and Motorola for example – have dropped the terms 'foreman' and 'supervisor', in favour of titles such as 'team leader', which is a visible manifestation of workforce empowerment.

For the manager this has led to an increasing emphasis being placed on project and teamwork, communications, customer awareness, auditing and quality procedures. The need to supervise, provide individual direction, motivate and control has diminished. Managers are being asked to facilitate events rather than lead; share responsibility and accountability rather than shoulder the burden; develop and administer participative planning and control systems. Such initiatives were at the heart of the British Telecom 'For a better life' programme, which was in effect a vehicle for change.

There may be a danger that managers, amidst all this activity, lose track of their key responsibility and reason for being there in the first place. Managers are there to ensure that both they, and the processes and activities for which they are responsible, add value to the organization as a whole. The manager of the twenty-first century is busy; they face challenging operating environments, multiple tasks and cross-functional responsibilities. In addition, they are increasingly encouraged to empower others and facilitate success. It is becoming less clear who is actually responsible for adding value. Is it the organization as a whole? Is it the systems? Is it a combination? Is it the manager?

READER ACTIVITY

Pause and consider the following questions. What is your experience of working within teams? Who was ultimately responsible? How well informed were you? Did you feel involved? Did the team achieve its objectives? Would you have tackled things differently?

Ensuring managerial value and the 'Trinity'

Value is added, in a managerial context, by ensuring that all organization systems, both tangible and intangible, are aligned with market requirements and are capable of being appropriately developed. In today's highly competitive environment, adding value is about ensuring the effective and sustainable management of change (see Mini Case 2.1).

Successful change requires adherence to three key managerial rules – the 'Holy Trinity'. The religious metaphor is merely intended to convey the importance of adhering to the rules. Those at the centre of significant change events must 'buy-in' to the process, without of course losing their objectivity, and believe with passion in the course of action about to be undertaken. If they don't approach their task with commitment, others are unlikely to be convinced, resulting in apathy and discord (Beer and Eisenstat, 1990; Kotter, 1995).

The Trinity may be portrayed diagrammatically as in Figure 2.1.

Figure 2.1   *The 'Trinity'*

Mini Case 2.1   GlenLight and Ericsson

The case of GlenLight Shipping (Boddy and Paton, 1998) dealt with the final and dramatic attempts of a long-established traditional enterprise to diversify into a potentially lucrative business. It hinted at one of the most frustrating obstacles that can confront a change agent – apathy. Disinterest in the proposed change is difficult to deal with as it manifests itself neither in support nor in opposition. In GlenLight the majority of the managerial stakeholders were too involved in maintaining the status quo and avoiding conflict. They had ceased to add value and had become apathetic; they most probably felt that events were no longer controllable and were happy to merely react.

The significance and immediacy of the change facing GlenLight, combined with the relative remoteness of the enterprise's principal stakeholders, hampered activities to secure ownership of the change amongst the workforce.

The case of Ericsson, Australia, contrasts markedly with that of GlenLight. The 1990s saw massive deregulation of the Australian telecommunications industry and for Ericsson this effectively threatened its privileged relationship with Telecom Australia (Telecom accounted for over 60 per cent of Ericsson's business). Over the years Ericsson had to a certain extent grown complacent, as business was easy to obtain and service. The new, deregulated environment would be far more aggressive and cost conscious. Ericsson had to develop a marketing focus, and fast.

The Chief Executive set about revitalizing the organization. A vision statement was developed and a leading change programme instigated. The programme was designed to articulate the vision and prepare the management team for the implementation of change. They developed 'mental tools for change' and charged their management with identifying a project that would act as a vehicle for transferring the tools to the workforce. Ericsson succeeded in adding value to its processes and people and thus protected and developed its market presence (Graetz, 1996).

All too often the process, or the activities associated with a change, assume more importance than the change itself. It is often far easier to 'talk a good game' and plan for a future event than to focus the mind on ensuring successful implementation. The first rule of the 'Trinity', *maintain your focus*, is designed to highlight the questions: why are we changing and what do we expect in return? It takes effort to maintain the focus in a dynamic managerial and business environment. Attention and commitment will diminish as time elapses. Interest can be maintained by forcing the pace; organizing special interest events; reorganizing the core management team; employing 'creative' communications devices; and above all else ensuring continued senior management support.

No less important than maintaining focus within the 'Trinity' is the second rule of *role awareness*. Understanding the nature of the term 'value added' assists not only in clarifying managerial roles but also in maintaining the focus. Change for change's sake seldom results in any meaningful improvements. Change is costly, disruptive and potentially dangerous; it would be unwise to embark on an 'adventure' without first establishing that success would be both probable and beneficial.

READER ACTIVITY

Do you have a career plan? Do you really know why you are reading this book? What are you hoping to achieve and why? If you know the answers to these questions and are happy with your replies then you probably have set, and are pursuing, your goal – read on!

The third rule of the trinity, *maintain your goal*, may seem obvious but it is often overlooked. Given that the focus is maintained and the roles remain clear, why raise the issue of goals? The effective development and achievement of business strategies, as described in numerous texts, depend upon successful implementation, which in turn is dependent upon the effective management of the resulting change. Focus and roles apply to the change at hand, but by considering goals the discrete change is placed in the wider context of policy and strategy. There is little point adding value to a system that is at odds with the strategic direction of the enterprise, or in maintaining focus on a target set between moving 'goalposts'. Change, whether strategic, tactical or operational, must be set in the context of general corporate strategy (see Mini Case 2.2).

Fundamental rules, useful though they are, provide no more than guidance to those managing complex changes. However, the value of such rules or edicts is enhanced within organizations where the cultural environment encourages creative and progressive solutions to pending business opportunities or threats (Peters and Waterman, 1982; Kanter, 1983).

The cultural web

Consider 'first impressions': many would argue that they are never wrong. Can you get a feel for a person, group, company or institution from an initial meeting? Could you attribute political leanings and social attitudes simply by observing an individual's car, clothes and look? By standing at the front door of a restaurant, pub, café or theatre, could

Mini Case 2.2   Hewlett Packard

Hewlett Packard is recognized as being a highly successful company. It led the way into open systems and was the first to adapt to reducing industry margins. It is an organization which at least on the surface adheres to the 'Trinity'. They have a clear goal articulated from the top, namely, to stay ahead of the game and be both aware and responsive to long-term trends. They strive not to lose focus by encouraging the enterprising spirit of the initial founders; innovation and drive are welcomed. Managers and staff in general are aware of their role, which is to ensure value to the end user. They stay close to the customer by organizing themselves into many multi-disciplinary and self-financing business units.

you get a feel for the likely level of service and quality that would be provided? If the answers to these questions are 'yes', then join the international stereotyping club. Stereotyping only exists because in the perceived majority of cases the initial impression is vindicated in some tangible way. Organizations can be classified, if only subjectively, by the way they 'feel' and 'behave'.

READER ACTIVITY

Consider the last bank you were in. How did it look and feel? Do you think that a deliberate effort had been made to create this feeling?

When you think of organizations such as Mercedes and Virgin, what images do they conjure up? How do these enterprises reinforce their image and why?

Organizations are cultures; they can be studied and manipulated as such. Just as the individual can adapt to their social surroundings, altering their appearance, beliefs and behaviours, so too can organizations (Kanter et al., 1992). However, it is worth emphasizing the importance of 'culture' as it relates to the creative management of change. Every enterprise, public or private, will possess a unique cultural blueprint, which dictates how it interacts with its environment and manages its people. Understanding the relationships between the cultural web and a changing environment greatly assists the organization to manage change (Johnson and Scholes, 1997).

In the 1970s British Airways lost touch with the aspirations and requirements of its potential market. An apathetic, take it or leave it, culture had developed. This was not too dissimilar to the prevailing cultures in British Leyland and the Fiat group. However, at British Airways, extensive customer awareness programmes along with a revamping of image and enhanced quality initiatives, undertaken in the 1980s, led and supported by their Chairman, Lord King, resulted in a

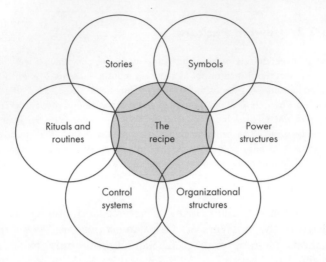

Figure 2.2   *The cultural web*

dramatic change in fortunes. A tangible cultural shift was greeted posi-tively by customers.

Johnson and Scholes (1997) argue that strategic developments can only be successful if they recognize and address the cultural aspects of the change at hand. Figure 2.2 illustrates the pivotal role played by the cultural 'recipe', the genetic blueprint of the organization, when explor-ing complex change situations.

Understanding the nature of any change is the key to ensuring both that the situation will be properly analysed and that a plausible imple-mentation strategy will be developed. The 'recipe' is made up of two categories of ingredients. The first is the physical or tangible, such as administrative systems; quality procedures; control mechanisms; organ-izational structures; dress codes; decor; communications systems; and written statements of aims, objectives, missions and philosophy. They are however only the manifestations of the second category. The intan-gible, 'soft' aspects of the 'recipe' may be thought of as the 'stock' of the dish. These ingredients are difficult to define but generally include factors such as informal value systems; interpersonal and group rituals; the politics of power; and the symbols of success. The cultural web of an organization is dependent not only upon the ingredients but also upon the manner in which they are mixed.

The web and the past

The web will protect itself, it will reinforce its values and relationships, and in effect it will resist change. Rosabeth Moss Kanter (1983) addresses this issue by asking the question: can we be sure what we are seeing is indeed the reality of the situation? History is written, or at least influenced, by the victors. Kanter suggests that to understand change, especially the 'softer', intangible aspects, the investigator must realize that what they are viewing or experiencing is the product of *post hoc* rationalization, a 'revised history' and a manufactured culture. How important is this? To predict the outcomes of any event it is necessary to understand the past and learn from previous mistakes and build on past successes. However, just as the historian must attempt to see beyond the victors' 'story', the manager, tackling a complex change situation, must investigate the true reality of past events. Reports, memos and documentation, along with personal and group recollections, will have been formed with a view to selling, justifying and embellishing previous courses of actions and decisions. The culture will protect itself. Also, organizations and their managers tend only to learn from their obvious failures. Successes are welcomed and hailed but not often fully understood.

READER ACTIVITY

Consider the following questions. Have you ever made a mistake and attempted to hide it? Have you ever blamed others for your failings? Have you ever done something because it was the 'done thing to do'? What memories do you cherish?

We all want to belong and to do what is best for the groups we belong to. This involves reinforcing shared values and projecting positive and successful images of ourselves. Organizations and their employees are no different.

Dig, seek the truth, and discover the reality of culture. Unlock the myths; examine the nature of the politics and power plays; research the failings of past strategies and determine the rationale behind the 'recipe'. Clearly culture and change are interrelated. How might the proactive and innovative organization be typified? Are there sets of culturally related attributes associated with effective change management?

Cultural attributes of change

Peters and Waterman (1982) and Kanter (1983; 1989) would suggest that there are common culturally related attributes associated with organizations recognized as being masters of change. The attributes may be presented as follows:

1   *A clear and communicated strategic vision*   People must know where they
    are going and why. Suppliers, customers and stakeholders obviously
    benefit from a clear understanding of the organization's philosophy,
    purpose and strategic undertakings. The vision, based on a thorough
    understanding of the operating environment and organization
    capabilities, sets the context for strategic developments, organizational
    cultures and management approaches and lays the foundation for the
    desired means of sustaining competitive advantage.

2   *Visible senior management involvement*   Sustainable change can only be
    achieved when senior management becomes visibly involved in the
    process. Executives must exhibit, and encourage within others, a bias
    for action (Peters and Waterman, 1982). The levers of change must be
    connected from the top to the bottom of the organization (Pettigrew
    and Whipp, 1993). The executive grouping, led by the chief executive,
    must support their change agents in their endeavours.

3   *People-based competitive edge*   In an increasingly bland corporate
    world, where products, technology, packaging and image are cloned
    and replicated, enterprises are finding it more difficult to identify a
    truly sustainable competitive edge. The people they employ, organize
    and develop offer a means of sustaining a competitive advantage
    that is dynamic, potentially unique and difficult to emulate. An
    empowered, autonomous, knowledgeable and participating work-
    force, encouraged to exhibit entrepreneurial tendencies, is more likely
    to respond to change and exploit potential opportunities.

4   *Marketing ethos*   No matter the nature of the enterprise's business, or
    the sector to which it belongs, it would be wise to maintain a watchful
    eye on the marketplace it serves. If it does not take care of its
    customers then someone else will. Everyone in an organization has a
    customer: satisfy the internal customer and build a 'marketing ethos'
    throughout the organization. Focus on the customer's needs and
    develop a culture designed to meet them.

5   *Consensus-driven management*   Driven by the previous four attributes,
    an organization would be wise to foster a shared view of the cor-
    porate ethos. It must strive to establish a consensus on the best course
    of action and the optimal means of achieving the desired outcomes. A
    shared perception is not easy to achieve, as there is always a
    tendency, especially for those in positions of power, to dictate rather
    than communicate. Gaining a consensus takes time and commitment.
    It involves the re-engineering of the cultural web and in extreme
    cases may require the wholesale dismantling of existing organization
    structures and procedures in an effort to jettison 'baggage'.

6   *Awareness and reflection of social responsibility*   By widening the
    definition of corporate stakeholder to include society in general, who
    after all in some shape or form may be regarded as the marketplace,
    corporations are now attempting to reflect societal expectations. In
    addition regulatory bodies, again seeing society as their market, are

endeavouring to ensure that enterprises of all types conduct their business in accordance with society's wishes. The cultural web is now, more than ever before, reflecting in a tangible way its responsibility to the environment, consumers, employees and the wider public.

READER ACTIVITY

Identify three well-known companies. Now do a little research. How do these companies stay ahead of the competition?

For example Gillette, through staying in touch with technology and the customer, ensure that they have at least 20 new shaving products in development at any one time. Pepsi, showing commitment from the top, have recently appointed a Director of Innovation for Europe. Virgin's Richard Branson brands all products with enthusiasm and commitment: he is the guarantee!

Recently a greater emphasis has been placed on the importance of communication within the cultural change framework. Achieving and maintaining the above noted cultural attributes require the organization to develop responsive communications systems (Pettigrew and Whipp, 1993). In addition, technological advances within the communications media are offering ever more interactive and imaginative means of 'getting the message across' (Morant, 1996). There is a widely recognized need to ensure effective corporate communication within what is effectively a constantly changing environment (Moorcroft, 1996; Richardson and Denton, 1996).

The role of communication

It is worth noting, from a change perspective, that there are a few well-defined guidelines that should be considered and followed when communicating change events:

- *Customize the message* The key here is understanding. Who is the audience? How will they react? What do they know? Ensure that the message has been encoded in a manner appropriate to the skills and knowledge level of the audience. Try not to use jargon and, if possible, place yourself in the reader's seat: would you understand the 'message'?
- *Set the appropriate tone* The interpretation of a communication depends upon both the content and the tone. Offence can often be caused if the tone has been perceived to be inappropriate, for

example, patronizing, flippant, condescending or impudent. Think before you act and always remember that the whole body sends the message: dress, body language, medium and the words set the tone.

- *Build in feedback* Communication is a two-way process. Assuming the message to be conveyed is not simply an instruction, a statement or a 'news item', then the sender must consider how responses are to be made. In change situations, given the need to allay fears and uncertainties, it is essential that the manager has some means of ensuring the message was received, believed, accepted and understood. Managers must plan, but remember they also must exercise some control. In change, follow-up and maintenance are essential.

- *Set the example* If you are asking others to respond to the communication, or brief their staff, ensure that as the sender you have done as requested. Be consistent, and at all times practise what you preach!

- *Ensure penetration* The medium selected to deal with the communication must be capable of achieving the required penetration within the organization. It must also reflect the time horizons of the change. Is real time communication required? Is written feedback expected?

The Philips executive team regularly utilizes the organization's personal television channel to communicate across Philips' global network. Glaxo Wellcome adopted a cascading distribution system; corporate communications are cascaded down and through the organization via networked employee groupings. Peugeot UK also adopted this approach. Here executive decisions receive a colour-coded urgency rating which determines the speed at which they must be communicated to the workforce. When Delta Airlines were faced with significant redundancies in 1994 they took positive steps to control and manage the situation. A communications centre, with freephone numbers, was set up to provide immediate responses to employee questions. Open forums were held in the organization, and vice-presidents were dispatched to allay fears. In addition, the senior management team visited all Delta sites within two days of the announcement.

READER ACTIVITY

Have you ever been misunderstood? Did you send wrong signals, or were they simply decoded incorrectly? Consider your communications skills: do they need improving? If so, then ensure that corrective action is taken; take the opportunities provided by your studies to practise in a non-threatening environment. Volunteer for presentations; lead the team; assist in report writing.

If organizations do not manage their communications, others will. The media, the unions, the 'rumour mill' and the competitors are only too willing to assist the 'silent' corporation in its time of need.

Effective communication, designed to inform, consult and promote action, will assist in overcoming both resistance to change and ignorance. Mobilizing the 'troops', while dealing with and overcoming resistance, apathy and ignorance, can be a daunting task for any manager. It is essential that organizations recognize the need to foster and develop the managerial talents required to facilitate change.

Resistance to change

An organization can create an operating environment, both internally and throughout its supply chain, which encourages an opportunistic stance to be adopted. However, no matter how welcoming an organization is to change, it will still face a degree of employee, supplier, distributor, stakeholder and consumer resistance to change. It may manage to reduce the frequency and potency of such resistance but it will never eradicate the fear of the unknown.

Why do people resist change? Quite simply because they fear the unknown and are comforted by the familiar. Also very often successes and power bases are rooted in the past and present, not necessarily in the future.

> It ought to be remembered that there is nothing more difficult to take in hand, more perilous to conduct, or more uncertain in its success, than to take the lead in the introduction of a new order of things. Because the innovator has for enemies all those who have done well under the old conditions, and indifferent defenders among those who may do well under the new. (Machiavelli, *The Prince*)

Kanter (1983) echoes Machiavelli's thoughts. She points out that it is always far easier to say yes, in the first instance, to a new idea, for in the early developmental stages its impact will be minimal. Once the development work starts to produce results then the detractors will appear and a host of negative comments and actions materialize. No matter the extent to which an organization has designed procedures, structures and cultures to encourage openness, responsiveness and innovation, there will always be detractors. All too often we forget that: 'We are not creatures of circumstance, we are the creators of circumstance' (Disraeli).

When facing an uncertain personal change it is easy to forget mankind's successes in shaping the world. Organizations, individuals and groups fear change for many reasons:

- *It can result in organization redesign*   Tampering with the design will modify, at least in the short term, existing power bases, reporting structures and communications networks. In extreme cases issues regarding security of employment will be raised and undoubtedly questions concerning redeployment and training emerge.
- *It creates new technological challenges*   New techniques, procedures and skills acquisition can bring out, no matter how briefly, the 'Luddite' that lurks just beneath our outer veneer of confidence. Never underestimate the 'power' of technological change. No matter how insignificant the change looks to the well informed it can have far reaching effects and consequences.
- *It confronts apathy*   A great many employees grow apathetic in their approach to working life. Careers falter, positions of apparent security and ease are achieved, competencies are developed, and the employee becomes apathetic to their working environment. They do what they do well, or have convinced their peers and manager that they do, and deep down they would prefer the status quo. Change may have the audacity to wake them up from their slumbers!
- *It permeates throughout the supply chain*   Change for change's sake is both foolish and potentially expensive. The effective and efficient management of the supply chain ensures that the final consumer is delivered a product or service that meets their expectations. Stakeholders within the supply chain, including the final consumer, tend to be sceptical of any change that results in the 'equilibrium' being disturbed. Management must be careful to ensure that the effects of a change, although beneficial to a particular member, do not cascade throughout the chain causing negative results further down-stream.
- *It challenges old ideas*   By their very nature organizations have traditionally encouraged stability, continuity and the pursuit of security. Continuity of procedures, services, products and staff leads to a stable operating environment. Remember that the basis of today's success lies in the past and this encourages management to reinforce the lessons of the past. For example, senior management do not retire, they take up non-executive positions on the board; non-executive directors are recruited for their past knowledge of the business environment; organizational design attempts to reflect the perception of historical success; recruitment policies endeavour to reinforce old beliefs by ensuring the appointment of like minded personnel. Success in the future will depend upon a management understanding the lessons of the past, but if too much emphasis is placed upon the 'history' then these lessons will simply reinforce old ideas.
- *It encourages debate*   Debate is healthy when well managed, but it does tend to identify those lacking in understanding or knowledge. Once again the assumptions of the past and those who promote them will be challenged.

READER ACTIVITY

Compile a list of words which you would associate with an impending 'technological change'. Classify them according to whether or not you consider them positive or negative (you may also denote them as neutral).

Once you have completed the task consider: how did you decide if they were positive or negative?

Managers must be aware of the impact of their actions. Resistance to change, as has been noted, can be reduced through creative organizational design and development, but it cannot be eradicated. Effective communication often holds the key to successfully unlocking the door to change.

Change needs to be portrayed in positive terms, a necessity to ensure long-term survival. In so doing gurus, chief executives, governments and individuals must be aware that not all resistance to change need be negative. Rational, principled and shared resistance to proposed developments may well signal that the 'common good' may not be best served by implementing change. For example, the design team who constantly fights cost cutting measures on the basis of maintaining product safety and performance levels should have their concerns openly and fully addressed. Had Ford done this in the 1970s the legendary case of the Pinto's safety-related lawsuits would have been avoided. British Airways' drive to regenerate the airline by focusing on creating the world's number one airline could have influenced staff decisions to engage in competitive actions against Virgin, which would be later described as a campaign of 'dirty tricks'. Change for change's sake, change for short-term commercial advantage or indeed change which may adversely affect the 'common good' should be resisted, not only on moral grounds, but also on the basis that the adverse long-term financial consequences are likely to outweigh any short-term gain.

The change agent or master

The term 'master of change' may be traced to Kanter (1983). However, there are many other terms that have been used to denote those responsible for the effective implementation of change: for example, change agents, problem owners, facilitators or project managers. The focal point of a change need not be an individual; a work group could quite easily be designated as a special task force responsible for managing the change. However, generally within, or above, any work group there is still someone who ultimately is accountable and responsible. What are the essential attributes of a change agent/master and are there any guidelines for them?

· Buchanan and Huczynski (1997) suggest the need to encourage participation and involvement in the management of the change by those who are to be affected. The aim is to stimulate interest and commitment and minimize fears, thus reducing opposition. It may also be necessary to provide facilitating and support services. These could assist in promoting an individual's awareness for the need for change, while counselling and therapy could be offered to help overcome fears. Management must engage in a process of negotiation, striving towards agreement. This is essential where those opposing have the power, and influence, to resist and ultimately block the change.

If consensus fails then one has little alternative but to move on to explicit and implicit coercion. Somewhere in between the two extremes management may attempt to manipulate events in an effort to sidestep sources of resistance. For example, they may play interested parties off against each other or create a galvanizing crisis to divert attention.

The techniques need not be employed in isolation. Kotter and Schlesinger (1979) emphasize that they may be most effective when utilized in combination. The core tasks facing a change agent or project manager, according to Boddy and Buchanan (1992), are to reduce the uncertainty associated with the change situation and then encourage positive action. They suggest a number of steps to assist:

1 *Identify and manage stakeholders*   Gains visible commitment.
2 *Work on objectives*   Clear, concise and understandable.
3 *Set a full agenda*   Take a holistic view and highlight potential difficulties.
4 *Build appropriate control systems*   Communication is a two-way process, feedback is required.
5 *Plan the process of change*   Pay attention to:
    • establishing roles – clarity of purpose
    • build a team – do not leave it to chance
    • nurture coalitions of support – fight apathy and resistance
    • communicate relentlessly – manage the process
    • recognize power – make the best use of supporting power bases
    • handing over – ensure that the change is maintained.

Are there any personal attributes that can be associated with the successful change master? Kanter (1983) suggests that masters exist throughout the organization (but are crucial at the top) and constitute in effect a latent force. Kanter typifies masters of change by their ability to:

• question the past and challenge old assumptions and beliefs
• leap from operational and process issues to the strategic picture

Mini Case 2.3   An NHS story

Boddy and Buchanan (1992) stress the need for control and feedback. This becomes crucial when communications are channelled from the managing group to other parties. A project manager, leading a team in a National Health Service trust hospital, assumed that information was being conveyed upwards by a senior member of medical staff. When it became apparent that no feedback was materializing the manager challenged the medic. It transpired that although initially agreeable to the assigned role of 'messenger' the medic now considered such a task as being one more associated with an administrator. More worrying, and much to the joy of the medic, the senior management team had not realized that it had not received any reports. Everyone was simply too busy to follow up all the initiatives they had sanctioned!

- think creatively and avoid becoming bogged down in the 'how-to'
- manipulate and exploit triggers for change.

Kanter (1989) further developed these thoughts. She suggested that the 1980s change master had to adapt to cope with the complexities of the 'post-entrepreneurial' organization of the 1990s; they had to become a 'business athlete'. Seven traits are associated with such 'athletes':

1 able to work independently without the power and sanction of the management hierarchy
2 an effective collaborator, able to compete in ways that enhance rather than destroy cooperation
3 able to develop high trust relations, with high ethical standards
4 possessing self-confidence tempered with humility
5 respectful of the process of change as well as the substance
6 able to work across business functions and units – 'multi-faceted and multi-dextrous'
7 willing to take rewards on results and gain satisfaction from success.

To summarize, the effective change agent must be capable of orchestrating events; socializing within the network of stakeholders; and managing the communication process.

Need the change master or agent be an internal appointment? Is it possible to acquire on 'loan' effective facilitators of change? The objective outsider has a lot to offer an enterprise engaged upon a change exercise. However, there is a need for competent internal change agents to be assigned to the project so as to ensure cooperation, effective implementation and successful handover upon completion (Buchanan and Boddy, 1992). The role envisaged for the external change agent, namely to assist in fully defining the problem; to help in determining the cause and suggesting potential solutions; to stimulate debate and broaden the horizons; and to encourage the client to learn from the experience and be

Mini Case 2.4 Mixed messages at Boart Longyear

In an effort to enhance performance, Boart Longyear, a mining machinery manufacturer, attempted to implement self-directed teams, capable not only of acting for themselves but also of facilitating and managing ongoing initiatives. Each team went through 60 hours of training, which covered leadership, decision making, interpersonal skills and facilitation. Despite the effort the teams were reluctant to take on the responsibilities, and the lack of leadership led to decision-making delays. A great source of frustration originated from the fact that the employees were far happier being told what to do.

With perseverance the teams began to perform: members contributed as they did not wish to be accused, by the team, of under-performing; former supervisors found a role as information providers and resource procurers; and productivity increased by 12 per cent.

ready to handle future situations internally; is complementary to that of the internal problem owner. It is the responsibility of the potential client to establish the need for an objective outsider, by considering their own internal competencies and awareness of the external opportunities.

To conclude, those involved in the management of change need to heed the above guidelines and attempt to acquire the desired attributes. However, they must not lose sight of the fact that change must be viewed as an event capable of causing multiple dislocations to the organization culture, structure, systems and outputs. Once again Leavitt's model, introduced in Figure 1.3, highlights the impact of organizational change and illustrates the interdependency of variables.

Change may be directed at any 'entry point' and have a resulting, possibly predictable, knock-on effect elsewhere. Understanding the complexity of this organization network is the first step in anticipating the likely response to any applied trigger for change. Chapter 3 attempts to come to grips with the potential identification and subsequent management of triggers for change.

3 Mapping Change

As we have seen in the previous chapters it is important that the nature of the change facing the organization, group or individual is defined according to its position on the change spectrum. The use of techniques such as the TROPICS test and force field analysis, along with the need to consider the role and position of the problem owner and any other associated change agents, have been discussed. Physical or mechanistic change, exhibiting both systematized technical attributes and a low degree of man–machine/systems interface, should be addressed by adopting a systems-based solution model from the scientific management school. On the other hand, more complex and generally messy change, involving personalized relationships and organizational cultures, warrants the adoption of a more people-based model from the organizational development stable.

The solution methodology associated with both ends of the change spectrum is therefore identifiable through a relatively limited examination of the change environment. Unfortunately most change occurs within what has been referred to as the 'flexi' area of the spectrum.

Messy change situations – those which may be classified as 'flexi' – present management with a multitude of complex, interrelated and conflicting problems and issues. The 'mess' resembles, in its complexity of relationships, the structure of a spider's web. The spider builds a complex structure which, if the imagination is stretched, may be regarded as its organization. The structure is organized in such a manner that it provides a collective strength that may be brought to bear against intruders, be they a potential lunch or an aggressive predator. An organization is built on a foundation of systems which, just like those of the spider, have a common primary role of some description and may respond in a like manner when faced by an intruder, or indeed change.

When the predator begins to snip away at the threads of the web its strength weakens. Initially the problem for the spider will be a structural one, classified as a hard change. As the threads continue to be destroyed, the change moves along the spectrum to the soft end. As the web disintegrates the primary objective becomes threatened and the spider will have to reappraise the situation. Once the destruction is almost complete, all that can be done with the remaining components of the system is to use them as a means of escape. For the primary objective to succeed all the systems must be pulling in the same direction.

The systems which constitute the organization in the 1990s are complex: they each have their own formal and informal objectives which, when managed effectively, achieve the primary objective. Change in any one system, or in its relationship with others, may therefore impact on the total structure and eventually on organizational performance.

To understand the nature of a change situation that falls between the two extremities of the spectrum, the systems and their relationships must be examined as a whole. When the interaction between the human resource and the system undergoing the change becomes complex, the need to fully define the change in terms of its interactions with existing systems, individuals, groups, departments and the organization as a whole becomes a necessity. How can management begin to cope with this complexity? The answer, in part, is to represent complex change situations in diagrammatic form and view the whole process of change in systems terms.

This chapter examines a number of tools that facilitate the thorough definition, analysis and communication of the impact of messy change. The management tools covered may be applied to either hard or soft change situations, and in so doing further the problem owner's understanding of the affected environment. They are often associated with systems change, owing to their origins in systems analysis and design. It would be foolish to limit their use to systems change alone for they can be profitably employed as a precursor, providing valuable diagnostic information, to the adoption of an organizational development approach.

The change problem may be viewed in terms of the systems and associated components and elements which it affects. Management can then represent the systems in terms of their physical and attitudinal characteristics alongside the principal relationships, in diagrammatic forms. Thus the inherent complexity of the problem is reduced to manageable dimensions through diagrammatic systems representation. Diagramming conventions, such as those used by systems analysts and programmers, need not feature in 'change diagramming'. What is required is consistency within studies and subsequently standardization within the management unit. If a standard format exists and is widely used by management then it should be adopted, possibly with modifications, within the planning and managing of the change process. What is important is that the diagrams assist in the definition, analysis and communication of the change event.

Do not let preconceived notions of the complex nature of systems diagramming prevent you from employing such a powerful communications medium and analytical tool. The diagrams described and demonstrated in the pages which follow have been selected for their simplistic, yet powerful, analytical characteristics. The principal construction and application rules which govern their usage remain more or less unchanged no matter the complexity of the problem. Formal conventions and terminology from the systems analyst's vocabulary have been intentionally ignored in an effort to reduce the entry barrier to non-systems readers.

No matter your background or future career path, your analytical and communicative competencies will be enhanced through effective utilization of diagramming skills. The simple techniques described in this section should be the starting point for experimentation in diagramming as an investigative tool and a communication medium.

If you followed the previous paragraphs, having had no cause to pause for a while to deliberate the meaning of a passage and/or reread to ensure understanding, then the written word has done its job. If, on the other hand, you had difficulty grasping the 'message' on first reading then the written word, or at least the author's usage of it, has failed. Diagrams can be used to simplify the written word; they assist in definition, understanding and communication.

Figure 3.1 attempts to communicate, in a logical and concise manner, the major points raised in the last few paragraphs. The diagram simply and concisely explains that forces act upon a change situation, which is in turn integrated with the dynamic environment; this amalgamation must be defined. By viewing the amalgamation as a system and using diagrams to assist definition, we have a tool to facilitate definition, analysis and communication. Diagrams are useful tools. Let us now consider their role in systems investigations more fully.

The role of diagramming in systems investigation

Organizations are composed of numerous interrelated systems and subsystems, which in turn may be subdivided into components and ultimately into indivisible elements. These systems are designed to ensure the accomplishment of organizational goals and must, if the goals are to be achieved, operate in harmony. Machinery, technology, procedures, policies, operatives, supervisors and management are, depending on the view being taken, either systems, components or elements. Once a change impacts upon the equilibrium of a system, it, along with any interrelated systems, will be disrupted and their performance impaired. Diagramming tools assist in defining, analysing and manipulating the systems environment.

There are essentially four reasons why management should adopt certain diagramming techniques in their pursuit of the effective implementation of change:

1   Diagramming, along with the systems approach, can bring a much
    needed sense of logic and structure to messy change problems.

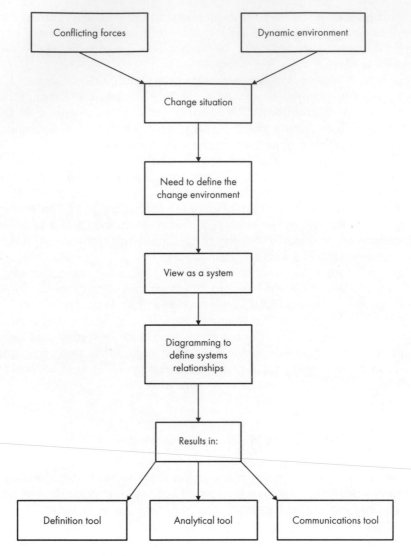

Figure 3.1   *The need for diagramming*

2   By adopting standardized diagramming techniques the problem owner will develop a clear and concise view of change environments and at the same time introduce a change handling methodology. This will simplify and standardize future change investigations, as well as provide the basis of systems specification and a relationships 'library'.

3   Unfortunately, verbal or long-winded descriptions of messy change tend to be messy in their own right. They are often ineffective in terms of their ability to provide the listener, or reader, with a clear

understanding and are generally limited in their use as analytical platforms for future deliberations. Diagrams assist the process of understanding by providing a clear and structured map of the problem and assist analysis and implementation by effectively illustrating potential developments and options.

4   The communication of ideas/options is an essential component of the change management process. Diagrams can assist the communications process by providing a standardized, impersonal and credible interface between concerned parties.

In any problem solving or systems analysis exercise one may find an effective role for diagrammatically based analysis. It is in a manager's interest to develop both a practical understanding of the available techniques and a level of expertise in applying and exploiting them. A range of diagramming tools is available for use by the change management practitioner, as illustrated in Table 3.1.

Table 3.1   Diagram types

Diagram types	Descriptor
Input/output	Shows the inputs to a system and the resulting outputs, as well as any feedback loops
Flow, process and activity	A linked representation of a series of steps, activities or events describing a process
Force field	A basic visual representation of the driving and restraining forces relating to a change event
Fishbone	Generally used to work back from a problem situation determining root causes
Multiple cause	As above
Relationship mapping	Details the relationships between 'hard' and/or 'soft' systems components
Systems mapping	Details the system(s) to be affected by a change
Influence charting (spider's web)	Charts the influences, and their linkages, on a particular system or situation

Diagrams may be employed to fully define the change process and are particularly effective when applied to the solution of complex messy problems which are capable of being considered in systems terms, those in the 'flexi' area of the change continuum, and, of course, hard physical problems. Figure 3.2 highlights each stage of the transition process in which diagramming techniques may be employed. For example, systems diagrams may assist in defining the existing steady state and may be followed by relationship maps, which would investigate the interactions between the steady state systems. Flow and process charts may both define the existing system and emphasize impact points associated with the proposed changes. All the aforementioned diagrams can be manipulated and studied to investigate the actual impact of the change; they also could be employed as communications aids. Action steps may be

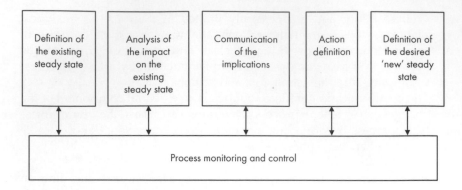

Figure 3.2   *Transition process chart*

developed through the use of networking diagrams; these would also be used to monitor progress, and once again all the diagrams could be utilized in defining the desired systems configuration.

Diagrams may be profitably employed by management when they are:

- defining and understanding the nature of those systems affected by the change (*before*)
- illustrating the means and stages associated with progress from the present to the desired situation (*during*)
- defining and understanding the nature of the desired solution/ situation (*after*).

In other words diagrammatic representations may be used to assist the problem owner when they are engaged in:

- specification/definition
- understanding
- manipulation/modelling/analysis
- communication
- implementation
- standardization.

Diagrams, or even interrelated listings, provide an effective means of defining a change event. There are a host of diagramming techniques which assist in the understanding of change, as detailed in Table 3.1.

Diagrams not only assist in defining change events but also offer a means of analysing, or plotting, developing situations; of specifying end points; and last, but certainly not least, of communicating both within and outwith the managing group. As long as the diagrams add value to the process of managing change they will have served their purpose.

By defining aspects of the system(s) undergoing change as above, the problem owner(s) will identify the extent to which the change will impact on: the relationships affected; the key influencing factors; the likely management team; and the potential reaction to the change itself. Diagramming not only facilitates definition but also leads to understanding because it allows the study of potential and actual behaviour, for both hard and soft aspects of the change.

A review of basic flow diagramming techniques

Three of the most common and revealing techniques employed by change management practitioners deal with 'flow' analysis. The first is the input/output diagram which provides an easy to follow means of investigating the input and output flows of physical materials and/or information with reference to any given system. The feedback mechanisms facilitating both control and performance measurement may also be included. Such a diagram is illustrated in Figure 3.3.

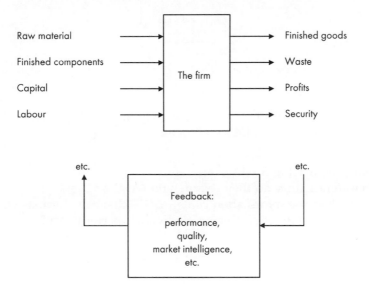

Figure 3.3   *An input/output diagram with feedback*

The second technique within this diagramming category is the traditional flow diagram, which permits the investigator to study the process steps and related activities, including interdependencies, associated with a particular system. Once again a pictorial representation provides a useful insight into a system at work, as the example contained within Figure 3.4 illustrates.

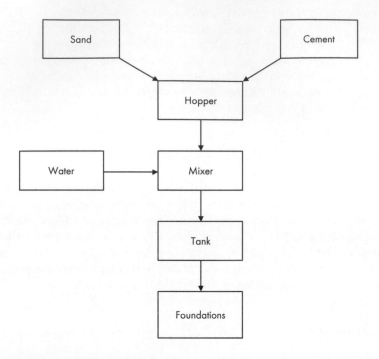

Figure 3.4   *A sample flow diagram*

Both the input/output and the flow diagrams may be further developed to incorporate such information as:

- Who does what and why?
- What information do they require and why?
- Where does the information come from – channels, formats etc.?
- What factors influence systems/individual performance?

The last diagram of this section addresses the 'softer' issues associated with systems investigation through the medium of 'flow' analysis. Activity sequence diagrams consider issues and stages of a process or elements of a system which are of a non-physical/technological nature. For example, consider the purchase of a car depicted in Figure 3.5. In such diagrams the activities associated with key decision points relating to a particular sequence of events are emphasized for subsequent study.

All three diagrams described in this section may be employed throughout the transition management process, to assist in the definition of the existing system or to indicate the steps which must be taken in achieving the goal. Finally, they may be used to help specify the desired outcome. Examples are given in Mini Cases 3.1 and 3.2.

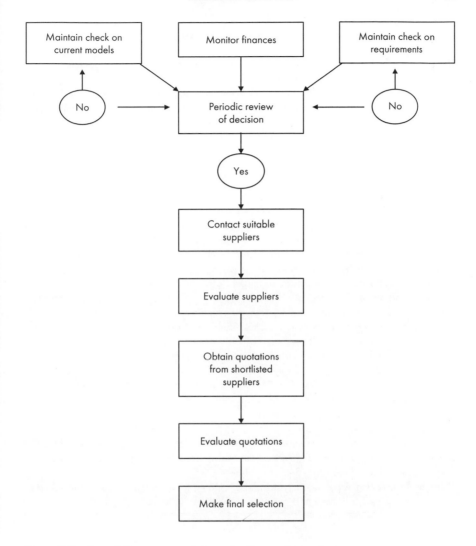

Figure 3.5   *An activity sequence diagram for the purchase of a car*

Systems relationships: the key to success

To fully understand the nature of a particular change situation, a problem owner must consider the relationships that exist between those
affected by the change. By developing a relationships map the problem
owner may begin to appreciate the systems interfaces and complexities
which are at work in the change environment.

By way of an example let us consider the relationship map in Figure
3.9 (see p. 65), which may have been applied when the UK steel industry
was undergoing privatization (it is not intended to be comprehensive).

Mini Case 3.1   Argyll and Clyde Health Board

The Argyll and Clyde Health Board, in accordance with their statutory obligations resulting from the introduction of the government White Paper entitled *Working for Patients*, were required to ensure that the processing of their Scottish morbidity records (SMRs) was enhanced in line with new performance targets which were specified within the White Paper.

The SMR is the document which records the details of each episode of care for a patient treated within a National Health Service hospital. The aggregated data for all patient transactions are used as the basis for research, epidemiological study and, possibly most importantly, as the basis for the planning and funding decisions taken by the centre for each individual Health Board.

Completed SMR data for each Scottish Board had to be lodged with the Common Services Agency (CSA) of the health service within two months from the completed collation of any given month's SMRs. The CSA collated the data for the 15 Scottish Boards and funding was subsequently allocated according to the number and types of patient treated. Prior to this, the performance target was somewhat more liberal, with SMR data for one year having to be submitted to the CSA by midsummer of the following year.

A computerized patient administration system obviated the need for paper SMR documentation and manual processing within the Argyll and Clyde Board. Its efficient operation was the ultimate responsibility of the Information Services Division (ISD). The ISD may be regarded as the problem owners in this case. Their computer centre, via the SMR standard system, processed the returns for remote hospitals.

The problem owner, who was located within ISD, produced the associated diagrams. They formed the basis for subsequent analysis of the existing systems conducted with a view to reducing SMR submission times. The diagrams constituted part of the problem definition phase and were used to illustrate the SMR production process. The activity sequence diagram, Figure 3.6, illustrates the preparation of SMR data and its subsequent transfer to the ISD processing centre. Feedback was required to validate centrally detected errors and queries. The input/output representation, Figure 3.7, depicts the entry of data into the SMR standard system. Once fully validated output had been achieved for each hospital it was aggregated and transferred to CSA for analysis.

The problem facing Argyll and Clyde will be returned to in Chapter 11, when the options for change will be considered and a solution identified.

The complex change situation that emerged from Mini Case 3.3 indicated that although at the core of the problem there was a significant system change, there was also likely to be a major organizational change. The identification of the need to integrate both schools of thought, systems and organizational, is a very common outcome of the diagnostic diagramming phase.

Systems diagramming

Having considered the problem of defining and understanding the basic influences associated with change, the next step is to investigate, in more depth, the actual systems affected by the change. Systems diagramming

Mini Case 3.2   Vitafoam and Kay Metzler Ltd

This case demonstrates the versatility of the diagramming techniques so far covered. Here a hybrid form of illustration is used to depict the change forces at work, a force field analysis, and an input/output graphic.

British Vita PLC, the parent company of both Vitafoam and Kay Metzler Ltd, wished to see a rationalization of both companies' operations. Amongst the many options available to the subsidiary organizations was a merger of operations at the current Vitafoam site. The problem owner, a member of the operational management team at the Vitafoam site in Paisley, Scotland, produced the diagram shown in Figure 3.8 (see p. 64) to assist in his understanding of the change forces at play in such a merger situation.

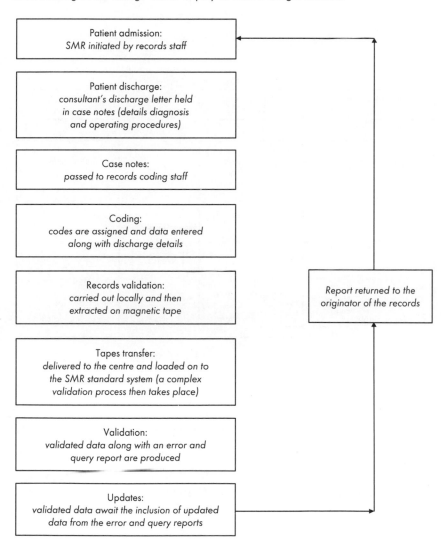

Figure 3.6   *SMR production (activity sequence)*

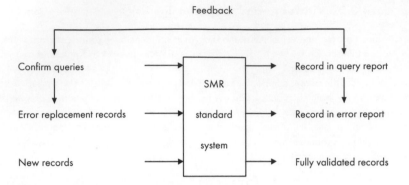

Figure 3.7   *SMR standard system (input and output diagram)*

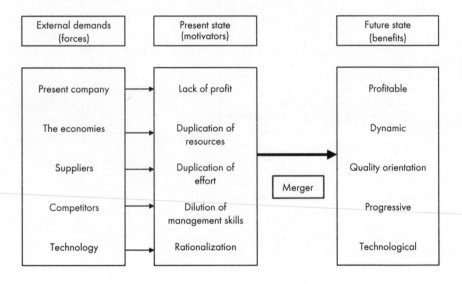

Figure 3.8   *Change analysis diagram*

is an essential component of the intervention strategy. The systems approach, through diagramming, brings a degree of sanity to messy change situations.

The principal diagramming techniques that will be employed within the intervention strategy model are as follows:

1   systems mapping
2   influence charts
3   multiple cause diagrams.

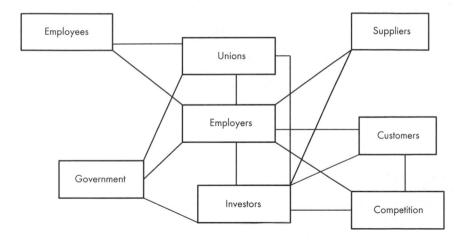

Figure 3.9   A sample relationships map

Each will be treated in turn and will be presented along with a practical case to illustrate their usage.

Systems mapping

Systems maps need not be complex or difficult to construct. Their basic function is to present a pictorial representation of the system undergoing the change and they can if necessary incorporate relevant interrelationships. The systems map is often employed in conjunction with the relationships map discussed in a previous section. The systems map identifies the systems and any subsystems associated with the problem, and the relationships map analyses the nature of the linkages between the systems, their components and their elements.

A system consists of component parts, or indeed subsystems, which in turn may be further broken down. Subdivision ceases once the element level has been reached, an element being incapable of further division. The systems approach is examined in more detail in Chapter 4. System maps can therefore be produced for all levels of the change environment. For example a map may be produced for the University of Glasgow Business School, a subsystem of the University of Glasgow, such as the one shown in Figure 3.11. This map could be further divided to show firstly the component parts of the Department of Management Studies, which could then in turn be further analysed. This is represented in the further subdivision shown in Figure 3.12.

The problem owner and/or the management team concerned with the handling of the change must decide at which level of analysis the process should cease. Not only does mapping highlight the systems involved but it also gives a clear indication of the parties who should be involved in

Mini Case 3.3 Caledonian Airmotive Ltd

Caledonian Airmotive Limited (CAL) was at the time a well-established company operating in the highly competitive international business of aero-engine overhaul. The company is the subject of one of the detailed system-related changes contained within Chapter 11.

As CAL will be dealt with in more depth in Chapter 11, all we require to know at this point is that the change dealt with the total reorganization of the accessory shop within their Prestwick site. This shop mainly serviced one-off maintenance jobs that did not pass through the rest of the works. It did however depend on many of the general manufacturing services. Therefore, it was not uncommon for the demands of the accessory shop to interfere with the efficient production flow of the mainstream manufacturing activities. Management decided to minimize disruption to mainstream engine overhaul by creating an autonomous accessory shop, which would be totally self-contained and no longer a source of disruption to other service groups.

The relationship map, Figure 3.10, was produced at an early stage in the change process to assist in determining the key players and establishing linkages between them.

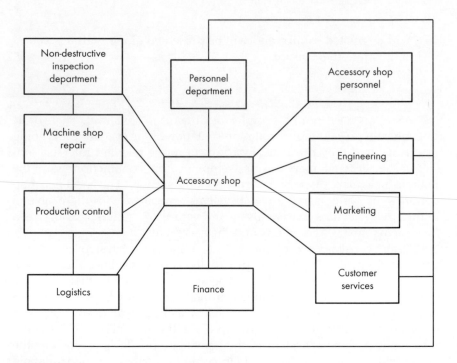

Figure 3.10 *Relationship map for the accessory shop change*

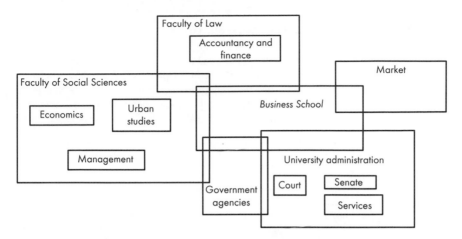

Figure 3.11   *The University of Glasgow Business School systems map*

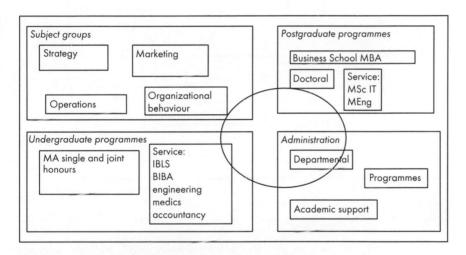

Figure 3.12   *The Department of Management Studies systems map*

the management process and at which point in the process they should
be brought in (see Mini Case 3.4).

Influence charts

The systems map is, in many ways, only of use when it is followed up by
the production of influence charts. Such charts illustrate influencing
factors. For example, what influencing factors or groups could act upon a
typical manufacturing firm? Figure 3.14 (see p. 69) depicts the potential
influences at play.

Mini Case 3.4   R. Terley Ltd (Texstyle World)

A manager from this company, an established retailer of a wide range of soft furnishings, when reviewing stockholding procedures, constructed a simple systems map. It is depicted in Figure 3.13. The map highlights the systems likely to be impacted upon by any changes to the warehousing computerized stock control system. The rationale behind the proposed changes will be returned to when considering multiple cause and effect diagrams.

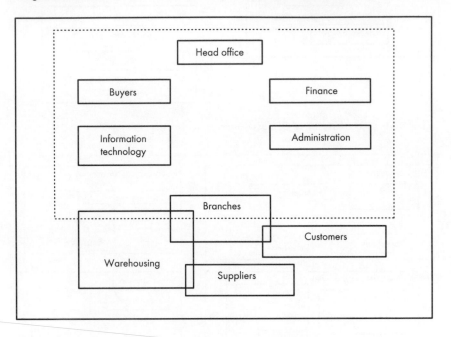

Figure 3.13   *Texstyle World systems map*

Influence diagrams connect the systems associated with the change and indicate lines of influence. Often, depending on complexity, both systems and influence diagrams can be shown as one (see Mini Case 3.5, see p. 70).

Multiple cause diagrams

A means of further developing the influence chart is to consider the causes associated with a change situation or problem. Multiple cause diagrams examine the causes behind particular events or activities and express them diagrammatically.

For example one may depict, as in Figure 3.16 (see p. 70), the factors which interact to create the energy costs within the home. From this figure the demand factors could be examined as shown in Figure 3.17 (see p. 71).

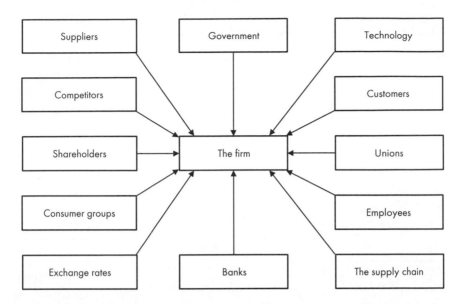

Figure 3.14 *Manufacturing influence map*

Multiple cause diagrams may be presented in a number of ways as illustrated by Mini Cases 3.6 and 3.7 (see p. 71 and p. 72). Such diagrams are of great value in determining the various factors that are behind a particular event. They identify 'cause chains' and assist in identifying the key elements.

A multi-disciplinary approach

Diagramming alone, although offering significant assistance to management, is unlikely to meet all our analytical and research needs in the field of change management. The successful management of complex situations calls upon many disciplines and the application of a wide range of theories and techniques: it truly requires a multi-disciplinary approach.

Environmental impact tests based on the previously detailed diagramming techniques, along with related investigative tools such as STEP (social, technical, economic and political) analysis, SWOT (strengths, weaknesses, opportunities and threats), scenario planning, Delphi techniques, brainstorming sessions and general auditing tools, assist in determining the nature of an impending change event. They commence the process of defining the change, but stop short of fully specifying its likely impact. That impact will be felt by the systems that constitute the organization and support its continued success.

Change can be managed by adopting a systems interventionist approach (see Part 2 'Intervention Strategies'), but only if this is done

Mini Case 3.5   Caledonian Airmotive Ltd

The change facing the accessory shop of Caledonian Airmotive has already been introduced in Mini Case 3.3. Figure 3.15 illustrates certain of the systems and factors that influenced this subsystem of the manufacturing establishment.

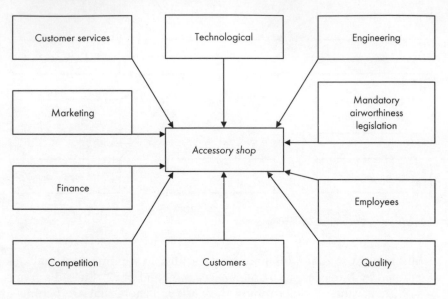

Figure 3.15   *Accessory shop influence map*

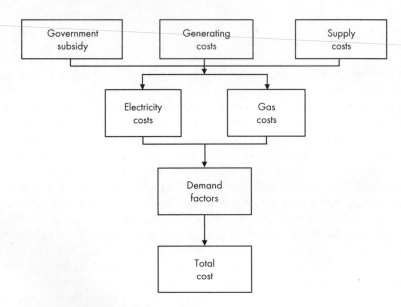

Figure 3.16   *Energy costs multiple cause diagram*

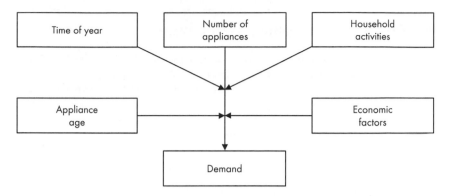

Figure 3.17   *Demand factors multiple cause diagram*

Mini Case 3.6   McGriggor Donald (Solicitors)

McGriggor Donald, a large law firm, upgraded its office IT systems. The problem owner was the Director of Administration and she produced the multiple cause diagram detailed in Figure 3.18.

Although rather simplistic, it does quite clearly indicate the reasons for the upgrade and in so doing pointed the way forward with respect to the required features of the new system. It also proved a useful means for assisting in the communication of the impending change to the office staff and acted as a focus for initial management/staff discussions.

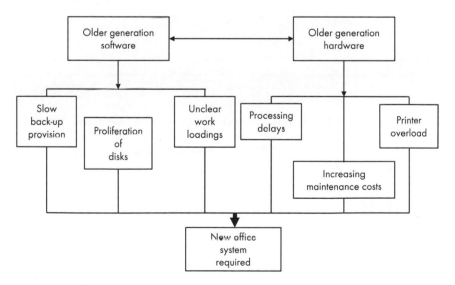

Figure 3.18   *Office IT system multiple cause diagram*

Mini Case 3.7   R. Terley Ltd (Texstyle World)

The Terley (Texstyle World) stock problem was previously introduced in Mini Case 3.4 and the associated systems map produced. The cause and effect diagram in Figure 3.19 neatly sums up the rationale behind the review of the existing computerized system. It utilizes a fishbone format.

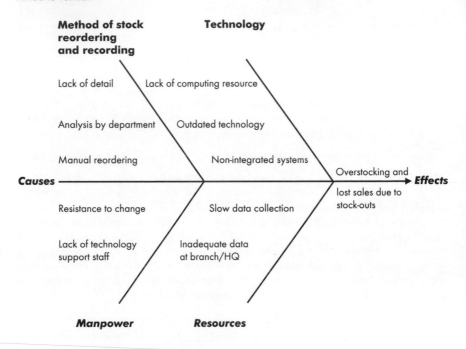

Figure 3.19   *Fishbone cause and effect diagram*

with the full knowledge that the 'softer' aspects of any complex situation must be built into the solution methodology. When one is dealing with a specific situation falling within the complex region on the change spectrum, the intelligent use of systems-based approaches will produce acceptable results. This is especially the case when environmental scanning suggests that both time and resources are significant constraints.

Major change events – those that are both complex and strategically focused – cannot be managed simply by applying interventionist models. However, intervention strategies can still assist in defining, investigating and planning for such complex situations.

When change occurs, the first questions that require attention are as follows. What exactly has been or will be affected? Can the systems and their subdivisions be defined? More importantly, however, how autonomous are the systems in question? The final practical examples relating to diagramming and change, as depicted in Mini Cases 3.8 and 3.9 (see p. 74), illustrate the value of adopting a diagramming approach when considering the impact of change.

Mini Case 3.8 British Airports Authority

The British Airports Authority (BAA) PLC recognized the potential benefits of harnessing the creative powers of the *team* as a means of further developing its competitive advantage and securing future success. To this end they instigated a 'freedom to manage' programme designed to stimulate change. The Terminal Three senior management staff at Heathrow, London, piloted the initiative. The team first identified the critical success factors as depicted in Figure 3.20.

These factors became the focus for further investigation by staff teams, led by an external consultant, with the aim of identifying what would have to be done to close the gap between the present position and the goal of achieving the freedom to manage. The pilot proved successful and was cascaded throughout BAA.

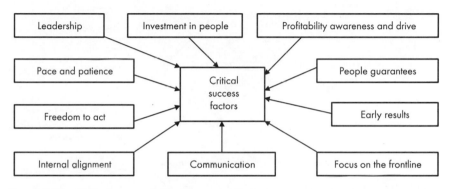

Figure 3.20 *Critical success factors*

READER ACTIVITY

Consider an airliner about to be struck by lightning. What electrical systems could it safely do without? List three:

1

2

3

Why the above? Hopefully, because you have selected systems which do not directly impact upon the ultimate purpose of the prime system, that is to fly (and land). For example, autonomous systems may include video facilities; catering services; cabin lighting; or the machine that goes 'bleep' in the cockpit!

Mini Case 3.9   Southern General NHS

The Cardiology Department of the Southern General Hospital NHS Trust assisted in servicing the European heart disease capital of the world, Glasgow. They did not, however, have any provision for cardiac rehabilitation. Such rehabilitation had been shown to be highly effective and reduced the likelihood of recurrence. In an effort to address this weakness, and in recognition that they were not the sole providers of cardiac care, the Trust, through its cardiology team, set about addressing the problem.

In an effort to understand the impact of change the team set about identifying the systems which would be affected by the introduction of a cardiac rehabilitation service. They produced the diagram illustrated in Figure 3.21.

By diagramming the systems implications of the proposed change, the cardiology team quickly identified the key players. In so doing they identified additional team members and those who must be kept informed; they had begun to manage the change.

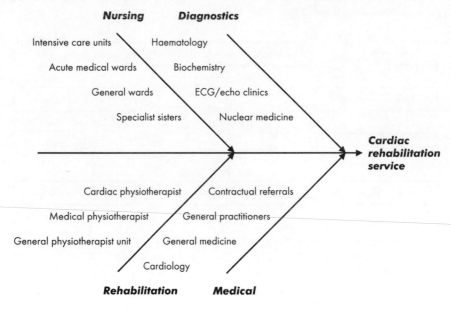

Figure 3.21   Cardiac change map

PART 2

Intervention Strategies

4 The Systems Approach to Change

In change management, the systems approach is the term given to the analysis of change situations that is based on a systems view of the problem. The intervention strategy model (ISM), which forms the basis of this chapter, is designed with the belief that messy change situations may be effectively managed through the application of systems thinking.

The application of the systems approach is not limited to the 'hard' end of the change spectrum. All management processes and structures may be described in systems terms. Therefore a systems analysis of the change situation, no matter how complex and people oriented the transition may be, will provide meaningful results for the problem owner(s). It would be incorrect to suggest that the application of an intervention model such as ISM to an extreme organizational change would produce in itself a detailed solution. It could, however, provide a framework for initial investigation, and/or a mechanism for more detailed analysis of specific change issues as discussed in Part 3 'The Organization Development Model'.

Prior to considering the actual framework of an intervention model it is necessary to develop an understanding of systems-related terminology.

What is a system?

From the perspective of managing change a system may be defined as being an organized assembly of components, which are related in such a way that the behaviour of any individual component will influence the overall status of the system. It is impossible to think of any physical mechanism or process that cannot be described in systems terms. Similarly, most managerial processes and functions may also be described in a systematic manner. All systems, physical or 'soft', must have a predetermined objective that the interrelated components strive to achieve.

Given that a system must have an objective and that it is interrelated with other systems associated with its environment, then the accomplishment of the objective must be of interest to all concerned. It is this shared interest that warrants the application of a systems approach. Any system that impinges on the activities of others must be investigated in the light of its associations. Changes in any given system will affect both its own internal workings and very possibly those of interrelated external systems. There is therefore a need to accurately define the system environment experiencing a change prior to the development of a transition path. This requirement highlights the importance of the previous chapter, which illustrated the use of diagramming techniques for the purpose of achieving systems definitions. Such techniques assist the problem owner in defining the nature and impact of systems-related changes from both a physical and an organizational perspective.

The motor car, when considered in terms of its basic transportation role, provides a simple example of interrelated systems dependencies, as Table 4.1 illustrates. The definition of the systems under study depends, to a great extent, on both the position of the reviewer in relation to the system and the purpose of the study. If the review is taking place from a position that is concerned simply with the car as a means of transportation, then the driver is a subsystem. However, a doctor assessing medical competence associated with the driver, or a manager selecting a delivery driver, may consider the 'driver' to be a total system in its own right. The fuel pump may be regarded as a total system by a mechanic working on a problem within its many mechanisms. The car itself may be seen as a subsystem if one considers the household and its operations as the greater system. The term 'element' is also introduced to describe the gearshift. An element is that part of a system or component which cannot or need not be broken down any further.

Table 4.1   Interrelated systems dependencies

Systems level	Status	Objective
The car	System	To transport occupants and associated artefacts
The driver	Subsystem	To manage and direct the system
The engine	Subsystem	To provide the car's driving force
The gearbox	Subsystem	To engage and influence the driving force
The fuel pump	Component	To provide petrol to the combustion chamber
The gearshift	Element	To facilitate driver/gearbox interaction

System objectives need not be singular, as they are in this example. The car's objective is to provide transport but this may be subdivided and thus provide a greater insight into the system as a whole. It is important to consider not only the prime objective but also any associated sub-objectives as they may be of particular interest to both internal analysis of the system under study and any other related external systems. Let us again take the car as an example and consider a possible objectives tree as shown in Figure 4.1. Transport may be the primary objective but economy and safety could be secondary aims, provided

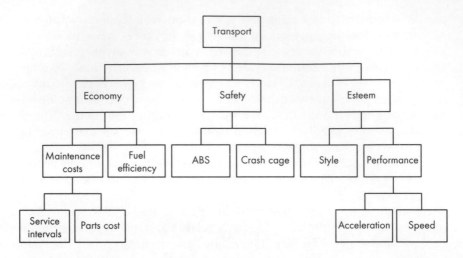

Figure 4.1   *Car objectives tree*

that the car still offers reasonable looks, adequate performance and personal esteem for the owner.

Objective trees, similar in construction to the one illustrated in Figure 4.1, are produced in most systems investigations. It is seldom enough simply to consider the primary purpose of a system or the macro-objective of a proposed change. The various elements of the associated change environment may place greater emphasis on particular sub-objectives; to ignore this possibility could lead to a problem owner poorly defining the relationships within the affected environment.

Systems autonomy and behaviour

Systems autonomy

The diagramming techniques previously introduced, along with the construction of objective trees, provide the problem owner with the ability to define the systems environment effectively, prior to and/or during a change event. Care must be taken to define the scope of the change environment in an accurate manner. To accomplish this, consideration and effort must be devoted to determining the degree of systems autonomy existing within the change environment. Within any given environment its systems and their internal workings will have both collective and individual boundaries. The problem owner must ensure that these boundaries are set when defining the change in such a way as to exclude any non-essential relationships. A change environment consists of all systems both directly and indirectly affected; it also includes all associated subsystems. It is part of the 'art' of systems diagramming to set the boundaries at the appropriate level – to include all relevant factors but exclude all irrelevancies.

It is therefore necessary for the systems investigator(s) to determine the degree to which the core system under investigation may be considered in isolation. Throughout an investigation we must constantly ask the following questions, bearing in mind the objective, nature and impact of the proposed change:

- How autonomous are the systems?
- What relationships exist?
- How relevant are they?
- Will developments lead to redefinition of boundaries?
- Can the complexities of the change environment be simplified?

READER ACTIVITY

Consider your next family holiday, or one from the past. Who must be considered and why, and what associated household-related systems must be adjusted?

The problem owner, wishing to conduct a thorough systems definition, must at all times remember the purpose of the study. Systems are not of interest because of their inherent physical structures, but rather for what those structures achieve – their aims, interactions and behaviour. Systems autonomy should be considered in light of the study objectives.

Systems behaviour

The consideration of the degree of autonomy associated with a given system determines its boundaries in relation to the study objectives. What is actually being considered is the behaviour of the systems with particular reference to the nature and relevance of their internal and external relationships. A study of systems behaviour requires that the following three process areas be reviewed:

1 the physical processes constituting the operational system
2 the communications processes handling the transfer of 'information' within and between systems
3 the monitoring processes maintaining system stability.

By reviewing the process linkages one may begin to determine the degree of autonomy existing within the various constituent parts of the system. It is how the system behaves, in relation to both internal and external change stimuli, that must be considered. A systems investigation should commence with a detailed specification and analysis of the change environment. Having determined the general environment, the investigator then focuses on eliminating irrelevancies. This is achieved by considering the study objectives with reference to the behaviour and autonomy of the systems under review.

READER ACTIVITY

Once again consider the holiday. How did the systems and their associated components behave? Did the dog howl at the thought of the kennels? Did junior jump with joy at the thought of Disneyland? Who stayed quiet and reflective? Did Sara not want to go because of the destination, or because she would have to leave her boyfriend in the clutches of Susan, her 'best friend'?

The intervention strategy

The previous chapters have examined both the nature of change and the means of coping with its inherent complexity. Now what is required is some means of handling, in a structured manner, the analysis and implementation of a change situation. An intervention strategy may be regarded as the procedural methodology for successfully intervening in the working processes of the original system. The ultimate result should be a stable new environment, which incorporates the desired changes.

The remainder of this chapter is dedicated to the introduction and examination of a practical systems intervention model, termed the intervention strategy model (ISM). This is very much a hybrid model which is firmly based on the traditional investigative techniques associated with the schools of operational and systems management. Elements and underlying premises associated with the systems intervention strategy (SIS) developed by the Open Business School and the total project management model (TPMM), which is the subject of Chapter 6, a product of the University of Glasgow Business School (Paton and Southern, 1990), have been incorporated within the ISM. All three models have been extensively tried and tested on countless practising managers and their associated organizations. ISM forms the basis of the 'Managing change' module in the Glasgow MBA, as does TPMM in the 'Operations management' module. In addition, both models have been employed on a number of successful consultancy projects. User feedback has at all times been positive and the models have found a place in many professional managers' toolkits.

In previous chapters, the basic investigative methodology associated with the operational and systems management schools was implicitly introduced:

1 objective clarification
2 data capture and performance indicators
3 systems diagnostics

4 systems analysis
5 determination of solution options
6 solution evaluation

7 solution implementation
8 appraisal and monitoring.

As we can see, the methodology consists of three phases. The definition phase defines the objectives and the general problem environment and sets the investigative framework. This is followed by an evaluation or design phase, of which the first step is to determine the most appropriate analytical and/or research procedures to employ. Having made this selection, the investigator analyses the data collected in the definition phase to produce a range of potential solutions. These solutions are then subsequently evaluated against the performance criteria associated with the investigation's objectives and an optimal solution is identified. The final phase is that of implementation during which the plan for introducing and monitoring the solution is devised.

Systems intervention models all share this basic three-phase approach. The actual terminology used to describe component parts of the model and the emphasis placed upon various elements within each phase may differ, but the underlying framework remains unchanged. However, the intervention strategies are much more than basic decision-making frameworks. They, for example, stress the importance of systems analysis, participative group work, iterative mechanisms, organizational issues and much more, as the following sections and the remainder of Part 2 will illustrate.

The ISM methodology emphasizes the linkages between the second and third phases. In particular the need to consider implementation issues within the design and evaluation phase to ensure acceptance of the change at a later date is stressed. The user is also advised to ensure the incorporation of the 'softer' issues associated with the project and where appropriate employ organizational development practices. The word 'system' has been deliberately omitted from the title, as the model can be applied to both specific systems-related change and more general management problem solving situations.

Change, be it technological, personal, organizational or operational, must at some point impinge upon a 'system'. A system's view of the process, operation, relationship and/or culture experiencing change is an essential feature of ISM. However, the word 'system' often alienates those of a non-technical background. ISM does not require the user to be familiar with systems analysis and design. The diagrams employed have been previously outlined and are neither overly technical nor complex, and their subsequent analysis need not be of a particularly quantitative nature.

By defining a change situation in systems terms, the problem owner may clearly define the nature of the change: those affected by the change, the boundary and scope of the change, the relationships affected by the change etc. A systems-based intervention strategy is a powerful change management tool.

The three phases of intervention

Successful systems intervention, or problem formulation and solution, requires the management team or the individual to proceed through the three interdependent phases until the management objectives have been achieved. The three basic phases of ISM are highlighted in Figure 4.2.

Problem initialization may sound impressive and conjure up images of a complex management process, but in reality its meaning is relatively simple. It means that a change situation has been identified and that the process of managing the change is about to commence. A problem owner and possibly a supporting group will have been identified and charged with handling the transition from the old to the new. Chapter 2 stressed the importance of ensuring that the problem owner was committed to the task at hand and possessed, or had access to, the necessary managerial expertise and skill to manage the transition process. For the purposes of this review of ISM the problem owner will be deemed to be the actual manager of the transition process. Those individuals, along with the problem owner, who eventually are identified as being part of the managing team will be termed the change agents. The nucleus of the management team will be formed during problem initialization. It may alter to reflect the environment affected by the change and the skills required in managing the problem.

The definition phase involves the in-depth specification and study of the change situation, from both a historical and a futuristic viewpoint. The second phase generates and evaluates the potential solution options. The third phase, that of implementation, develops the action plans which should successfully introduce the outputs of the design phase. Owing to the inherent dynamic nature of operational, organizational and business environments, it is essential that, during each of the phases, the systems affected be constantly monitored. This should occur on both an internal and an external basis, to ensure the validity of associated assumptions,

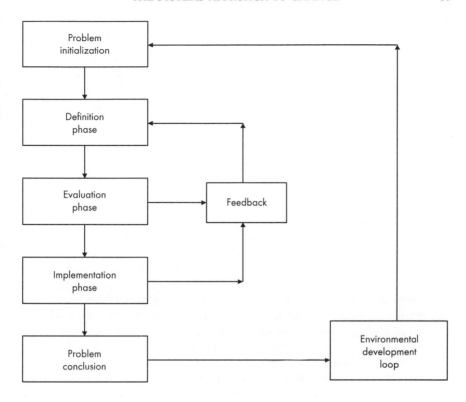

Figure 4.2   *The basic phases of the intervention strategy model (ISM)*

objectives, information and analysis. At any point, it may be necessary to iterate back to an earlier stage for the purpose of incorporating a new development, or factor, which may influence the outcome.

Iterations are an essential feature of an effective change or problem management strategy. For this reason, it is often advisable to conduct a 'quick and dirty' analysis of the change, prior to a more formal and detailed investigation. This should reduce the need for numerous time-consuming iterations once the 'intervention' has formally commenced.

Figure 4.2 shows an environmental development feedback loop, linking the final outcome, the 'new environment', with that of the 'initial situation'. The purpose of this loop is simply to illustrate that the change cycle is never complete. Dynamic environmental factors will, over a period of time, necessitate additional change and so the process will once more commence. As operational, organizational and competitive environments continue to develop, management must adopt a proactive stance, thus anticipating and managing the inevitable change to their advantage. The ability to handle, in an effective manner, the transition between 'steady state' situations should be regarded as a potential source of competitive advantage.

The intervention strategy model (ISM)

The individual stages associated with each phase of the model are shown in Figure 4.3. The adoption of the model will provide a means of managing the change cycle in a structured, logical, interactive and visible manner. It facilitates the total planning and control of a systems-oriented change.

A number of important points must be noted relating to the effective and efficient use of the model prior to investigating each of the individual stages. They are as follows:

- Iterations may be required at any point, within or between phases, owing to developing environmental factors. Once the desired position has been reached, further environmental developments may cause the transition process to be re-entered at some later date.
- Problem owners and any other associated change agents should be involved throughout. It is essential they are committed to the initiative as they are the driving forces.
- There is a tendency to rush through the diagnostic phase, with problem owners basing assumptions on their own brand of 'common sense'. Time spent getting it right first time is seldom wasted. Specification and description are crucial to the understanding of a change situation.
- It is always advisable to attempt to produce quantifiable performance indicators in stage 3, as they will simplify the evaluation process in stage 6.
- It is virtually impossible not to start thinking about options during the diagnostic phase, especially on a 'live' problem. There is no harm in this, but do not skip stages. Put the options aside until stage 4.

Having generated a host of options, some form of screening must take place. Often one will find that certain options may be eliminated, for implementation reasons, or because they are dependent upon uncontrollable factors. Such options should be removed prior to more formal evaluation. Occasionally, options may have been entertained for 'political' reasons. For example, suggestions that are less than suitable may have to be tolerated to avoid alienation, or because they come from key players who expect to be listened to and acknowledged. Such options may be edited out at this stage; they may be lost or forgotten for long enough to allow more plausible alternatives to take hold.

The options and solutions generated and evaluated within the second phase need not relate to individual and unrelated entities. It is often the case that chains of interrelated options and solutions have to be dealt with and care taken to ensure they are evaluated as a total entity.

The distinction between the second and third phases is rather blurred. The second phase concludes with the option evaluation. The implementation phase commences with the development of implementation

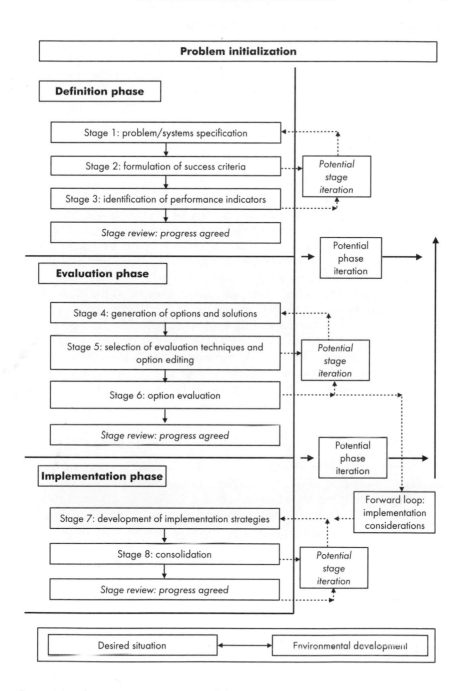

Figure 4.3   *The intervention strategy model*

strategies. However, for effective implementation to take place it must itself be considered during the evaluation phase. Options may on occasion have to be considered in the light of their ease of implementation. Users of ISM must be prepared to jump forward during the evaluation phase to consider implementation.

The stages of ISM

The key to successful change management is firstly the identification of the appropriate problem owners and secondly the selection of a management methodology to provide the means of handling the transition. Provision of adequate resources and support is crucial. It is worth noting that key, possibly senior, stakeholders might not be on the team directly addressing the change; however, they must be kept informed of developments and their support secured and managed.

Assuming the players have been identified, they must decide on their subsequent course of action. ISM should be selected when the impending or existing change situation exhibits tendencies towards the hard end of the change spectrum. It should be noted that the systems approach could on occasion be employed to tackle the initial stages of softer organizational problems. Long-term solutions would not be generated, but the problem owner would have 'kick-started' the change process and this can be useful when time is of the essence.

Definition phase

Time spent defining a change event – its nature, impact and repercussions – will pay dividends as the management process develops. Accurately describing the change allows the managing team to adjust membership if required; assess cultural impacts; examine, through system mapping techniques, relationships, attitudes and causes; and begin to address the change holistically.

Specification then moves on to the formulation of the success criteria. The principal objectives are identified, along with any sub-objectives and/or constraints, and against each are assigned success criteria.

STAGE 1: PROBLEM/SYSTEMS SPECIFICATION AND DESCRIPTION   Management must, through the problem owner(s) and with the assistance of interested parties, develop their understanding of the situation. The change, or problem, must be specified in systems terms and the complexity reduced so as to isolate and determine the systems interactions, relationships and cultures.

It is at this stage that one employs the previously outlined diagramming techniques as a means of assisting definition and analysis. Meetings and interviews will be conducted, experience sought and historical data examined, in an effort to construct an accurate picture of the present system and the likely impact of the changes. As this is likely to represent the first formal notification of the change one must tread lightly, unfreeze the present system in such a way as to minimize the likelihood of resistance and non-cooperation. Mistakes made here in communicating the impending change to interested parties will create both immediate and future difficulties. The problem owner requires cooperation if the true nature and impact of the change are to be defined. In messy change situations, diagramming and defining the change must be seen as a group activity.

STAGE 2: FORMULATION OF SUCCESS CRITERIA   The success criteria associated with a particular change situation may be defined in two ways. The first, and most common, involves the setting of objectives and constraints. The second is merely a corruption of the first in that it generates options, or paths, which are tagged on to the original objective. For analytical and communicative purposes it is always best to produce objectives and constraints. They are simpler to understand and can be more readily associated with performance measures. Options are messy to deal with and have to be broken down at a later stage to determine specific measures of success.

An example of an option masquerading as an objective could be a phrase such as 'Improve productivity by reducing manning levels'. A solution or option has followed the objective. This tends to result in the problem owner(s) focusing in on this option without fully considering alternatives, a dangerous and unimaginative course of action.

Objectives may be derived from the rationale behind the change and constraints generally emerge from the resources that have been allocated to the task, or more accurately the lack of them. It would be fair to say that the normal constraints facing management in change situations are time and money. Constraints may also be traced to both the nature of the systems and the cultures affected. Even when objectives and constraints appear to be clear and unambiguous the problem owner(s) must ensure that any less obvious sub-objectives, along with any associated constraints, have been identified.

It is always advisable to construct a prioritized objectives tree, with associated constraints incorporated. Figure 4.4 illustrates such a tree. It considers the objectives and their ranking which may be associated with the need to upgrade the size of the family home owing to a pending 'population explosion'. Priorities are numbered, with the number '1' indicating the greatest priority. Constraints are shown in parentheses. Figure 4.4 is only a first draft, but it could quickly develop into a complex network of interrelated objectives.

This objectives tree can, during the evaluation stages 4, 5 and 6, be developed further to include the options for achieving the objectives. In

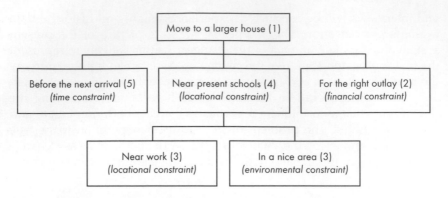

Figure 4.4   *Prioritized objectives tree*

turn the generated option paths can then form the basis of an implementation strategy.

STAGE 3: IDENTIFICATION OF PERFORMANCE MEASURES   Having decided
what the objectives of the exercise are, it is necessary to formulate appropriate measures for each one. If this is not done at this point, then how can
the problem owner evaluate the options generated subsequently?

Where possible it is best to identify quantifiable measures, such as
costs, savings, volume, labour and time. When this is not possible then
the measures should be graded in some way, e.g. seeding or ranking
could be employed. Measures can be entered on the objectives tree, thus
providing one descriptive representation of what is to be achieved and
how its success will be measured. This provides an ideal focal point for
the subsequent evaluation phase and also communicates in a logical
fashion the aims of the change.

READER ACTIVITY

Consider a forthcoming change, at work, at home or in another arena of
personal activity. Now complete the following:

- Through diagramming identify the key players, their relationships and
  lastly their anticipated reaction to the proposed change.
- Identify the primary objective of the change and any associated sub-
  objectives; for each identify a valid measure of success.
- Identify and relate any constraints associated with the project.
- Develop the above by conducting further environmental tests, for
  example, TROPICS, SWOT or STEP.

Now, briefly detail how you would proceed: who would be involved, how
would you structure the option evaluation phase, and where would you
place the change on the spectrum?

Table 4.2   *Option generation*

Attitude surveys	Ideas writing
Brainstorming (experience)	Interviews
Comparison analysis	Market research
Delphi	Supply chain research
Desk research	Story/scenarios telling
Focus groups	Structured meetings
Gap analysis	Talking wall

Evaluation phase

The definition phase should have highlighted the key players in the change process: they should, in some way, be involved in the generation of potential solutions to the problem. However, dependent upon the outcomes of the definition phase, they may need to be joined by additional stakeholders: indeed, some of the original team may have to be dropped.

STAGE 4: GENERATION OF OPTIONS OR SOLUTIONS   A wide range of techniques (Table 4.2) is available to the problem owner(s) which assist in option generation. It is outwith the scope of this text to investigate these techniques; however, the reader will see many of them detailed and practised within this and other chapters.

Many of the benefits associated with adopting a collective solution methodology will be lost if the groups and teams involved are not operating effectively. Very often, especially when those coming together do not generally function as a work team, it is best to engage in some form of structured team building. This should firstly break the ice, and secondly raise the level of performance. Facilitating the learning development process is crucial to the success of group-based approaches. Vennix (1996) develops this point and proposes adopting systems-based dynamics into team building, a focus on structure and process to gain results.

It is important not to take too blinkered a view of the change during the option-generating sessions. A variety of possibilities and opportunities should be considered. There is no need to worry about 100 per cent relevance, as any sub-optimal options may be screened out in the subsequent evaluation.

The participating individuals and groups must see such sessions as being constructive and influential. They should not become cosmetic smokescreens for the tabling of preconceived options. If this happens, those involved may withdraw support and take a more reactive stance. To this end sensitivity must be shown towards the promoter of even the most ridiculous options.

STAGE 5: SELECTION OF APPROPRIATE EVALUATION TECHNIQUES AND OPTION EDITING   Having identified the potential options or solutions, which may of course be presented as 'strings' of options rather than discrete solutions, the investigator must then evaluate them. Firstly, a brief comparative study of the options and the predetermined success criteria will act as initial screening devices. It is important not to alienate those who have contributed suggestions. Secondly, a range of evaluation techniques must be selected and applied, for example:

- Examination and manipulation of the previously developed diagrams should assist in determining the impact of the solution option(s) upon the systems environment.
- Physical and computer simulations may assist in determining operational viability – especially in situations where real-life experimentation could be 'costly'.
- Investment, cash flow and cost–benefit analysis should assist in determining the likely return on investment and the projected cash flows.
- Project management techniques, such as network analysis, will test the potential benefits, time scales and resource implications of implementation.
- Environmental impact analysis may be employed to establish the 'hidden' environmental cost of adopting particular solutions.
- Strategic and cultural fit must be considered: will proposals match intended strategic developments and does the existing culture support the changes?

This initial formal screening should eliminate sub-optimal options, as well as develop an understanding of the interrelationships and order of option paths and linkages. Remember that options need not be stand-alone activities: they may form paths, courses of activities that must be considered as a group. The analysis within this stage need not be quantitative. Subjective assessments of an option's suitability may be conducted when there are non-quantifiable performance indicators. Subjective assessments are best conducted in an open and participative manner, thus ensuring that accusations of bias and skullduggery are minimized.

STAGE 6: OPTION EVALUATION   This stage constitutes the final hurdle of the evaluation phase. Here, options are evaluated against the previously determined change objectives, in particular the performance measures previously identified in stage 3.

A tabular format may be used to conduct the evaluation. Objectives, along with their associated performance measures, are entered as a prioritized listing on the left. Individual options and/or option chains are entered along the top. Factual data and/or calculated weightings are

Table 4.3   *Evaluation table*

Objective/measure	Priority	Option A	Option B	Option C	Option D	Optimal
Cost (£)						
(constraint: < £25K)	3	10K	22K	15K	12.5K	A
Performance:						
0–60 mph (seconds)	1	10	8	8	12	B
top speed (mph)		99	130	116	109	
Safety	4	Low	High?	High	Medium	C
Esteem	2	Low	High	Medium	Medium	B

entered in the appropriate box corresponding to the option's performance against a particular objective measure.

The example shown, Table 4.3, illustrates the use of such a format for the selection of a new family car based on four objectives and a choice of four models (the options). The safety and esteem objectives can only be assessed against subjective values derived from data gleaned from the motoring press. A grading system would have to be employed. Given the indicated priority for each objective, the selected model would be B. Modifications to any of the variables can be easily introduced and the priority system altered to illustrate greater differentials. For example, let us assume that the driver, owing to a recent addition to the family, increases the priority on safety to 1 and that on cost to 2, while down-grading performance and esteem to a negative digit. The selection may then alter to model D.

This simple example illustrates the visual impact of the tabular presentation and indicates how it may be used as a focal point for discussion and the consideration of 'what if?' scenarios.

The process of option evaluation must be conducted with reference to subsequent implementation. A forward loop is incorporated within the model to emphasize the importance of this factor. This can be formally addressed by ensuring that implementation objectives are built into the original objectives tree, thus resulting in the production of at least sub-jective measures of success relating to implementation issues. Unless implementation objectives or constraints, with their associated measures of success, have been included in the definition phase then the strategy will be untested against the rigours of implementation. Will it be accepted? Are staff trained? Has it been fully communicated and understood?

Implementation phase

Assuming all has gone well, the foundations of an achievable strategy to deal with the change will have been laid. One danger – and practitioners will testify to its prevalence – is that too much time will have been spent on developing a solution and too little left for implementation. In such cases all the good work will have been in vain. The 'trinity' of change, previously noted, must be adhered to throughout the application of ISM. Stay focused, remember the goal and ensure task completion.

STAGE 7: DEVELOPMENT OF IMPLEMENTATION STRATEGIES   By this stage in the change management process, or in any other form of problem analysis or systems investigation, the detailed foundations of a successful conclusion to the project have been laid. Objectives are clear and current, options are selected and reviewed and the system is well defined and understood. Now all that is left is to package the findings into a coherent whole and introduce the changes to the system.

It may sound simple, but it never is. It is at the point of implementation that the full impact of the change will be recognized by all those likely to be affected. Only now will the problem owner discover the extent to which a shared perception was reached. In problems with truly 'hard' systems there will be little or no resistance and the physical change will go ahead, but as one gravitates towards the 'softer' end of the change continuum the risk of latent resistance is always a worrying factor.

To ensure the successful implementation of change via ISM the following key success factors must be adhered to:

- The foundation of effective change management lies in a comprehensive definition of the change situation: 'act in haste and repent at leisure'.
- Participation of those likely to be affected is crucial.
- Change calls upon a wide range of competencies to be employed. A team-based approach is likely to produce the best results, assuming it is 'facilitated' by a skilled exponent of change.
- Visible and tangible senior management support is essential.
- An open mind must be kept, effective communication must be striven for and the change must be 'marketed'.
- Sensitivity and understanding should be displayed when dealing with those who may feel threatened by the change.
- Failure to provide the resources, development and training required to handle the change will be disastrous: prepare staff to cope.
- Organizational structures and forward looking strategies which welcome change and see it as an opportunity will greatly enhance the environment for change and thus ease the change agent's task.

There are essentially only three basic implementation strategies available and they are as follows:

1 pilot studies
2 parallel running
3 big bang.

Pilot studies provide the greatest opportunity for subsequent review of the change. Assumptions and procedures can be tested, arguments developed and the likely future acceptance of the fully implemented change increased. But they also delay full implementation, and they allow those who may wish to resist the change to adopt delaying tactics. In addition, the environment does not stand still; delays to implementation may render the original solution sub-optimal and therefore necessitate a review of the whole process.

Often the proposed changes will have a dramatic effect not only on those parts of the system directly affected but also on all associated systems. Under these circumstances one may adopt a parallel-running implementation strategy. Slowly phase out the old system as the new becomes more reliable and understood.

Big bang implementation maximizes the speed of change but it can also generate the maximum resistance to the change, at least in the short term. Like most things in life, compromise generally provides the answer, and a blend of the three strategies is normally found.

Later chapters will deal with the development of implementation strategies in more depth, from both a systems and an organizational development perspective. But for the present, remember that to gain a shared perception of a problem, and commitment to its solution, it is essential to involve those affected by it in the decision-making process and to ensure that they have the knowledge, skills and tools to handle the change.

STAGE 8: CONSOLIDATION   Armed with an implementation strategy designed to maximize the probability of success and acceptance, the agents introduce the change; but we have not yet finished. Old systems and practices, just like old habits, die hard. It takes time for a new system or change to be fully accepted. Skilful communication, visual support from above and provision of adequate support to those affected, are required throughout this stage. Initial changes must be followed up, and both protection and enforcement of the new system will be required. It is up to the problem owners, the agents of the change, to nurture the growth of the new, while encouraging the peaceful demise of the old. Implementation is not the end of the process. Lessons learned must be openly discussed and communicated. Mini Cases 4.1 and 4.2 provide examples.

The 'quick and dirty' analysis

The impression may have been given that the adoption of ISM will force the change agents into a protracted period of consultation, negotiation and deliberation. In many instances the nature of the change will be such that its magnitude will necessitate a lengthy and meticulous transition

Mini Case 4.1   British Airports Authority

Having identified a need to change, to match organizational, managerial and employee strategies with those of the business, BAA faced the question of how to the energize those responsible for managing the future within an environment which challenges the past and threatens their position.

BAA ensured that their empowerment programme was driven and owned by their middle to senior management team. To ensure that their customer focused business produced results they intended to empower staff, democratize the communications processes, and ensure business results. Such moves can threaten the position, authority and stability of the middle management team, which is ultimately responsible for implementation.

BAA ensured that middle management were at the centre of the design, development and implementation of their 'freedom to manage' programme: they owned it, they transferred it to others, they developed their 'new' role and they guaranteed personal and organizational success.

Mini Case 4.2   Vision

Implementing change obviously calls upon both basic and advanced planning and control techniques. However, managing significant change events requires the energizing of many disparate individuals and groups to achieve the predetermined goals. Richard T. Pascale (1994) identifies the need to 'manage the present from the future' when dealing with major 'transformation' programmes. He suggests that British Airways in the 1980s, Thomas Cook in the 1990s, along with many others such as Haagen-Dazs, recognized the need to project their goals and identify achievable, yet challenging, visions of the future. From these visions a set of goals was identified and projected backward in time to the present; each organization then determined whom, what and when to move forward. They took only what was needed; they left the baggage of the past behind.

Successful implementation of change is dependent upon many variables. However, if one encumbers the prime movers with the emotional and moribund baggage of the past then they will pull and push it with ever increasing loathing towards future goals. It is far better to free them to select the best of the past and transport it to a future ideal.

process. In situations where either the nature of the change is such that its impact will be limited, or the time scales involved dictate a speedy conclusion to the problem, or both, the application of ISM may be conducted in what may be termed a 'quick and dirty' manner (Q&D for short). A small group can drive themselves through the model and arrive at a solution which may not be the optimal one, but it will at least have addressed and incorporated the key factors associated with the change environment.

A Q&D analysis can also be a useful starting point for the change agents tackling a more complex problem. It will indicate key factors and potential barriers to change. It will highlight the principal players and give an indication of resource requirements. Such an analysis will at an early stage set the scene for things to come and provide the change agents with a valuable insight into the complexities of the transition process.

The iterative nature of the model

A principal aspect of the model is its iterative nature. Although the model has been described in a stage-by-stage sequential manner, one must not forget the feedback loops. These have been incorporated into the design to facilitate the return to previously completed stages in the light of environmental changes. In addition, each phase is concluded with a review activity. The first two phases conclude with an agreement from those involved that the stage sequence is complete and all agree with the decisions and conclusions reached. Ownership of the problem as it develops is thus maintained. The final phase concludes with a debrief activity. What were the management lessons associated with the transition process, and how can things be improved the next time?

To date, this chapter has mainly highlighted the 'macro' aspects of the model's iterative nature, in particular the need to be aware of the continuous cycle of change which affects all systems. But the need for what may be termed 'micro' iterations also exists. Such iterations take place during 'real time', while the transition process is actually occurring. The model design incorporates feedback loops between each of the stages so as to emphasize the importance to the user of constantly updating and monitoring the system environment.

Environmental shifts which affect the basic definition of the system(s) undergoing change must be incorporated into the first phase of the model, and their impact assessed. If the impact is such that the system definitions and relationships are altered then this must be appropriately incorporated in the subsequent stages of the model. Iterations may not all result in a complete reappraisal of the definition phase. The feedback may be from the implementation to the design phase; such would be the case if resource allocations altered prior to implementation and rendered a selected solution path redundant.

Living with reality

The reality for most managers, in today's changing world, with limited resources and time, is that they are simply 'snowed under' with work. Although they know how to manage change they simply do not have the time to do it justice. If applied on a 'quick and dirty' basis, possibly with only a core team involved and a competent and motivated change agent, then ISM can often show a clear way forward. It may not produce an optimal result for the long term, but it may secure short- to medium-term results. The following quote may help justify such hasty action: 'Details are the vermin that destroy great work' (Voltaire, 1698–1778).

Managing the future

Managers, organizations and the societies they serve would be foolish, fatalistic, if they failed to realize the necessity of planning for the future. Planning for planning's sake must be avoided. The ultimate failure of centralist planning initiatives, such as those adopted by the Soviet Union and China, and by many corporations in the 1960s and 1970s illustrate the need to be responsive. Plans must be flexible and in tune with the environment in which they are implemented. Operating environments, in the broadest sense of the term, need to be understood and managerial actions need to reflect their complexities and intentions.

There is no evidence to suggest that the rate and the nature of change are likely to alter dramatically. Technologies, industries and societies will continue to converge. Organizations will continue to seek strategic alliances and maximize the benefits associated with a well-managed supply chain. Managers and employees in general will be judged, as they are now, on their ability to cope with and manage change. Adaptability, continuous improvement, lifelong learning and sustaining competitive advantage remain the watchwords.

Corporate winners, whether public or private enterprises, will have fostered and maintained a desire to succeed through progressive, dynamic and challenging initiatives. Strategies and cultures that welcome, address and imaginatively manage change will continue to triumph. We will return to the need to maintain a competitive edge, and indeed to the following quote, in Parts 3 and 4 of the book.

> The first law of the jungle is that the most adaptable species are always the most successful. In the struggle for survival, the winners are those who are most sensitive to important changes in their environment and quickest to reshape their behaviour to meet each new environmental challenge. (Cotter, 1995)

5 Cases in Intervention

The previous chapter concentrated on the technicalities of the intervention strategy model (ISM). Each phase and its associated stages were described in a sequential manner. The iterative nature of the model was highlighted, which facilitates the return to earlier stages in the light of changes in either internal or external environments. Key points concerning the model's application were emphasized. The need to consider some of the models and techniques associated with Part 3 of this text, namely organizational development and design, which deal with the 'softer', people issues, was raised. Effective implementation can only be accomplished when both participation and commitment have been sought and won.

This chapter aims to illustrate the detailed use of ISM by introducing a number of short case studies from a range of 'real-life' practical applications. They will be presented in a sequential manner in accordance with the ISM's format.

The definition phase

Stage 1: problem/systems specification and description

Chapter 3 dealt with systems diagramming and in general the definition and initial analysis of change situations. There is therefore little point in dwelling on this area of systems definition. Stage 1 should produce a clear and concise definition of the affected systems and their relationships. To illustrate this point let us briefly consider the systems change described in Mini Case 5.1.

Stages 2/3: formulation of success criteria and identification of performance indicators

Having fully defined the change environment as far as is possible and necessary, we may enter the next stage. Mini Case 5.2, taken from ABC Ltd, details the objectives, constraints and measures developed to assist in solving a particularly 'hard' problem.

Mini Case 5.1   British Gas

An example from the purchasing department of British Gas (Scotland) PLC illustrates how a systems problem should be entered. A policy decision was made and justified at the corporate level of the company, to the effect that the stockholding of items termed 'one-time buys' (otherwise denoted OTBs) would commence and that the more frequently used OTBs would be held at two central locations. The aim of this exercise was to reduce the delivery time of such items and thus improve the quality of service to the end customer. Traditionally, these were items ordered by purchasing clerks directly from suppliers as and when requested. The numbers involved and the frequency of orders did not, on a regional basis, justify internal stockholding.

The policy change, designed to improve delivery performance, would result in the bulk of the OTBs being held in a central warehouse facility with the regions ordering directly. Delivery time, about 15 days when ordering directly from the manufacturer, would be reduced dramatically.

The purchasing manager, in effect the problem owner, was directed to manage the change and had an imposed target date to work to. He quickly identified another two key change agents and brought them on to the team: firstly the spares buyer who had line responsibility for the clerks who dealt with OTBs, and secondly the purchasing department's own systems development officer. They then, as a group, set about defining the exact nature and impact of the change. The first steps they took on entering and defining the change were as follows:

1   The ordering clerks were notified of the proposed change and the rationale behind it and the process was explained.
2   A flow chart was developed by the change agents, with the assistance of the clerks, which detailed the internal OTB ordering system (in effect a subsystem of the total ordering system) to assist in the understanding of the existing process.
3   The change agents then constructed an activity sequence diagram to determine how the new system would impact on the old, thus determining the scope of the change.
4   Next they produced a systems map detailing both internal and external systems associated with the OTB ordering process.
5   A relationship map was then developed to aid their understanding of the nature of the linkages between the systems involved.
6   An investigation then took place into the relative magnitude of the conflicting forces that existed, to determine their effect on the likelihood of success. Force field analysis was employed.

On completion of the sixth step the change agents had a clear picture of the systems involved and their relationships and status. By this point it was obvious to all concerned that they were faced with a reasonably 'hard' systems change, with minimal people issues. The clerks' function would be retained and retraining was unlikely to be significant. This case, along with the diagrams mentioned above, will be dealt with in more depth in Chapter 11.

Mini Case 5.2   ABC Ltd

This case involved the possible automation of calibration and monitoring systems on an engine test rig. The problem owner, namely the test controller, defined the problem and cited the following reasons in support of an ISM-based solution:

1   *Time scales*   As soon as possible to maintain competitive advantage over other test facilities.
2   *Clear objectives*   The introduction of an automatic recording system to a test rig with the purpose of reducing costs and improving the quality of data.
3   *System boundary*   Clearly defined and limited to the test facility.
4   *Source*   Internally driven by the testing facility management.
5   *Control*   Essentially fully under the control of the testing facility management.
6   *Resources*   Limited financial budget.
7   *Motivation*   A high degree of interest and commitment existed amongst staff.

The above review of the nature of the change facing the test controller deals with the issues raised by the TROPICS test introduced in Chapter 1.

All the above factors were considered, with the term 'motivation' being employed loosely to cover the areas of perception and interest. Diagrams were produced which vindicated the initial assumption that this was indeed a 'hard' systems change. Subsequent production of the objectives and constraints listing, along with the associated performance measures, also indicated a straightforward systems change. The products of ISM stages 2 and 3 are shown in Table 5.1.

Table 5.1   *Objective and performance measures for ISM stages 2 and 3*

Objective	Performance measure
(a) Quality improvement	% of correct data
(b) Test time reduction	Hours
(c) Reduced calibration time	Hours
(d) Removal of manual inputs	Hours
(e) Reduced fuel usage	Gallons
(f) A more reliable system	% downtime
Constraints	
(a) Cost	£, limited hardware and software budget
(b) Resistance	Cooperation, potential employee/union resistance (recognized but not acted upon)

It is at this point that ABC Ltd strayed from the ISM path. Like-minded engineering managers who focused on the technical aspects of the system constructed the diagrams. They entered the formulation stage as one and did not think forward in sufficient detail to the implementation phase.

The millwrights, who were the shop floor operatives most directly involved in the existing manual process, were not fully briefed or adequately consulted during the planning process. The 'softer' issues were not identified in the definition phase as the emphasis had been on technical specifications and systems. The result was that the management of the project was impeded just as the implementation phase was being entered. The cooperation of the operatives and their union could not be relied upon. Insufficient attention had been paid to the operators' perception of a loss in status due to the automation of their task and the possible resulting redeployment of their resource.

The situation was resolved by an iteration back to the definition phase to incorporate the 'softer' elements of change into the overall systems definition. The implementation was put on ice until the involvement and retraining of the operatives had been effectively incorporated into the solution.

The evaluation phase

Stages 4/5: the generation and editing of options and solutions

As we noted in Chapter 3 there are a host of techniques available to the problem owner to assist in both the generation of options and their subsequent reduction of numbers. The appraisal and subsequent selection of the evaluation techniques employed, and their degree of sophistication and method of application, will depend almost wholly on the nature of the problem and the availability of resources.

The ABC Ltd example introduced in Mini Case 5.2 followed the ISM protocol as outlined in the following.

OPTION GENERATION   Owing to the perceived need for haste, given the expressed desire to maintain the firm's competitive edge, the generation of options was conducted via a single brainstorming session led by the test controller. Representatives of the following groups took part, their presence being justified by their key positions within the original systems definition:

- computer systems
- instrument technicians
- engine performance analysts
- testers.

This group produced the following list of options:

- hire or buy equipment
- in-house designed system
- externally designed system
- partial system – data collection only
- complete system – no manual intervention
- external equipment maintenance
- in-house equipment maintenance
- tester operated
- tester operated with instrument technician back-up
- tester operated with staff back-up.

The reader should note that this list is not as extensive or as detailed as that produced by the team during their option-generation session. The technical nature of many of the options and their explanation was such that their reproduction would simply lead to confusion.

OPTION EDITING   Having generated the options, the group then set about editing out those which were unsuitable or at least impracticable given the existing system environment:

Table 5.2   Option evaluation (test rig)

Objective	Buy	Rent	Data record only	Data record and transfer	Complete system	Tester and technician
				Options		
Improve data quality	N/A	N/A	90%	95%	98%	98%
Reduce testing time	N/A	N/A	1 hour	1 hour	1 hour	N/A
Reduce fuel consumption	N/A	N/A	150 gal	150 gal	150 gal	N/A
Reduce calibration time	N/A	N/A	0 hour	0 hour	8 hours	N/A
System reliability	N/A	N/A	N/A	N/A	N/A	2%
Reduce costs	N/A	N/A	£50K	£75K	£100K	N/A
	N/A	N/A	*	*	*	N/A
Reduce manual input	N/A	N/A	0 hour	2 hours	2 hours	N/A

N/A denotes not applicable.
* Rental costs would be approximately 30% less than the associated purchase cost.

Option	Rejection criteria
Tester operated with staff back-up	Shift working problems
In-house system design	Insufficient expertise
In-house equipment maintenance	No facilities

As we can see, there is no need to become involved in complicated procedures and protracted discussions. These options were eliminated without recourse to any form of financial analysis.

Stage 6: option evaluation

Following on from the editing stage, the group moved to the evaluation of the remaining options. The data required to formally evaluate the options were gathered and generated by the problem owner and the other change agents. Much of the information came from financial and operational analysis of existing in-house data and literature provided by equipment manufacturers. Various break-even analyses were conducted to establish both costs and performance profiles for all the options. The necessary information along with the objectives and options were collated and presented in a tabular format as shown in Table 5.2.

The agreed solution was as follows: the recording system would be externally designed and 'complete', allowing auto-calibration and recording of data to be directly transferred to the mainframe computer. The equipment would be hired and operated by the tester with support from the instrument technician.

The implementation phase

The importance of this phase must not be underestimated. One of the most frequent failings associated with poor change management occurs at this point. The problem owner, along with any other relevant change agents, having just completed a major project evaluation, possibly very effectively, may rush into the implementation without fully preparing the way ahead. Implementation strategies are required which address issues such as timing of events, scheduling of activities, acquisition and delivery of resources and the development of the human resource support structures. Implementation issues need not be left until the final stages of ISM. They will naturally emerge during both discussion and evaluation of options and solutions. Previous discussions regarding sound implementation strategy emphasized the need to build implementation issues and objectives into the actual evaluation process.

There is much more to developing an implementation strategy than engaging in network-based planning exercises and the construction of elaborate control charts and budgetary monitoring devices. No one would deny the value of such techniques or the importance of seriously considering the harder issues. However, the vast majority of competent managers are capable of dealing with both the planning techniques and monitoring mechanisms, either directly or by seeking expert assistance when required. The technical aspects of project planning are not generally associated with project failure. It is the 'softer' people-based issues that can have a detrimental impact on the successful implementation of a project.

The two cases chosen to highlight the implementation phase have been selected not for their complexities of planning but rather for the emphasis they place on the management of people. The importance of this was also illustrated in a study entitled *The Glasgow Management Development Initiative* (Brownlie et al., 1990), the investigators contacted many employers and their managers, through both focus groups and questionnaires, in an effort to establish the health or otherwise of management development. By far the most sought-after category of development was managing people. Managers themselves know that the key to success lies in their ability to effectively manage people in an enterprising manner towards the fulfilment of mutually agreeable objectives.

Stages 7/8: develop implementation strategies and consolidation

The first case, Mini Case 5.3 on Froud Consine Limited (FCL), demonstrates the benefits of generating a shared perception of a problem and ensuring that the principal players are 'onside' prior to implementation. To make sense of the implementation phase, we must join the case at the conclusion of the formulation phase.

The change situation in Mini Case 5.4 was previously referred to in Mini Case 3.3 where examples from Caledonian Airmotive were used to demonstrate diagramming techniques. The company will also be referred to in Chapter 11. Mini Case 5.4 deals with the company's implementation strategy for the modification of the workshop area.

Mini Case 5.3   Froud Consine Ltd (FCL)

FCL is a medium-sized engineering company involved in the design, manufacture and installation of high-technology test equipment. Babcock International (BI) acquired the company in 1985. Prior to the BI takeover, FCL had experienced a succession of management teams endeavouring to improve the firm's performance, mainly through diversification. The company found itself providing a service as well as a product, but did not successfully restructure its manufacturing and management systems accordingly. FCL was a traditional engineering company; they had their own way of doing things and had managed to survive in their original base in Worcester for almost a century.

The problem owner, part of a four-man management team from BI, was faced with an organization set in its ways and fast developing a substantial inertia to change. There were of course many issues that the BI team addressed, but for this example the emphasis will be placed on the objective of improving the commercial control of contracts in line with the increasingly important customer-servicing requirements.

As one might have expected from the project objective and the nature of the company, the change was not going to be one of simply updating a few physical management systems. There would be a number of complex organizational issues. This was recognized within the management of the change process and every effort was made during the early stages of the systems change to identify and involve the principal parties who would play a key role in securing the successful adoption of the change. Although the organizational issues were significant, the management team opted for a systems-based solution methodology. In the aftermath of a takeover and faced with tight schedules the aim was to secure immediate improvements with minimal opposition. The more protracted and open organizational development solution methodologies were not considered to be positive factors in this particular change environment. This is not to say that BI did not wish to see organizational change, but at the time of the takeover this was seen as being a longer-term objective. The option evaluation table, Table 5.3, produced by the problem owner along with the change agents, reflects the importance of organizational issues within this particular change environment.

Table 5.3 *Option evaluation (restructuring)*

Objectives	A dedicated contract management function	Improve administration effort and employ progress chasers	Place contract responsibility on functional department heads
Contract control	Responsibility defined; good chance of success	No single point of responsibility	Difficult to view the whole problem; poor chance of success
Cost control	Requires contract budgeting system	No budget responsibility	No overall contract cost control
Customer service	Single contact point	Multiple contact points	Multiple contact points
Team spirit	Facilitating role; independent of functions	No effect	No cross-functional benefit
Internal communication	All significant communication via contract manager	Possible improvement within functions only	Possible improvement at middle management level only

The preferred option was the establishment of a dedicated contract management function. As Table 5.3 illustrates, all the generated options dealt with the organizational issues associated with the proposed change. ISM produced a solution to what at least was superficially a non-systems problem. It identified the optimal route forward and by ensuring, in the traditions of best practice, that the principal change agents were involved and committed from an early stage, it simplified the process of implementation.

Implementation was dealt with as follows:

1 Detailed planning to establish the new function, conducted by the BI team and the proposed contract managers.
2 Immediate transfer of staff from their existing functions (see point 3).
3 The transferred staff, 10 in total, acted as 'product champions'. These individuals had in the past, out of necessity, been acting as contract managers for large orders. As a result they were keen to promote the concept and generated a great deal of enthusiasm in others. In addition they both possessed a practical knowledge of the existing systems and understood the organizational issues.
4 The contract managers, within their new department, developed the control systems.
5 Resistance to the change was minimal, as the new systems did not replace any existing control mechanisms. Remember that this function had not previously existed.

Over a period of time the contract management function established itself and in so doing produced a dramatic improvement in the handling of contracts. BI involvement continued until the change had been consolidated. They acted as an external driving force providing the change agents with authority and encouragement.

Mini case 5.4   Caledonian Airmotive Ltd

An autonomous accessory workshop was the desired outcome of the following implementation strategy:

1 Parallel running of the proposed autonomous system along with the existing integrated set-up designed to minimize production disruptions.
2 Building modifications to create purpose-built space for the new facility.
3 Installation of an additional testing facility to ease capacity problems.
4 Selection of additional supervisors for the new facility, with recruitment taking place from the existing systems personnel to minimize employee resistance.
5 Erection of a new storage area to service the facility.
6 Selection and training of store personnel.
7 Additional training of the mechanics about to enter the new autonomous working group.
8 Final organizational change.

The sequential nature of the implementation strategy reflected the physical aspects of the change. Training and development, points 4, 6 and 7 above, ran alongside the physical construction activities. Discussions dealing with the finer detail of the organizational change were also scheduled to take account of the construction completion date. As would be expected, the greater emphasis on physical systems within the Airmotive case produced a typical project planning solution of a sequential nature, but people issues were identified and received attention alongside the technical aspects of the change.

Iterations

The example taken from the ABC testing facility (Mini Case 5.2) illustrated a typical iteration. Too great an emphasis was placed on one aspect of the problem, in this case the technical features of the proposed system, which resulted in a key systems relationship, namely the role of the operatives within the new system, being overlooked until implementation loomed. In any project dealing with new and/or complex issues, iterations are inevitable. The ISM methodology recognizes the need to formally introduce mechanisms which facilitate a number of feedback loops, and which may be utilized without casting aspersions on the abilities of the project management team.

All too often, especially in the West, failure is taken in its literal sense. However, if one takes a broader view, a more informed view, then failure can be seen in a far more positive light. If we can learn from our 'mistakes', build on the lessons learned, and do better next time then we have not failed, we have learned and improved. Iterations are built into ISM both in recognition of the dynamic nature of change and to legitimize 'failure'. Managers often fear admitting they got it wrong the first time: in change, as in life, the ability to admit omissions, possibly errors, and then act positively to resolve the situation should be admired, not ridiculed.

READER ACTIVITY

Identify a forthcoming project within your workplace or your social circle, and apply a forward looking ISM analysis. Do not involve anyone else. Try to anticipate likely outcomes and stakeholder positions. Revisit your analysis at a later stage: did you get it right first time and could you have done better?

---

6 Total Project Management

Project managers, or practising managers with extensive knowledge and experience of project-based management approaches, have often expressed the view, when first faced with ISM, that they have no need for yet another investigative methodology based on the traditional phases of definition, design and implementation. They generally consider themselves to be proficient in the use of network and budgetary-based planning techniques and fully understand associated decision-making processes. However, with a little prompting they will very quickly admit that the problems they face when managing a complex project, a transition from one state to another, a change in effect, are often traceable to people-related management issues. When they are then forced to examine the planning and control tools they employ in project management, along with their decision-making methodologies, they realize that they do not incorporate the features necessary to integrate the organizational complexities with the physical planning mechanisms.

Even in the twenty-first century, many organizations, or at least divisions within them, do not fully recognize the need for holistic, people focused, change management. The ISM, described in Chapters 4 and 5, may be considered too 'soft' an approach. Many managers may readily identify with the rationale behind its design, but consider the emphasis placed on a holistic systems review and participative style as simple common sense – a common sense that they acknowledge but do not necessarily observe.

Staff at the University of Glasgow Business School, in particular Geoff Southern, detected an interesting development in the 'Operations Management' module. People undertaking a practical assignment, designed to examine and improve the relationship between operating practices and business strategy, were employing investigative techniques, namely ISM, from the 'Managing Change' module. The prevalence of ISM within the assignment, which should have employed more traditional project management approaches, was such that it was decided to investigate the rationale behind the shift towards this new approach. Focus groups were organized. The participants expressed the view that existing network-based planning tools, computerized or not, did not fully address the 'softer' problems raised by the assignment.

However, many participants operating within more traditional organizational cultures, in which in many respects 'Taylorism' and 'Fordism' were alive and well, felt uncomfortable with what was obviously a useful tool.

In response to this change trigger, work commenced on developing an integrated model, which was later to be called the total project management model or TPMM for short. The basic aim of the TPMM is to present to the project manager a package which integrates the participative features of ISM and the mechanistic planning tools associated with a more scientific management approach. A model such as TPMM cannot teach a manager to manage in a more participative manner – this is the task of management development and training – but it can highlight the points within a typical project life cycle when a more liberal and open management approach should be employed (Firth and Krut, 1991).

'Project manager', as far as TPMM is concerned, is the term used to denote the individual charged with handling a specific project. They therefore in the course of normal events need not hold the title 'project manager' in a functional sense. They may or may not be skilled in the application of project planning techniques. However, the assumption has been made that they will be aware of their existence and seek out, when appropriate, project team members skilled in their application. Such assumptions concerning the capabilities and knowledge bases of professional and appointed project managers are in the authors' view valid, given the nature of TPMM's target audience, namely, professional managers engaged in a programme, formal or otherwise, of managerial development and self-development.

This chapter will introduce the TPMM and develop its key features associated with both personal and organizational development in such a way as to lead into Part 3 of the book, which deals in more specific terms with organizational design and development.

The value of total project management

The introduction to this chapter noted that project management has traditionally been treated as a systematic process with the emphasis placed on the physical planning process, rather than on the actual practical non-technical managerial problems associated with the implementation of the plan. The planning process has been in the past and often continues to be, according to the feedback from MBA participants, solely conducted by those deemed to be directly responsible for the 'management' of the project. This project team will consist of planners and possibly technical experts with specific expertise associated with the project at hand. They will not experience the actual implementation of their plans from a managerial viewpoint. Many of the individuals and groups who will be both affected by and involved in the implementation of the planning outcomes are excluded. Yet surely it is this 'excluded' group who will ultimately determine the degree of success associated with the venture?

An example which rather dramatically illustrates this need for consultation involved the construction of an office block in the mid 1970s. The clients for whom the office block was to form a new headquarters, through their architects and consulting engineers, specified and subsequently had installed an air-conditioning system. Such systems were not common in Scotland at this time (although the year-round tropical climate does make them a necessity!) and people's knowledge of them was therefore limited. On occupying the premises the clients' staff, the ultimate users of the system, discovered that the windows did not open, and created such a fuss that at considerable expense to the client a large number of windows were removed and replaced with the standard opening variety. No one, from the clients to the contractors, had ever thought of asking the users what they desired in terms of workplace design. If they had, they might have discovered the need for some form of direct control over the working environment. The end-users were never told that one of the advantages of air-conditioning, namely the automatically controlled working environment, negated the use of independently controlled window openings.

A holistic investigation of the project boundaries along the lines advocated by ISM and TPMM would have indicated the need to consult the end users. By involving the users in the planning process and engaging in a programme of explanation as to the rationale behind the use of air-conditioning, the project managers might have reached some form of agreement and/or compromise prior to installation. Resistance to change is greatly minimized when employees feel that they have exercised a degree of control over potential outcomes.

READER ACTIVITY

Pause and consider situations in which you have actively participated in resisting a proposed change. Were you fully aware of the rationale behind the change? Did you feel involved in the decision-making process? Were you an 'afterthought'?

Complex projects

At what point does a project cross the 'boundary' from mechanistic to complex? There is unfortunately no simple answer to this question. Earlier chapters dealt with the classification of the nature of change and the subsequent definition of a change environment. A project manager should employ the techniques and follow the procedural steps outlined in these chapters. This will permit the change and/or project to be placed reasonably accurately on the change spectrum. The greater the tendency towards the 'softer' end of the spectrum, the greater the probability that the project falls into the complex category. In such cases a purely 'hard' approach will not provide an optimal solution; that is not to say that the project will fail to be implemented, just that it will not arrive at its conclusion without creating a great deal of controversy and resistance. Any disruption to a project causes concern as delays generally mean that some form of penalty, often financial, will be incurred.

One of the most important factors which differentiates a complex from a mechanistic physical project is the degree of dependency placed on the cooperation and acceptance of those directly affected by the outcomes of the planning process. The successful implementation of complex projects will ultimately depend on the effective management of organizational issues throughout the total planning process. Characteristics associated with complex and mechanistic projects are compared in Table 6.1.

Table 6.1   Comparison between mechanistic and complex projects

Complex projects	Mechanistic projects
Unclear objectives	Clear objectives
Large number of activities	Limited number of activities
Activity sequences and boundaries are unclear	Clear activity sequences and boundaries
Activities tend not to be technically oriented and/or the technical aspects are not well defined (e.g. new communications technologies)	Activities are technically oriented and the technical aspects are well defined and understood
Activities have indeterminate durations and resource requirements	Activities have a fairly determinate duration, and resource requirements are at least approximately known
Activity successes are largely dependent upon mobilizing and motivating people	Activity successes are linked to known technologiesand systems, with limited human interfaces

The success of the project management process depends on the appropriate selection of a planning methodology. By fully defining the project in systems terms, the manager gains an insight into the complexities associated with the planning process. In situations where the project activities work towards the achievement of a specific and well-defined objective, and where the technologies, along with the environment, are equally well defined, then traditional planning tools should suffice. If any doubt exists as to the nature of the problems facing the project team and/or the environmental impact is difficult to define, then it is always safer to adopt an intervention-based strategy such as TPMM.

The total project management model (TPMM)

TPMM recognizes that a technically oriented approach to the management of complex projects must be augmented by the adoption of 'softer' people-centred planning mechanisms. As already stated, projects consist of both technological (or systems-based) and organizational (or people-based) elements. A systems-based planning technique is needed to handle technological or physical change; after all, it is in fact the systems that are being manipulated. However, adopting a purely systematic approach to the 'people' components of the project environment is likely to lead to subsequent difficulties during the implementation phase. TPMM addresses both 'hard' and 'soft' issues, by focusing on the technical and more physical aspects of a project from a systems point of view, and by adopting techniques associated with organization development (French and Bell, 1990) to address 'softer' aspects. Both areas are thus treated in an integrated manner, utilizing cross-functional teams, drawn from key areas of the project environment, who will bring to the problem a range of appropriate managerial skills and knowledge bases (McCalman, 1988).

The TPMM is an iterative and systems-based planning technique, which integrates 'softer' management philosophies and techniques into a traditional project management process. The model is outlined in Figure 6.1. Again the familiar three-phase format, similar to that adopted within ISM, is employed, with terminology and activity modifications to reflect the specific emphasis on project management as opposed to the management of change.

The first phase is almost identical to that of the ISM, with the only change being the addition of a formal step dealing with project validation. The evaluation phase of ISM has been replaced with that of planning, which, although it accomplishes a design process, does so through a prescribed networking technique, without the need for option generation and evaluation. In a project the activities will be defined in the first phase. Implementation is dealt with in a similar manner in both models. Table 6.2 outlines the principal factors addressed within each phase.

The following sections will address each phase from both a project management and an ISM perspective.

Phase 1: project definition

The first step in managing a complex project is to define its scope in terms of primary mission and associated objectives, constraints and performance measures. This involves conducting a detailed examination of the project environment in order to help optimize subsequent management decisions relating to the project plan. It is achieved by making a detailed, systems-oriented analysis of the project environment

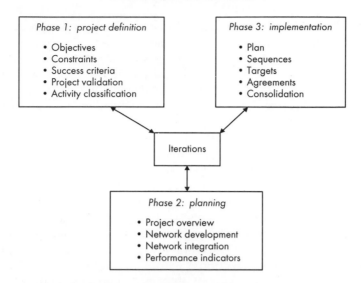

Figure 6.1   *The total project management model*

Table 6.2   *TPMM phase descriptions*

Factors addressed	Techniques employed
Phase 1: project definition	*For example:*
Definition of the current position:	Brainstorming techniques
• Specification of environment	Team building
• Evaluation of the project	System diagramming
• Definition of the project owners	Factor ranking
	Decision trees
Definition of the preferred position:	Investment appraisal
• Project objectives	Stakeholder analysis
• Resource constraints	Competence analysis
• Resource requirements	
• Success criteria	
• Activity classification	
Phase 2: planning	*For example:*
• Integrated project plan	Gantt charts
• Performance indicators	Cash flow analysis
• Potential iterations	Critical path methods
	Resource scheduling
	Investment appraisal
Phase 3: implementation	*For example:*
• Presentation of the plan	Charting methods
• Application and monitoring of review systems	Process charts
• Potential iterations	Cumulative spend charts
• Autopsy of the project	Variance analysis
	Exception reporting
	Socio-technical change models

in association with any individuals or groups who have a vested interest. Within this analysis the activities and resources required to complete the project will be identified and detailed. In stressing the need for such an environmental analysis, TPMM is no different from ISM, and similar techniques would be employed in accomplishing the definition.

TPMM possibly emphasizes the need to indulge in team-building activities to a greater extent than ISM. This reflects the fact that project managers are often dealing with environments that change in terms of their composition from project to project. As TPMM suggests, the best way of ensuring that organizational issues are incorporated into the plan is to create and develop a cross-functional team representing key system areas and relationships from the project environment. As this team is likely to vary between projects, every effort must be made to ensure a team approach to the planning process is developed (Boddy and Paton,1998). To this end TPMM advocates the use of brainstorming techniques and planning sessions, within the definition phase, which emphasize a participative team involvement in specifying the project in terms of objectives, constraints, resources and environmental factors. Given the diverse nature of the project team, in terms of their hierarchical position, disciplines and roles, a non-threatening and open means of generating information for the definition phase is required (Paton et al., 1989).

READER ACTIVITY

Have you ever been in a group situation where you felt uncomfortable with regard to offering your ideas, solutions and thoughts? Why was this the case?

What could the facilitator and/or group leader have done to encourage participation?

Could the process have been modified to encourage the 'team' to come forward with ideas? For example, non-attributable 'talking wall' approaches can allow respondents to remain anonymous.

Could the facilitator have adopted a less threatening and/or confrontational approach? We do not pay enough attention to facilitator training and development. Interpersonal skills and facilitation techniques/approaches are often ignored; a manager, or team leader, is apparently meant to pick them up as they go along. This is, sadly, rarely the case.

Project validation, involving investment appraisal techniques, within the first phase of analysis is not normally associated with ISM. It is employed to deal with a change that possibly, for many reasons, cannot be avoided. A project manager often finds it necessary to justify future actions by either proving the need to go ahead or validating someone else's initial proposals. TPMM also identifies the project activities and resources required within this first phase; these will be required to complete the network plans associated with the next phase.

Phase 2: planning

Having fully specified the project environment in the initial diagnostic phase, the project team can now progress to a formulation phase, during which they will be confident of their system's assumptions, targets and resources. By evaluating the plans produced at this stage against the previously defined performance measures, the team will be able to evaluate planning alternatives effectively. In addition, since the total project environment has been considered, they should be aware of and ready to deal with any obstructions that may delay implementation.

The planning process itself consists of four steps.

1 *Project overview*   This is conducted by the project team and consists of the identification of major components, key events, component relationships, and human resource requirements (Boddy, 1987).
2 *Network development*   This is conducted by a component team (i.e. a subgroup of the project team) identified during the previous step. This stage consists of task definition, resource requirement definition, and then network design (Lockyer, 1991).
3 *Integration of component networks*   This is conducted by the total project team and consists of potential iterations back to component networks, formulation of the total project network, and referral back to objectives and measures identified in phase 1.
4 *Performance indicators identification*   This again is conducted by the total project team and consists of identification of specific performance indicators and iterations back to phase 1 and step 3. The indicators will be used for control and assessment purposes.

The planning phase of TPMM follows the traditional project planning route, utilizing networking techniques, to facilitate the actual physical planning of the project. The actions required to address the organizational issues identified within the definition phase, along with any others discovered during this phase, should be incorporated into the network planning process. These may include educational and training programmes and/or the limited involvement of additional key players in the actual planning process. In the similar ISM phase there is unlikely to be such a clear path to follow as one must first determine the potential solution paths and appropriate analysis techniques, prior to even considering sequencing solution options.

Phase 3: implementation

The final phase, that of implementation, consists primarily of the 'mechanisms' to present the plan to relevant parties, and to put in place the necessary monitoring and correction systems. It is reached only after exhaustive examination of the environment has been completed, and the results are incorporated into the planning stage. As factors concerned with implementation are part of the planning process they will have already been considered earlier. Hence the presentation and monitoring mechanisms already developed to ensure successful implementation are integrated into the plan, and are more likely to be easily administered and understood.

Implementation involves the integration of the network analysis exercises of phase 2, together with a thorough appraisal and action plan concerning any organizational issues, such as education, development and negotiation identified in earlier stages. Consolidation in the case of TPMM involves the project manager in monitoring the control mechanisms and taking corrective action as and when required. TPMM must deal with similar implementation issues to those addressed in ISM.

All too often project planning teams reach the final hurdle of 'implementation', only to find that a lack of consultation in the earlier environmental definition has led them to neglect a key factor associated with successful implementation. By fully specifying the problem in systems terms and subsequently analysing the interactions to identify areas of interdependence and resistance, the project team will have the ability to forecast and deal with potential difficulties during phases 1 and 2. The major difficulties associated with implementation hopefully will have then been removed. Mini Case 6.1 provides an example.

If 'external' business and organizational developments alter the project environment between phases 1 and 3, then the TPMM model, with its built-in iterations, can backtrack and incorporate the developments. Phase 3 ends with a post-mortem of the TPMM cycle; any lessons learned may be identified and incorporated into the project team's subsequent planning processes. The net result of the adoption of the TPMM philosophy will be effective project management allied to the development of an integrated design team. The use of socio-technical models to effect the final implementation is included to emphasize the point that TPMM, just as ISM, may require to employ, when dealing with a particularly messy change situation, techniques and processes associated with organizational development and design.

Administrative and organizational points

TPMM is a multi-disciplinary approach to the process of project planning. A cross-functional team, bringing its own managerial skills

Mini Case 6.1   Moving Office

A finance company, based in a city centre, identified a number of commercially related factors or trends which led them to decide to relocate to an 'out of town' site. For example, clients were moving HQs 'out of town'; technological advances were reducing transaction costs and simplifying the communications process; city centre costs were escalating; and lastly, but not least, it was anticipated that a purpose-built 'greenfield' site would both improve the quality of working life and offer the opportunity to further enhance IT capabilities and productivity. A team consisting of divisional heads, supported by IT specialists, set about identifying a site and planning the move.

Staff were kept informed but the communication process was rather one-sided and always put a positive 'spin' on the move. The management team conducted a thorough and professional review of the situation; it was a 'textbook' exercise in best evaluation planning practice. However, ultimately the move cost more than expected and took far longer to implement than was originally envisaged.

Staff, when finally faced with the reality of the move, objected on two accounts – neither of which had been explicitly voiced during the planning process. Out of town meant that they would be cut off from the 'buzz'. The city centre offered a way of life, good pubs, restaurants and entertainment, combined with quality shopping – all of which were seen as being far more appealing than a greenfield site full of cows, fast food outlets and superstores! Further, how did you get out of town? The commuting links were poor; therefore you had to use a car – not nearly as appealing as jumping on a train, bus or tube!

The move went ahead. It had to: contracts had been signed and commitments made. However, given the critical timing of the emergence of staff doubts, namely immediately prior to the move, there were inevitably going to be some hard 'face to face' negotiations. Staff had to be compensated for the move; car lease schemes were introduced and flexitime was adopted.

The project team should have taken a more holistic view; they were more concerned with the logistical task at hand than the overall change. Delays and additional costs may have been avoided, or at least reduced, had a more holistic view and approach been adopted.

Another, less dramatic example of an office move offers further evidence of the need to think and act holistically. This move concerned a small training establishment. They were only moving a short distance, within the same office block, utilizing the same services, and essentially it was a case of business as usual. The project manager did every thing right. A detailed plan ensured minimal disruption to service. The staff knew of the move. They knew where they were going and when. They also knew why and agreed fully with the rationale and benefits associated with the move.

So how could things go wrong? The project manager had overlooked a number of 'key questions'. Who was going to get the window seat? Who was going to face the door? How would seating plans be decided? Once again, up to the point of the actual physical move everyone had remained quiet and had fully cooperated with the overall design and layout of the new facilities.

After much debate and behind the scenes activity the matter was resolved. Seat allocation was decided by the drawing of names out of a hat, with prior agreement that there would be no subsequent mention of the subject. Initially there were many petty grievances, but by focusing attention on the fairness of the selection method and the unanimous prior agreement, the project manager rode out the storm!

and environmental knowledge, progresses through an integrative and interactive planning process, led by an accomplished facilitator, to produce a project plan geared to a total solution. This multi-disciplinary and cross-functional approach to project planning, along with the required establishment of a team approach, often necessitates extensive management development of the core project team. The provision of technical planning skills is not enough, and managers must be made aware of, and provided with the skills to cope with, the 'softer', people-related issues associated with effective project management (Boddy and Buchanan, 1986).

Project planning is conducted in a dynamic environment; the variability of both external and internal factors necessitates that the TPMM concept incorporates iterative feedback loops. Iterations, as mentioned previously, are particularly important during the implementation phase, but they may occur within and/or between any of the aforementioned phases. They may be seen as the reaction to the dynamic nature of associated variables. Iterations may be minimized through the development of a proactive stance by the project team. Changes in the environment associated with the project must be managed and incorporated within the developing plan (Wright and Rhodes, 1985).

Total project management, as in the case of the intervention strategies previously discussed, may be regarded as a hybrid planning tool. Its component parts are not revolutionary; it is the packaging of the systems and organizational disciplines into a cohesive whole that creates the positive results. Such a complete planning package, when effectively managed, cannot fail to increase the likelihood of successful project implementation. It also reflects the changing nature of today's management structures and strategies. Total quality programmes, customer awareness initiatives, just-in-time and the globalization of markets must surely necessitate the development and implementation of innovative planning procedures that reflect management's overall strategy. Networking techniques, computerized or not, can no longer be seen as an independently sufficient means of achieving effective project planning.

Organization development and design: their role in systems interventions

In both the ISM and the TPMM much is made of the need to ensure participation and involvement, with the aim of achieving firstly a shared perception of the problem and secondly commitment to finding a solution. A systems-based solution methodology cannot achieve this without recourse to management techniques and processes associated with the field of organizational development and design. Unless the change or project is of a particularly 'hard' nature, the problem owners and project managers must endeavour to encourage those affected to accept the situation and thereafter assist in implementing a solution to the problem.

Adoption of the 'softer' management approaches within a systems-based investigative framework should encourage the management team concerned to integrate, involve and 'share' more fully with those at the sharp end of the change.

Let us now consider five factors which influence the way in which people respond to change:

1 *Involvement* Involve them in the process by explaining the nature of the change and discussing its implications in an open and frank manner. Gain participation by seeking out and fostering their ideas.
2 *Communication* Communicate – don't lecture – by means of: meetings and discussions; presentations; and education and training.
3 *Perceptions* Consider people's worries. Think about: individuals' objections and how one could deal with their fears; the benefits of the change and how they could be sold.
4 *Resources* Recruit and transfer in advance to allow assimilation of the new environment and facilitate training.
5 *Schedule* Avoid scheduling the change and/or associated activities during work peaks: inconvenience can lead to resistance.

These factors must be integrated with the 'harder', systems-based approaches. In earlier chapters, organizational culture was noted as an important factor in promoting a climate of change, along with the need to formulate a proactive stance towards change and therefore encourage it to be viewed as an opportunity rather than a threat. Opportunistic and proactive actions are encouraged within cultures that exhibit enterprising features and open structures that foster challenging ideas. The creation of such cultures is far beyond the remit of systems-based intervention models. The power of the intervention model as a change management tool increases dramatically when it is employed in a progressive and cooperative environment. The organizational development chapters that follow in Part 3 detail and discuss the rationale, strategies and approaches associated with accomplishing 'softer', people-based change.

To provide a link between the systems intervention model and that of organization development, we recommend that the reader study Figure 6.2. This provides analysis of a step-by-step guide to managing change used by one of our case study organizations, MTC Ltd. Figure 6.2 examines the people element of change as part of a total systems approach where the emphasis is on preparatory work for change. The harder issues

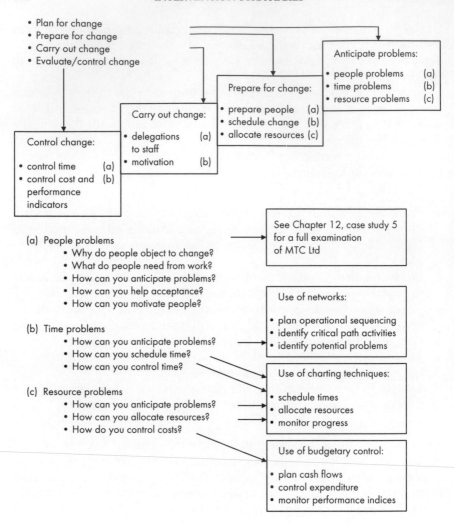

Figure 6.2   *A step-by-step guide to managing change*

addressed are grouped under resource and time problems. These groupings reflect the more technical features of the TPMM and are used to manage the control, planning and implementation of the change project in conjunction with the people problems.

PART 3

The Organization Development Model

7 People Management

The bulk of the scientific evidence suggests that the more the individual is enabled to exercise control over his task, and to relate his efforts to those of his fellows, the more likely he is to accept a positive commitment. This positive commitment shows in a number of ways, not the least of which is the release of that personal initiative and creativity which constitute the basis of a democratic climate. (Thorsurd, 1972)

You firmly believe that sound management means executives on one side and workers on the other, on one side men who think and on the other men who can only work. For you, management is the art of smoothly transferring the executives' ideas into the workers hands. (Matsushita, 1988)

More employees need to take a greater interest and a more active role in the business. More of them need to care deeply about success. Companies achieve real agility only when every function . . . when every person is able and eager to rise to every challenge. This type and degree of fundamental change, commonly called revitalization or transformation, is what more and more companies seek but all too rarely achieve. (Pascale et al., 1997)

An examination of any of the current, vogue examples of 'successful' companies reveals that two underlying themes are ever present. Firstly, there is an emphasis on meeting, to the highest standards, customer satisfaction. The quality criterion is what guarantees success in any business you care to mention. Secondly, the successful organization, no matter which country it comes from, how long it has been in existence, or what products or services it produces, takes care of its people. That is to say, success comes from customer satisfaction which is generated from motivated people. The ability of an organization to manufacture products or provide services rests on its ability to gain commitment from the people within that organization. This seemingly simple process is complicated, however, by the approaches adopted by managers within organizations in terms of their behaviour and attitudes towards the individual.

There is the potential for conflict in all organizations. In fact, conflict occurs on a daily basis. The argument with your secretary over a report that is needed for the board meeting; the screaming match between marketing and the factory floor; the formal warning given for consistent lateness; are all examples of conflict between individuals who theoretically share the same objectives. Buchanan and Huczynski (1997) view this as a potential organizational dilemma:

> Many of the 'human' problems of organizations can be identified as conflicts between individual human needs, and the constraints imposed on individuals in the interests of the collective purpose of the organization.

Similarly, March and Simon (1958) note that:

> An organization is, after all, a collection of people and what the organization does is done by people. Therefore . . . propositions about organizations are statements about human behaviour.

The simplistic logic in these statements is only lost on us when we begin to view organizations as something more than what they are. When the issues are confused by organization structure, management roles and the role of technology, we begin to lose sight of what the real basics are. If we build organizations for performance, then it is the people within such organizations that deliver the performance we require.

Part 3 of this book, and this chapter in particular, deal with three fundamental concepts:

1 Organizations are about people.
2 Management assumptions about people often lead to ineffective design of organizations and this hinders performance.
3 People are the most important asset, and their commitment goes a long way in determining effective organizational design and development.

People in organizations can be provided with the opportunities for growth and development if the organization itself is designed to do so. It is the recognition of this which drives the basic principles of organization development (OD). We introduce here the concept of design and development within the organization as it relates to people. The organization development model (ODM) is not new, nor is it radically different from the writings of many of the leading authors in the field. What it does do is to place design and development in the context of managing change. To do so requires that people, as well as structures and systems, change and this leads to the potential for conflict. Avoiding conflict is as much a state of mind as it is a manageable process. If the manager believes in employee involvement, the freedom to exercise control over tasks, then the design element should reflect this. The difficulty, as Konosuke Matsushita points out at the beginning of this chapter, is that a lot of managers in organizations in the Western world believe in the division of labour – the separation of initiative from performance of the task, thinking from doing, manager from employee. This raises a number of questions which this and the following three chapters will hope to address. For example, why does this type of thinking still occur at the beginning of a new millennium? Why is it so prevalent in Western economies? Can organizations develop into learning entities? What are the consequences of adopting these approaches? And lastly, can we do anything about it ? Part 3 seeks to address these questions by looking at how and why an organization development model is needed. We begin by looking at why some form of people management is necessary in all organizations. From there we go on to look at the concept of organization design and various reasons why OD is not paid enough attention.

The latter part of this chapter begins to look at some of the presumed weaknesses of Western management. In particular it addresses managers' perceptions as they relate to the desire for control in organizations, the way in which they perceive design as an analytical exercise, the lack of resolution to delegate responsibility, and the lack of philosophy and values about the organization. These are serious accusations that are laid at the door of managers in organizations in the Western world. They reflect a level of truth associated with them. Management in Western economies to a large extent still operates with traditional forms of work organization which are epitomized by the application of assembly style manufacture. This may be a gross generalization, and some of you may work in what can be termed enlightened companies. But many will not, and this is what we need to address. One answer is to look at how other countries do it. The quote from Matsushita (1988) at the beginning of this chapter continues as follows:

> We are beyond the Taylor model; business, we know, is so complex and difficult, the survival of firms so hazardous in an environment increasingly unpredictable, competitive and fraught with danger, that their continued existence depends on the day to day mobilization of every ounce of intelligence.

Our first justification is based on the assumption that firms look for alternative models of design and behaviour where they perceive that a need exists. In the past the need for change did not exist; the old ways of manufacture brought profitable returns. This is no longer the case. The reasons are related to the growth of competition from abroad. Managers are beginning to ask questions of themselves and their organizations based on the need to search for solutions that will ensure competitive survival in the marketplace. Until the crisis which hit the 'tiger economies' in 1997, the West viewed the development of countries such as South Korea, Malaysia and Indonesia as examples of economies producing and managing in a better way. Many firms in the industrialized

West operate traditionally because they know of no other way. This is the way that it has always been done, and it brought profitable return. However, when the marketplace demands change, for example products geared to specific customer needs, traditional concepts such as the long production run or the provision of a service regardless of customer need are no longer feasible, and change is therefore needed.

Second, we wish to see firms actively address these organizational and managerial issues in a positive sense by looking at alternatives – by using the intervention strategy and organization development models to consider options, and by implementing changes which make for effective organizations. We all have a vested interest in the survival and growth of organizations. By overtly opening up the discussion in this way we hope to suggest that there is a need to look at organization design and development and view it as being as important as product development. It is only in this way that managers begin to recognize its importance for effective performance.

Why manage people?

Extremism is a popular concept in management. Both in the theoretical underpinnings and in the everyday practice, analogies are used which portray the two extreme elements of management characterized by an either/or exchange deal: good and bad management practice, hard and soft management techniques, manufacturing versus marketing trade-offs, technology or people. The reality is a continuum which Simon (1957) recognized as bounded rationality: that is, all managerial decisions are made by individual rationality based on economic (business) and social (humanistic) concerns. One of the outcomes of these concomitants of economic and social rationality is that there is a dependence and an independence among individuals in organizations.

McGregor (1960) argued that the individual in American industry existed in a state of partial dependence:

> Authority, as a means of influence, is certainly not useless, but for many purposes it is less appropriate than persuasion or professional help. Exclusive reliance upon authority encourages countermeasures, minimal performance, even open rebellion.

If this was true of the American organization of the 1950s, then it is also true of Western societies in the new millennium. The power of the individual has assumed greater prominence over the past decade, fuelled by the cult of entrepreneurialism, the alteration in the demographic make-up of the working population, the increasing educational awareness of the workforce, and the erosion of the middle management layer in organizations. What we have in existence in today's society is a workforce which matches ideally that propounded by the early organization design and development writers:

> *Inter*dependence is a central characteristic of the modern, complex society. In every aspect of life we depend upon each other in achieving our goals . . . the desirable end of the growth process is an ability to strike a balance – to tolerate certain forms of dependence without being unduly frustrated. (1960: 27)

This is one of the major issues concerning the management of people today: how does the manager tread the fine line between complete dependence of the individual on the one hand, and complete independence on the other? This brings us back to extremism again. Down one path (dependence) is the conceptualization of the individual as specialist in the organization process. This is the Tayloristic view of structure and design of the firm – everyone in their place. Down the other path, many would see the manager's worst nightmare: organizations without management. As was hinted at earlier, the reality is the middle ground, what McGregor would refer to as interdependence.

The need to effectively manage people is the desire to attain what is termed the 'helicopter' approach to management, that is being able to take the longer-term view without becoming involved in the day-to-day operational issues. These are workforce issues and are most comfortably dealt with at that level. One manager explains how this process should work, and why it doesn't:

> Let me give you an example of how you manage it. It's dead easy and the analogy is so straightforward that even some of our managers can understand it. You have an important meeting to get to on Monday afternoon and you discover that your car isn't working on Friday night. What do you do? Obvious, you contact the garage first thing Saturday morning, get them to come round, take it away and fix it for you. You also find out if they can get it back to you later that day or Monday morning. You then go ahead and make alternative plans for your meeting if necessary, plan what you are going to do at the meeting, and in reality enjoy the rest of the weekend. You now enjoy the Chablis over a good meal on Saturday night, oversleep Sunday morning, spend the afternoon over *The Sunday Times* etc. etc. What you don't do, and this is where you get the message home, is stand over the mechanic while he repairs your car, telling him what to do. He knows what to do for Christ's sake!
>
> If it's good enough as a personal example then it's good enough in a workplace scenario. The manager has to let go. He has to let the people for whom he is responsible get on with their own jobs, secure in the knowledge that they have the competence, the capability and the commitment to deliver the goods on time. This leaves the manager free to do other things, planning is an example, dealing with customers and suppliers, both internal and external to the business. The difficulty we have is that so many of our managers find it

painful letting go of the everyday reins of what they consider management. It's basic insecurity on their part, they have to be seen to be doing something and overtly managing the work is the best showpiece they have, it's silly really.

One of the key elements of managing change now and in the future will be to develop this 'hands-off' management approach. Peters notes that:

> In this new role, the middle manager must become: (1) expeditor/barrier destroyer/facilitator, (2) on-call expert, and (3) diffuser of good news. In short, the middle manager must practice fast-paced horizontal management not traditional, delaying, vertical management. (1987: 369)

Similarly, Kanter stresses the importance of change in organizations, away from formalized structures and rules towards greater personal commitment:

> In the traditional bureaucratic corporation, roles were so circumscribed that most relationships tended to be rather formal and impersonal. Narrowly defined jobs constricted by rules and procedures also tended to stifle initiative and creativity, and the atmosphere was emotionally repressive. The post-entrepreneurial corporation, in contrast, with its stress on teamwork and cooperation . . . brings people closer together, making the personal dimension of relationships more important. (1989: 280)

The difficulty with these visions of the future is that making the change is painful, and not too many managers truly believe that the changes are essential to business survival. Why is this the case? If there is any truth to what we are saying here, then why don't managers want to make the necessary changes that ensure survival, growth, customer satisfaction and success? The answers have a self-accusing, almost frightening tone to them.

We have met the enemy, it is *us*

Most managers when they look at their employees see a need for control. Tom Peters summarizes this approach quite eloquently:

> You have to ask yourself what you see, what you really see when you look into the eye of a front-line employee. Do you see a ne'er-do-well that needs that span of control of 1 to 10 prevalent in your organization, that'll rip you off if you turn your back for more than three or four nanoseconds? Or do you see a person that could literally fly to the moon without a face-mask if only you would just train the hell out of them, get the hell out of their way, and give them something decent to do? (quote from 'Tom Peters – business evangelist', 'Business Matters', BBC Television)

It is this concept which lies at the heart of the control versus commitment argument of management. From an organization development perspective, organizations are about people, about their development, enhancing their performance and building the organization on that performance. The essence of rigid control is an onerous one. It is obvious that every organization needs a set of rules and guidelines against which individual and group behaviour is judged. However, in most modern organizations, these tools and methods are traditional. No matter how well refined and expertly applied, they are insufficient mechanisms for the development of the organization towards higher standards of performance. Why? Let us look at a common and persistent example.

Task fragmentation is a popular system in firms (Buchanan and McCalman, 1989: 11). It can have a number of advantages for the organization that applies it. The individual employee doesn't need too much expensive, time-consuming training; those who leave are easily replaced because the job is simple to learn; employees can do their tasks at great speed and less skill is required, hence lower-paid workers. For the manager it is also easier to control employees who undertake simple tasks. However, fragmentation also has a number of serious drawbacks. For one, the job is repetitive and boring. The employee working on a fragmented task has no idea what their contribution to the organization as a whole is. This boredom costs money – absenteeism, apathy, carelessness, even sabotage. The employee develops no skills which can lead to promotion, a greater degree of contribution, or higher standards of performance. But, it is these facets which are exactly what we require from every employee to allow the firm to survive and grow in the global economy of the future. And yet, the procedure for fragmenting manufacturing or service tasks is common and accepted in most industries today. Telephone call centres are the latest example of task fragmentation to be established, this time in the service sector (McCalman, 1996).

One therefore has to ask oneself: why are these techniques and practices still applied so widely? Many of the management theories developed in the last century are now widely known and practised. However, many of these, Taylorism for example, are inappropriate for today's organizations. Designed in the early part of the twentieth century, they work on assumptions that are out of date. So in this sense we practise the wrong stuff, and many Western organizations stick by these theories as if they were tablets of stone. For example, companies are structured in bureaucratic forms: rules, procedures and role allocations are established throughout. How can companies like Compaq, Microsoft or Sun Microsystems come from nowhere to become the world's leading multinational enterprises in the space of 15 years with a fraction of the manpower that other electronics companies employ? The reason is that they allow their people to make decisions. They are founded on the belief that success is a people factor.

There has recently been a growth in interest in the concepts of work organization and development. The reasons for this are fairly straightforward. The circumstances that organizations face today are related to speed and flexibility of response to changing market situations. Management concern is associated with being able to deal with changing markets, how to make best use of sophisticated levels of technology application, and how to meet the rising expectations of customers as they relate to quality, reliability and delivery. This means that issues related to the people element of firms become more important. As Kanter notes:

> You watch human resource policies now, move in British firms, from being a sort of backwater, 'they're the people who do the paperwork', to being a much more significant piece of strategic thinking for the firm because everybody is going to compete for people in the 1990s. In fact the quality of people is going to make a bigger difference than the quality of products or the quality of services. (quote from Rosabeth Moss Kanter, 'Business Matters', BBC Television)

Buchanan and McCalman (1989: 6) argue that these issues have meant a movement has occurred in the management of people in organizations. This movement is away from 'personnel administration' (the hiring and firing) and towards 'human resource management' (development of the individual in the organization). As problems have become more serious, what was traditionally accepted as the boundaries placed on work organization have been widened. One could postulate that human resource management is no longer acceptable unless it is accompanied by organization strategy and improvement. The argument here is that traditional personnel departments have become involved in people and organizational development at the same time to assist the organization in dealing with more complex issues. Effective people management affects the overall operating profitability of the organization and must therefore involve management at all levels from the boardroom to the shop floor.

There are important issues at stake here. In earlier chapters we have emphasized how systems could help resolve what we classified as hard issues – questions such as technology allocation and priorities. In Part 3 we also want to place emphasis on the concept of what would be considered by many as soft issues. The concern here is with people management as part of the 'big picture', getting the best from the human resource. These are not incidental issues. Effective human resource management makes money, guarantees profitability and ensures effective performance. We may classify these as soft issues by comparison to systems but the returns on getting it right in terms of organizational development are as equally important as the issues dealt with in Part 2. The significant questions associated with people management are:

- How do we manage people to best effect?
- What systems do we put in place to ensure that this effective management of the human resource occurs?
- To the extent that effective human resource management systems have been widely known since the 1930s and 1940s, why are these systems and styles not applied?

The answers have a familiar, self-analytical tone to them: we manage organizations according to our perceptions about the individual and about the organization. We don't apply models where we believe they are likely to upset the apple-cart. In other words, *we have met the enemy – it is us*. The answer to the question 'Why are these systems not applied?', is that there is a fundamental problem in the way managers think. It may be a rather simplistic way of putting it, but managers design and run organizations. If these organizations are unable to compete in the marketplace, then the design is wrong and the blame ultimately rests with those responsible for that design. This is what Konosuke Matsushita was getting at in the quote at the beginning of this chapter. In this sense the battleground is over the correct and appropriate division of labour. Megson (1988) argued that:

> Six major issues seem to be at the core of building organizations that perform exquisitely. These in my experience are the major educational hurdles we have to overcome if our quest for more effectiveness is to bear further fruit.
>
> 1 *The way we think is THE root cause.*
>   We use analytical and mechanistic thinking inappropriately. With organizations we need to use systemic and synthetic thinking instead.
>
> 2 *Our models of organizations are too limiting.*
>   Produced by analysis, they run on analysis. Machines are their analogues.
>
> 3 *We have no purpose.*
>   Preposterous? Organizations are inward looking and purpose can only be found beyond their boundaries. So if we don't look in the right place for purpose we will not have the right one, which is as bad if not worse than none at all.
>
> 4 *We have no vision or sense of mission.*
>   Without this any organization cannot achieve really high performance.
>
> 5 *We lack the resolution to delegate.*
>   We simply do not treat our subordinates as we expect our bosses to treat us – and if they feel 'less than' their contribution is 'less than' as well.
>
> 6 *We have no values or philosophy.*
>   Values relating to work and people are not explicit, or shared, they do not address the part people play in the scheme of things.

As a result, there are a number of elements associated with the choices that are made in relation to people management in organizations today.

First, because the root cause is the way we think, we tend to use models for organization design which are too limiting for our needs. Managers use and concentrate on the machine theory of design and place capital equipment above and before people in the design element. The machine system analyses the problem, produces the desired design and installs that design, in-company, by analysis. The difficulty here is that the reason for designing the organization in this way is to meet an internal purpose, when purpose is to be found beyond the boundary of the firm. An example of this would be where managers design systems that are technologically driven but ignore human contribution and/or customer demands.

Second, very little time and attention is paid to the concept of design from an organizational perspective. The research and design of a *product* can take years from initial idea to final product delivery. Market research, advertising and placement of that product can command massive budgets in ensuring that everything is right when the product hits the marketplace. The amount of time spent *designing a new organization system to cope with change* is minimal, if it takes place at all! It is more often than not done *on the back of an envelope,* with little consultation with those likely to be affected by the changes involved, and little consideration given to the likely outcomes of the change. The reasons for this are related to the way managers think about their organizations. Analytical and mechanistic thinking are encouraged (especially at most business schools and on most MBA programmes) when they are highly inappropriate. If an organization is an organic system then systemic and synthetic thinking are necessary.

Third, the behaviour of managers in organizations suggests that there is a distinct lack of resolution to delegate within organizations. This was referred to earlier on, and the examples by Thorsurd, Matsushita and Pascale et al. explain the impact that this has. There is an unwillingness to treat subordinates in the same manner that managers expect to be treated by their own superiors. This has knock-on implications for motivation. Place yourself in the position of a front-line operator. Ask yourself the question: 'If I am treated as "less than" by my immediate boss, then is it surprising that my response in terms of commitment is "less than"?' If the answer is no, which it should be, then managers have to ask themselves, 'What types of hellholes have we as managers created?' (Tom Peters, 'Business Matters').

Fourth, managers lack any form of systematic thinking about core values and philosophy. They have few beliefs concerning the nature of work and people that are explicit, shared and identify the part that people in organizations play. If you don't understand yourself how you want your organization to operate, then how can others see how they fit into it?

It is these issues which need to be addressed in order to create a clearer understanding of what the big picture is, and how people fit into it. This leads us on to Chapter 8, which details the organization development model and how it can be used. The remainder of this chapter takes each of the comments associated with the main management issues outlined above and explains them in more detail. We look at why these issues occur, how they manifest themselves in organizations, and what is needed to change. The accounts given here are largely prescriptive in the sense that we specifically set out what is being done wrong, and what is required to make it right. They are also set in fairly provocative and challenging terms – deliberately so. We want you to think about them, see if they are true, see if they apply to your organization, and then think what can be done to resolve them. However, we have also attempted to be descriptive and to present particular events and circumstances that the manager would be expected to come across during the course of their job. You should be able to sympathize and associate with these. You should also be able to recognize and begin to think about the changes that are needed. One important point needs to be emphasized here. Suspend your initial judgements and your firm belief that 'This wouldn't happen to me, so I can ignore it.'

The models we use are too limiting

The way the manager thinks is very much conditioned by their approach to the management profession. It is most readily summed up in that well-worn (and flawed) sentiment that 'It's management's right to manage.' The noun 'right' in this instance connotes a prerogative, authority or desire to control or dominate. The right is that of position power in many instances and is based on nothing more than title. This is reflected in the traditional Tayloristic model of organization popularized in the early twentieth century. This views people, especially those on the shop floor, as machine parts, elements, factors of production, cogs in the larger machine. In this sense, the individual only needs to know as much as is necessary to play their part in the process. It is the manager's role to organize, control and coordinate the bigger picture.

There are three reasons why models such as Taylorism retain their popularity. First, they are easy to apply. Taylorism, the division of labour, task specialization etc. appear as a plausible and cheap set of techniques. The ideas are fairly straightforward by comparison with some of the models which are linked to organization development. Specialization, for example, increases the amount of work that progresses through the system. It also simplifies the production element, for everyone has a place and everyone should be in that place: 'It is always easier to blame workers who have the wrong skills, wrong attitudes and wrong values, than to blame a systematically prepared job specification' (Buchanan and McCalman, 1989: 12).

Second, it perpetuates status. The status is that which Taylorism affords to managers. A greater degree of responsibility taken on by the workforce, who can control the performance of meaningful sections of an organization's operations, begins to threaten the legitimacy of management. It is easier (and more comforting to status) to have individual workers who have little or no identification with the whole organization and who have no idea how they fit into the bigger picture. Taylorism fragments tasks, hides contribution and maintains managerial status.

Third, managers are unaware of alternative forms of design and development for their organizations. This is the not the manager's fault. The alternatives are couched in such obscure language (and journals) that their wider applicability is lost to the manager, and thus the credibility of such alternatives is eroded.

One of the difficulties with the old-fashioned view of management was that it failed to recognize the full potential of the individual in the organization. For most organizations survival and growth will stem from the full utilization of the intelligence, skills and commitment of the workforce. It is essential to perceive the labour element of production as an asset value instead of a factor cost.

It is not surprising that approaches to the concept of design are not new in organizations. The fact that firms have been in existence for 150 years or more would suggest that at some time during this period a body of knowledge on how best to organize and design the firm would have built up. There are a number of approaches that can be considered. Many are couched in the period in which they developed, and many show the signs of age. However, there are schools of thought which try to integrate differing variables associated with design to effect more appropriate forms of business performance.

Four models are briefly outlined in this section. We freely admit to not doing them justice here, and the reader may look elsewhere for more detailed explanations. The models have a historical, sequential development, beginning with machine theory or scientific management (Taylorism) and developing through the human relations movement, the contingency theorists and finally the organization development movement.

Scientific management (Taylorism)

One of the first models of organizational and management behaviour was that developed in the early part of the twentieth century by Fredcrick Winslow Taylor. The concepts of what is now widely referred to as 'Taylorism' lay in the division between manual and mental work in the organization. The basis of Taylor's theories was that work could be divided into subunits or specializations which could be performed by individuals. Taylor started from the basic principle that work could be scientifically determined and that 'one best way' to perform a task could be found. This would then be made standard practice and the individual and organization would benefit. We do not have the time or space here to go into the details of the model but would recommend you read any general organizational behaviour textbook for an introduction to Frederick Taylor and the concept of scientific management.

The human relations movement

The second school of thought related to organizational effectiveness and behaviour stemmed from the studies of Elton Mayo and Fritz Roethlisberger at Western Electric's Hawthorne plant near Chicago during the 1920s and 1930s (Roethlisberger and Dickson, 1939). Whereas the scientific management studies of Taylor focused attention on mechanistic, machine theories of organization, the Hawthorne studies drew attention to the humanistic approach and in particular to group behaviour and relations among group members and between group members and management. Effective performance was associated with understanding the linkages between the individual, their role among other members of the group at the workplace, and the degree of independence given to the group. In the human relations movement, increasing individual satisfaction within the group led to increased performance and greater organizational effectiveness. The human relations movement was also important in recognizing job design and the working environment as key variables in organizational performance.

The contingency theorists

By the early 1960s further research in the area of organizational behaviour suggested the development of a series of contingency theories based on an open-systems concept or view of the organization. These organizational theorists advocated no single form of organizational structure or style of management. Concepts such as structure and managerial style were dependent on the organization's business and its environment, or numerous other influencing variables. There were a number of contingency theorists, each with their own specific view of the influencing variables which determined the way an organization was designed. We shall look at two pairs of authors in particular: Burns and Stalker, and Lawrence and Lorsch.

In an examination of 20 British firms during the 1960s, Burns and Stalker identified two types of effective organization – mechanistic and organic. Both types were effective under different circumstances. The mechanistic firm prospered in stable markets whereas the organic firm succeeded in rapidly changing markets and technologies. The mechanistic organization has the following characteristics:

- task differentiation and specialization
- hierarchy for coordination of tasks, control and communications
- control of incoming/outgoing communications from the top and a tendency for information to be provided on a need to know basis
- interaction and emphasis placed on vertical reporting lines
- loyalty to the organization and its officers
- value placed on internal knowledge and experience in contrast to more general knowledge (Burns and Stalker, 1961: 119).

By contrast, the organic organization was characterized by:

- continuous assessment of task allocation through interaction to utilize knowledge which solves real problems
- the use of expertise, power relationships and commitment to total task
- sharing of responsibility
- open and widely used communication patterns which incorporate horizontal and diagonal as well as vertical channels
- commitment to task accomplishment, development and growth of the organization rather than loyalty to officials
- value placed on general skills which are relevant to the organization (1961: 120–5).

Burns and Stalker's research work was important in the sense that their studies identified differentiation between types of organization. It also stressed the belief that the organization could change its design, structure and approach in relation to its environment.

In a similar vein, the basis of Lawrence and Lorsch's (1967; 1969) analysis of organization was that structure and management depended on the environment the firm found itself in. Because of this, the more complex the environment, the more decentralized and flexible management needed to be. Patterns emerged which suggested that the nature of *differentiation* occurring in the organization determined the degree of centralization or decentralization that took place. This differentiation could be measured by an examination of:

- formal structure (rules, regulations, procedures etc.)
- certainty of goals (are they clear and easily measured or uncertain?)
- the timing of feedback (are results seen in the short or long term?)
- interpersonal interaction (level of interpersonal and intergroup communication and cooperation).

Let us look at this in practical terms by considering the example of the structure and management of firms in the hardware and software sectors of the electronics industry. Both the internal and external environment for software manufacturers is extremely complicated. Firms deal in the concept of, and trading of, pure knowledge – the expertise of their software writers. Policy is largely flexible, being a function of current demand in many instances. Instantaneous feedback and interpersonal communication are a way of life. Structure is largely informal (for example, Microsoft has relaxed dress codes, and single-status parking and restaurants). The environment changes rapidly and therefore the organization has to be able to monitor and react quickly to changes. This suggests a more informal, decentralized form of organization and management.

By comparison, in many of the hardware sectors of the electronics industry, e.g. defence and avionics goods, there is a more stable environment. Structures are more formalized, as are reporting and communication procedures. Although, by comparison with other industries, change may be perceived as rapid, there is a tendency for more centralization, longer-term goals, and precise policies and procedures.

Which of these types of design, structure and management are correct? The answer, according to Lawrence and Lorsch, is that they both are because they both fit the organization's environment. One of the key elements to emerge from the work of Lawrence and Lorsch was that predictability of the task was a basic condition variable in the choice of organizational form. That meant that both internal and external criteria had to be taken into consideration.

The organization development model

The next chapter deals specifically with the historical development, systems and application of organization development. However, it is important here to emphasize that it is a design model that has been developed extensively over the last 30 years. A wide body of literature exists on the subject of organizational development and design. It is important here to classify what we mean by organization development and the concerns it attempts to address. Warner Burke (1994) classifies OD as 'a planned process of change in an organization's culture through the utilization of behavioural science technologies, research and theory'. The importance though is that:

> OD practitioners are concerned with change that integrates individual needs with organizational goals more fully; change that improves an organization's effectiveness, especially human resources; and change that involves organization members in the decisions that directly affect them and their working conditions. (1994: 11)

OD provides us with a model in which the importance of relating work to people is fully recognized. They no longer become cogs but are an integrated part of the organizational equation. Figure 7.1 is a schematic

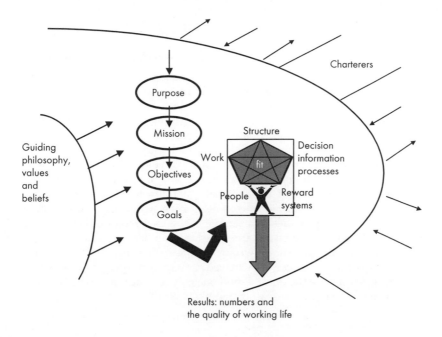

Figure 7.1   *The organization development model at Digital (Megson, 1988)*

representation of this. The first point to note is that it is a bounded model. It places the organization within an environment (this pays heed to the work of Lawrence and Lorsch) represented by 'charterers'. The word 'charterer' is used to convey importance to those outside the organization, those that give the organization its reason for being and can take it away. Mechanistic models of organizations ignore them or assume that their needs, having previously been established, do not need to be reviewed. However, for survival, organizations need to identify expectations of charterers, and synthesize these into a statement of purpose.

Our organizations have no purpose

If the accepted design norm is that most organizations are/were designed using the process of analytical thinking – breaking the job down into constituent parts for task specialization – then this machine analogy finds its purpose by reference to an internal focus. However, as many organization theorists point out, the purpose of an organization is found outwith its own boundaries, in its ability to react with and to its environment. Therefore, design which focuses too much on internal issues is looking in the wrong place. This becomes clearer when we look at the purpose of organizations.

READER ACTIVITY

Take a couple of minutes to think about your own organization's purpose.

You may have come up with some interesting conclusions. The first reaction is normally a straightforward one. The purpose is to make a profit, to provide a needed service or to stay in business. Simplistic, yes, but hardly definitive. Delving a little deeper may bring you to the provision of goods and services of high quality that serve customer needs. This is getting closer to the reality of an organization and its purpose which is provided by the external environment and is directly linked to results and performance. What the organization has to take into account is that the conflicting expectations of the external environment (customers, share-holders, suppliers, governments etc.) need to be synthesized into a single statement. Megson provides an example of the importance of establishing purpose: 'Purpose has to be on target because all other organization design flows from it. An unclear or wrong purpose ruins further design and effectiveness can no longer be achieved. A wrong purpose can be worse than none. With none the quest to find one may continue, a wrong one may stop further search and so seal its doom' (1988: 10).

Sherwood (1988) argues that one of the features of high-performance organizations is the definition and organization-wide awareness of purpose:

> A shared sense of purpose entails sharing a vision that is based on a clearly stated set of values describing both the organization's mission (purpose) and the methods for realizing it. An organization's vision provides energy and direction. . . . It empowers individual employees and forms the basis of a planned culture.

Organizations have to be able to define their purpose in clear, unam-biguous terms which enable them to create a precise design to fit the purpose. The most effective means of doing so is to look to the external environment to find the purpose of the organization (provision of product on time, negotiation of supply contracts that benefit both sides etc.). This provides the work that an organization needs to accomplish, and then the organization executes the work. The other variables in Figure 7.1 operate to assist in the accomplishment of purpose. Define the purpose, do the work, achieve the result and effective performance follows. This appears too easy. The reality is that design is complicated because of what we have argued earlier. We are not geared towards thinking in these terms. Pasmore notes that:

> Neither managers nor employees are prepared for this task at the beginning of a redesign effort. Most have never worked in a flexible organization of the kind I am describing or read much about alternative ways of organizing or how to

approach change. Some have never thought about these things before, and a few don't ever *want* to think about them. . . . If people know only what history has taught them, they are prisoners of the past. (1994: 46–7)

These concepts of defining purpose and organization redesign are seen as 'woolly' and too far removed from reality and the everyday pressures of work. We would argue that this is because many organizations lack the vision or sense of mission to think in these terms.

Our organizations lack vision or sense of mission

The mission statement in organizations is a popular tool for clarifying operational strategy. Mission, in an organizational sense, is for the people working in that organization to develop. The level at which mission is defined determines awareness and commitment to it. The most popular form of mission definition is that provided by the boss; it's quick but shuts out the rest of the organization. Mission defined by a senior management team takes longer but the payoff is more powerful. Mission determined by the whole organization is rare, takes an enormous amount of time, and may prove impossible to develop. Whoever sets it, mission is about aspirational values within the organization. By not sharing these aspirations the opportunity to build an effective organization is lost. In developing vision and mission the organization also has to look at the needs and wants of the individual. People do not get energized unless they see their own needs and wants in parallel with those of the organization. If purpose tells the organization what it needs to do, then mission gives the organization what it wants to do as well. There are opportunities to structure work that has to be done to fit the purpose in ways that meet individual needs. However, these needs are often ignored. Organizations require to develop their mission, to tap into the talents and energies of the people within them.

Managers lack the resolution to delegate

Many managers do not treat their subordinates as they expect to be treated by their bosses. As a manager, the expectation is that your immediate superior will give you space – you can manage yourself – true? However, managers expect obedience from those who work for them. Managers see themselves as committed to the organization and to its purpose as well as their own. Yet managers expect loyalty from subordinates without considering their needs and wants. The manager expects to use their talents to the full, yet tells people what to do. As a manager you see yourself as open, candid and courageous, yet we see subordinates as 'less-than'. This results in shutting off employees' candour and makes disagreement and argument feel like a test of courage or a career decision. There is a need to empower subordinates so they see themselves as equals.

In Chapter 8 we will look at some of the practical applications of organization development. One of these is the use of autonomous or semi-autonomous work groups where employees are empowered to take responsibility for their own actions in a workplace setting. However, this is difficult for the manager to deal with because it involves a 'hands-off' approach. The structure of these work groups sets up the requirement for employees to be treated as equals. Managers have trouble with this because most of them do not really believe that they are or can be equal. Because of this managers do not have the necessary values which are consistent with the concept of delegated responsibility. Without this there is never full commitment, and hence the potential of employees remains unexplored.

Organizations have no values

This is a mistake. Everyone has their own values and philosophy which guide them through life. However, in an organizational setting what is lacking is a shared set of values and philosophy. Philosophy and values relate to how organizations deal with their beliefs about people and work. These fundamental beliefs and philosophy guide the design of organizational life. They need to be defined and shared with organizational members in order that people understand and make sense of their working life – how and where they fit into the big picture. Megson, in describing the guiding values and beliefs at Digital, comments that:

> They are based on a *Philosophy* that I describe as follows:
>
> People are the most important asset we have. They want and need to grow. Without growth interest wanes and talents waste away. With growth interest flourishes and talents develop. People really do care, they do exquisite work – if it is designed to enable them to grow.
>
> *In other words, personal growth is the engine that drives organization performance.* (1988: 16)

It is the ability to put these guiding values and beliefs into practice which is at the heart of the organization development model which we deal with in the next chapter. The key is to design work that fits people and not the other way round. If we accept that effective performance comes from people being energized towards their needs and wants as well as those of the organization, then the design has to take account of this.

The concept of design in organizations

All firms have to consider the element of design. To the extent that every firm exists, it has a design associated with it. The small business operating out of a garage and employing 10 people has a structure and is designed according to the owner's wishes. The corporate multinational operating across five continents and employing 400,000 people also has to consider design. The commonality is associated with the attainment of standards of performance and the need to deal with complexities of size and division of labour (Galbraith, 1977). The organization has to conceive an approach to satisfy the attainment of a number of factors. There are three factors: • the goals and purposes for which the organization exists; • the patterns of labour division and coordination of different units within the organization; • the people who will do the work (Galbraith, 1977: 5). The concept of design in organizations is associated with establishing a fit between these three areas of choice. The essence of design is the assessment of fit between the three areas, the examination of alternatives where the fit does not operate effectively, and the implementation of those alternatives in the form of a new design.

The examples given in Mini Cases 7.1 and 7.2 (see pp. 140–3) best illustrate the need for fit and the concept of organization design.

The role of politics in orgainzations

One of the main reasons for the failure of many change management programmes is the resistance to change people within the organization put up. Managers and workers see a proposed change path and put up barriers. What causes this resistance? Bedeian (1980) argues that there are four common causes: parochial self-interest, misunderstanding and lack of trust, contradictory assessment of the impact change will have, and a low tolerance for change. Organizational politics is the means by which many attempt to resist or affect change.

In examining the politics of organizational change Buchanan and Badham (1999a) suggest that political behaviour is acceptable and 'can serve organizational goals as well as personal career objectives; and that while specific actions may appear unacceptable when considered in isolation, political behaviour is potentially defensible in context'. Similarly, Appelbaum and Hughes (1998: 85) argue that, far from having a negative connotation, political behaviour is quite neutral and can be either helpful or harmful to members of an organization or the organization itself. Gunn (1994: 33) suggests that what is of concern is the high costs of allowing people to use the political system to mask their self-serving actions. Whether the manager wants to get involved in the politics of career progression is obviously an individual choice; however, they must acknowledge that it exists or they will potentially become

Mini Case 7.1   Bell Atlantic and participative change

In 1991 Rosabeth Moss Kanter conducted an interview with Bell Atlantic's CEO Raymond Smith who, on his appointment, had seen the urgent need for change. He realized that the growth of his company's core businesses would not sustain it into the competitive global economy of the twenty-first century. Smith designed four initial strategies to improve Bell Atlantic's position:

- improved efficiency
- improved marketing to protect market share
- new products and services
- new businesses operating outside the United States.

The culture of Bell Atlantic had grown out of a long-standing monopoly with a centralized organizational structure. As a result, managers did not understand the initiative, innovation, risks and accountability necessary to meet the new business goals set by Smith. The company also indulged in parochial, cross-departmental competition which raised costs and prevented new initiatives.

Plans were made to seek to change the behaviour of the organization to realize Smith's strategies. He was personally involved in the design of seminars in which 1400 managers spent half a week discussing and debating what the values of the new organization should be. Five values were eventually agreed upon:

- integrity
- respect and trust
- excellence
- individual fulfilment
- profitable growth.

Some of these are essential to underpin organizational development efforts, e.g. the individual should be treated with respect and dignity.

Once the company values had been agreed, Smith realized that the organization needed to move from general statements to concrete behaviours and work practices. Through participative management, Smith defined the obligations of the managers to the organization and encapsulated these in a formal document, 'The obligations of leadership'. Bell Atlantic took a year to get the required understanding and commitment from its management.Once this was done, an organized programme of internal communications for all employees was developed, outlining obligations to each other, the opportunities ahead and the need and reasons for change.

The emphasis of the organizational structure was on teamworking and quality because Smith believed that: 'In a large business the most important determinant of success is the effectiveness of millions of day-to-day interactions between human beings. If those contacts are contentious, turf-orientated, and parochial, the company will flounder, bureaucracies will grow and internal competition will be rampant. But when employees behave in accountable, team-orientated and collegial ways, it dramatically improves group effectiveness.'

These activities led to the design of 'the Bell Atlantic Way', an organized, participative method of working together that allowed everyone to maximize their contribution to team goals. Smith announced a 10-year transition to this way of working. Forums were designed to introduce the Bell Atlantic Way to 20,000 managers and from there to staff. He wrote to all employees defining the basic business problems, the strategies identified to resolve them, departmental goals and individual objectives. Reward systems were then initiated, which focused on team and individual results.

When Smith unveiled his new organization, individual departments were empowered to create the organization they thought would be most efficient. The 'champion programme' was also introduced at the same time to identify potential corporate entrepreneurs, train them and develop their ideas into new businesses.

After these changes had been implemented, Smith noted that people were no longer parochial or territorial but were more accountable and more team oriented. Some 36 champions were accepted into the programme and by late 1990 there were 33 products and services in the pipeline, several near to commercialization.

The techniques Smith used at Bell Atlantic map well onto the perpetual transition management model outlined in the introductory chapter, as shown in Table 7.1.

Table 7.1   *Bell Atlantic approaches*

Theory	Practice
Trigger layer	Core businesses would not sustain the company in the competitive global economy of the twenty-first century
Vision layer	Development of four strategies Articulate five values of the company The obligations of leadership
Conversion layer	Communications programme to all managers and staff defining the business problem, strategies to resolve it, departmental goals and individuals' objectives Definition and practice of 'the Bell Atlantic way'
Maintenance and renewal layer	Reward systems Business measures, e.g quality and customer service Development of the 'champion programme'

Kanter argues that competitive pressures are forcing organizations to adopt new, flexible strategies and structures. Bell Atlantic's move towards empowered, flexible teams seems to be an example of this.

---

disillusioned by the process (Standing and Standing, 1998: 313). It can also be argued that getting involved in politicking in an organizational context is part of normal behaviour. Stone argues that: 'When people have a choice between a rational decision and their ego, they always choose their ego!' (1997: 23). Therefore, the prevalence of political behaviour is the norm rather than the exception (Buchanan and Badham, 1999a). In some senses it may also be seen as desirable. Frost and Egri (1991) argue that political behaviour is both inevitable and necessary in stimulating creativity and debate and that it should be seen as a positive mechanism for change.

Power and politics have generally been under-researched in organizations. Thompson and McHugh (1995: 132) suggest that most textbooks

Mini Case 7.2   A new telecoms enterprise and dictatorial transformation

Dunphy and Stace (1990) argue that incremental and collaborative or consultative modes of change implementation often generate conflicting views and ideas which are not always reconciled. As a result such change strategies are time-consuming. They argue that there is a role for dictatorial transformation and forced evolution in such situations. A newly formed telecoms enterprise provides an example of where dictatorial transformation and lack of participative change management have not worked well. If a programme of coercive or dictatorial change is adopted, as Dunphy and Stace suggest, with no communication programme or planning for change, then the effort may well be doomed from the start. Kotter (1995) explains that 'without motivation, people won't help and the effort goes nowhere'. This view is also supported by evidence for the failure of many change management initiatives. Reasons often cited include:

- *Poor communication* – Giving information gradually is risky.
- *Misunderstanding of what change is about* – Change is a journey, not an event.
- *Lack of planning and preparation* – Management may look only to the end result, not at the required steps to get there.
- *Lack of clear vision* – If staff do not know where the company is going, how can they get there?
- *Quick-fix option* – Change means more than a T-shirt, quality poster, coffee mug, seminar or newsletter.
- *Legacies of previous change* – May have developed a sceptical, risk-averse culture.
- *Goals set too far into the future* – Short-term wins are essential for success.

The new telecoms enterprise's main objective was to become a leading regional telephone operator. In 1994 the company was an informal adhocracy moving towards a functional structure. The advantages of such a structure were its flexibility and ability to cope with changing circumstances. This was outgrown as the company increased in size, launched more products and acquired more companies. The move from business into residential markets also had a major impact on the organization and the company developed a function-based bureaucracy with control centralized through the CEO. Merging other acquired companies into the new structure became increasingly more time-consuming. The company did not use change management techniques to manage its transitions and no change agents operated within the organization.

In 1997 a staff survey was undertaken by management. Some of the responses seem to highlight the effects of rapid change within the organization.

Question: how frequently do you feel stressed at work?

Not at all	8%
Every few months	23%
Every few weeks	28%
At least once a week	32%
Every day	8%

Short temper, poor or careless work were cited as the main expressions of stress, with 18 per cent of those asked saying they occasionally became ill as a result of stress.

Question: What is the most important management action that could be taken to reduce workplace stress?

Discussion and communication	32%
More staff	19%
Improved resources	16%

Question: indicate whether you think the following culture statements are true of the firm

The organization is honest, open and trusting.

Very true	12%
Quite true	41%
Not sure	34%
Not very true	11%
Totally untrue	2%

These findings appeared to suggest lower than desirable trust levels. To explore this further additional cultural-related questions were asked concerning:

- whether staff felt empowered
- whether promises were delivered
- whether management 'walks the talk'
- whether teamwork and cooperation were natural
- whether staff felt personally responsible for the success of the enterprise.

These questions received similar ratings. The 'walk the talk' culture statement scored badly, with nearly a third of the company saying it was not true and nearly half saying they were unsure.

Employees did not feel involved in the company as much as they might otherwise have been if communication was good. Values of teamwork and respect etc. were not lived or communicated throughout the business from the top down. This factor perhaps explains some of the scepticism regarding cultural statements and indicates that there could be a role for organizational development to play.

In the case of the new telecoms enterprise, where organizational change was dictatorial and unmanaged, problems have occurred. The implication of this seems to be that a participative approach could be more successful.

Finally, there may be a role for academics and managers to work together in developing successful approaches to organizational change. Bennis (1996) notes that: 'while the French moralist may be right that there are no delightful marriages, just good ones, it is possible that if managers and behavioural scientists continue to get their heads together in organizational revitalization, they might develop delightful organizations – just possibly.'

ignore power and politics or subsume them under other headings such as leadership. Similarly, the literature on change is fairly scathing of organizational politics in general. Although dealing with change from a number of different stances, most of the literature lacks substance when it comes to discussions of political activity. The exceptions are authors such as Yates (1985), Pettigrew (1985; 1987; 1988) Pfeffer (1994), Hardy (1996) and Buchanan and Badham (1999a; 1999b).

The main recognition of the importance of politics comes from the contextual/processual approach to change (Pettigrew, 1985; 1987; 1988; Dunphy and Stace, 1988). By recognizing that change is non-linear, the contextual/processual approach focuses on the enabling and constraining characteristics of change and hence on the political arena in which change is made. Lee and Lawrence argue that: 'There is much power in being able to affect the political context, often more, and with longer-term effects, than possessing strong power bases and adopting effective strategies within the context' (1991: 143).

Other fields of change management are less willing to accept the processes and behaviours associated with organizational politics. In reviewing the field of organization development (OD), Buchanan and Badham (1999a) argue that authors in this field either deny the relevance of 'power-coercive strategies' or recommend action within a legitimate domain of politics. Here individuals are advised to pursue the moral high ground for organizational wellbeing instead of 'dirty tricks' and other dubious tactics for self-enhancement (Greiner and Schein, 1988; Egan, 1994). Similarly, managerial humanism attempts to deny the existence of, neglects or disdains the politics of organizational change and the activities of managers therein (Klein, 1976). In drawing comparisons between humanist management and existentialism, Stone (1997: 45) argues that whilst humanism attempts to provide individuals in the organizational setting with a safe environment for self-exploration, existentialism recognizes the confrontational nature of organizations.

Yet there is a need to draw attention to organizational politics as it affects the management of change. Buchanan et al. (1997: 15) provide evidence that 70 per cent of managers felt that the more complex and wide-ranging change was in an organization, the more intense the politics became. Similarly, these managers felt that the change agent who was not politically skilled would eventually fail.

One of the main difficulties in looking at politics in organizations is in gaining access to research evidence associated with the behaviours of individual managers in this area. There are two key aspects to this: image and legitimacy. In terms of image, managers dislike discussing subjects such as organizational politicking because they believe that it reflects badly on themselves as managers and their organizations publicly. Rationalism rather than power-plays therefore legitimizes decision making: 'Managers often tend to rationalize their activities in terms of technical skills and choose to ignore the influence of politics' (Standing

and Standing, 1998: 311). Therefore gaining access to such information is
a potential minefield. The main difficulty is that within organizations,
politics relies on informal behaviours and an oral tradition. It is rare
for political activities or deals to be documented. Managers place less
significance on the role of politics by attempting to rationalize their
behaviours and actions. Political behaviour is therefore highly unstruc-
tured and difficult to access.

Conclusion

The concept of design in organizations has to be congruent with people.
Work needs to be designed in a manner in which people are engaged in
meaningful tasks. The organization must fit work to people, not the other
way round. Anything less is sub-optimal, it doesn't guarantee high
performance. When designing the organization, we must consider how
the work of the individual employee adds to the purpose of the enterprise. Work has to contain within it elements that achieve business
purpose and can be measured. For example, in manufacturing, the
mechanistically determined fragmentation of tasks means that the
individual employee knows their own job very well but not the whole.
This means that people miss the impact that interactions have on their
surroundings. The traditional mechanism for responding to this lack of
interaction is supervision. The supervisor provides the overview and
direction to the task players. Today the pace of change is such that this
level of supervision is questionable. It is an inadequate use of employee
capabilities and is overmanning gone mad. Work that is designed to
allow the employee to build a product, test it and ship it provides
contribution and meaning. People understand where they fit into the
system, and performance is easy to assess in terms of results that are
important – quality, cost, time to customer etc. It provides the employee
with work that demands commitment.

   This is largely where we came in. Management in organizations today
is largely people management. If people are the important asset,
effectiveness is related to:

- how managers perceive the individual
- how people relate to one another
- how we get the maximum contribution
- how we go about changing from a situation which is seen to be
  ineffective to one which ensures higher standards of performance.

In Chapter 8 we set out the organization development model as an
approach to managing change. It is one which lays emphasis very much
on people issues. In this chapter we have tried to lay the groundwork in
a challenging manner. We doubt whether organizations are as black as

the picture we have painted in terms of purpose, mission, delegation etc. But when dealing with the people element of managing change it is important to continually question why we are doing things. It is how we perceive people that matters. It is how we perceive the organization that matters. It is how we perceive the manager's role that matters. We are fortunate to live in an era of rapid change. It gives us the *raison d'être* to ask questions, try new concepts, and most importantly be aware of the pervasive nature of change. The goals associated with the soft issues such as organization development are related to communication within the organization, to decision-making styles and systems, and to problem solving. The values are humanistic and are aimed at developing maximum potential for the individual, the group and the organization as a whole. The requirement is for the encouragement of open relationships in the organization. Understanding the importance of people is the first step.

8 Organizations Can Develop

In the last few years, more and more organizational leaders have realized that it is not enough to carry out piecemeal efforts to patch up an organization problem here, fix a procedure there, or change a job description. Today there is a need for longer-range, coordinated strategy to develop organization climates, ways of work, relationships, communications systems, and information systems that will be congruent with the predictable and unpredictable requirements of the years ahead. (Beckhard, 1969)

Let us make no mistake: the cultures of consent are not easy to run, or to work in. Authority in these organizations does not come automatically with the title; it has to be earned . . . based . . . on your ability to help others do better, by developing their skills, by liaising with the rest of the organization, by organizing their work more efficiently, by helping them to make the most of their resources, by continual encouragement and example. (Handy, 1989)

Perhaps the greatest competitive challenge companies face is adjusting to – indeed, embracing – non-stop change. They must be able to learn rapidly and continuously, innovate ceaselessly, and take on new strategic imperatives faster and more comfortably. Constant change means more organizations must create a healthy discomfort with the status quo, an ability to detect emerging trends quicker than the competition, an ability to make rapid decisions, and the agility to seek new ways of doing business . . . the only competitive weapon left is the organization . . . winning will spring from organizational capabilities such as speed, responsiveness, agility, learning capacity, and employee competence. (Ulrich, 1998)

Plus ça change? There is almost a 30-year span between Beckhard, Handy and Ulrich yet the issues being addressed have not really changed all that much. Beckhard, writing in 1969, identified that the business environment of the time had to deal with quite a few changes. This included internationalization of markets, shorter product life cycles, the increased significance of marketing, relationships of line and staff management, new organization forms, and the changing nature of work (1969: 5–6).

Issues don't really change over time, only their degree of importance. How many of the changes identified by Beckhard are crucial today? We would argue that they all are.

READER ACTIVITY: APPROPRIATE CONSIDERATION OF CHANGE

In the twenty-first century a number of changes are likely to have a serious impact on the way your organization does business. Consider for example the following trends.

AN AGEING POPULATION   In 1990, the UK population totalled 57.3 million with 19 per cent aged less than 15 years old. People in the 45–60 age bracket made up 16 per cent of the population, while the old, those over 75, made up only 6.9 per cent. By 2000, this age distribution will have changed markedly, with the youngest age group making up 20 per cent of the population, the middle-aged 18.5 per cent and those over 75 7.4 per cent.

The structure and size of the population has a major influence on the economic wellbeing of a country. Population demographics have a serious bearing on the profitability of certain industrial and service sectors.

TECHNOLOGY GONE WILD   The development of computing and information technology will continue to spiral and this will create significant reductions in geographical and temporal space. The time distance between Europe and the Far East will diminish to become insignificant.

Computing systems will become the main form of doing business through the Internet, and technological advances will cause business to become less labour intensive. Advances in medical technology will mean we live longer and continue to be active long into what is now considered old age.

ENVIRONMENTAL PROTECTION   Being able to develop business ideas at either the micro or the macro level will have to be undertaken within rules of sustainability and protection of global resources such as the oceans and the atmosphere. Firms will be publicly prosecuted for infringements and those that can illustrate environmental enhancement will gain competitive advantage.

FLEXIBLE APPROACHES TO THE WORKPLACE   Not only will work become increasingly more mental than manual, the concept of the workplace itself will alter radically. As fewer people are employed in manufacturing, the service sector will design and implement methods of working that remove the concept of a physical working environment and place this within the realms of technology.

People will no longer be employed by a single organization but will develop consultancy approaches to their work. This will lead to the development of lifelong learning patterns paid for by the individual themselves.

MANAGEMENT AS A CONTROL PROCESS WILL CEASE   As individuals take on greater and greater levels of personal responsibility for the outcomes of their work, the need for traditional forms of management will end. Managers, to the extent that they exist, will act as coordinators of independent staff and will be judged on their ability to attain a number of performance criteria such as inspirational capabilities, visionary sense, and the ability to delegate.

What are the major implications of these changes for organizations in the next century?

In Chapter 7 we seemed to indicate that there was a great deal to be done in the area of organizational development in Western firms. Our argument was that because of the nature of managerial behaviour, the full level of effective performance of an organization was hampered. The major element of this behaviour was reflected in approaches to the management of change. More often than not these are non-participatory, lack clear goals and objectives, and are undertaken in a piecemeal fashion. Our suggestion in this chapter is that the element of people management via organizational development programmes is not given the same level of importance, or thought, as that attached to product development or market research development.

READER ACTIVITY: APPROPRIATE CONSIDERATION OF CHANGE LEADS TO EFFECTIVE RESPONSES TO OPPORTUNITIES

Let us look at some of the implications of the trends highlighted in the previous reader activity. Most organizations during the next century are likely to be affected by changing demographic patterns to a greater or lesser degree. Three examples serve to show the crucial nature of being aware of the need for proactive change within organizations.

Private pension firms will increasingly take advantage of the mismatch between the working population and those moving to retirement. As governments struggle to manage the gap between tax inflows and outflows the private sector will service the individual's needs. The development of individual pension and savings plans will catapult pension firms into even greater prominence.

Two of the major beneficiaries of an ageing population are likely to be pharmaceutical giants and health care companies. An ageing population spends more per capita on health care than any other section of the population. Organizations such as BUPA face a drain on their resources as an ever ageing population begins to take advantage of the health care schemes that individuals have contributed to over the years. Similarly, there is a growth opportunity in nursing homes that cater for an older population but do so in a professional manner. However, a generally healthier, more health-conscious population might not be such a drain on firms in the health care sector. The National Health Service in the United

Kingdom currently struggles under the strain of too few resources trying to cope with increasing demand. Will an ageing population bring about greater levels of privatization? Some may find it morally indefensible to remove the socialist icon of 'from the cradle to the grave' but others will identify opportunities for exploitation. The politics are not at issue here. The concern is what type of change response one contemplates – proactive or ostrich?

In retailing, an increase in the middle-aged sector of the population may hold benefits for companies that specifically target this range of the population. Marks and Spencer won't go to the wall, assuming an attractive product and service mix, in the next decade because its traditional customer base is in the 30+ age group. Companies such as The Body Shop, with ecological and environmental reputations, will match up well with a more environmentally aware population.

The importance of change management is not the extent to which these trends are accurate or will actually come to fruition. The importance lies in thinking about the implications of issues such as demographics on company performance 10 years down the road. How many of you, when thinking about demographics, thought about the impact on recruitment on organizations?

In dealing with the often 'messy' problem of people management, many settle for the easy route of ignoring the problems and hoping that performance will somehow be maintained. What we argue in this chapter is that, given the current economic climate, organizations can no longer afford to ignore the human element as part of the change process. All change in organizations is about people. Technological change includes a people element. Product design or improvement is likely to affect those who have to manufacture the products or provide the services. In this sense then, the people side of change cannot be ignored. Nor should it. We firmly advocate in this chapter that firms begin to use more refined mechanisms for instigating change that consider, include, seek out and involve those likely to be affected – the organization's members. What we recommend here is the use of an *organization development model* (ODM). However, in doing so we are not attempting to break new ground. The techniques that we describe and explain here are neither unique nor innovative. These techniques have been well known for at least 30 years, but not so well practised by organizations. The techniques of the ODM, however, will require a change in emphasis in management thought. First and foremost, they require recognition that change implementation involves people and that gaining their involvement and active participation will assist the likelihood of success.

There are three areas that we will concern ourselves with. First, we look at where organization development stemmed from. To do so involves an analysis of the work of a number of writers in the fields of behavioural and social science, what they suggest and how this impacts the individual, management and organization as a whole. Second, we detail what we mean by the organization development model and how it can help organizations to manage change more effectively. Third, we comment on guiding values and beliefs that assist the movement towards effective performance.

Sorry, there are no route maps

Handy (1997) comments that those firms that succeed tend to have a number of characteristics:

> The corporation is changing. The research on long-lasting and successful organizations suggests that what enables a corporation to succeed in the longer term is a wish for immortality; a consistent set of values based on the awareness of the organization's own identity; a willingness to change; and a passionate concern for developing the capacity and the self-confidence of its core inhabitants, whom the company values more than its physical assets.

To be able to meet future challenges managers need to create (or more realistically recognize the existence of and channel) commitment from the workforce towards new working relationships and more effective performance. Effective performance comes from having a committed workforce. This is accomplished by allowing people to have a sense of belonging to the organization, a sense of excitement in the job, and by confidence in management leadership. The difficulty with excellence programmes, as authors such as Peters and Waterman have found out to their cost, is that although many management writers are aware of where organizations should be heading for in the future, there are no route maps. We can describe the processes by which change should take place and the issues that need to be considered by management and workforce alike, but you cannot buy a stencilled guide to change management for your own organization – it doesn't exist.

Many managers, while accepting the overall argument about the need for change in organizations and the development of new organization structures and management styles, would like to see some substance. There is a common belief that there is a lack of adequate guidance on how to transform an organization and its employees, at all levels, in this direction. What we will stress is that the change movement process is not effortless. However, when one pays attention to the experience of change as it is lived, a more comprehensive perspective of change emerges (Buchanan and McCalman, 1989: 50–7). One of the best ways of doing this is to look at examples of change management situations in some detail, analyse how and why they took place, and learn how to apply the benefits that accrued elsewhere.

What we attempt to address in this chapter is the process of organizational development from a people point of view. The model that we put forward here – the organization development model – is not a panacea. It is the description of an approach, a school of thought on change that has developed largely since the late 1960s. In this sense, we offer a set of descriptive commentaries. However, we justify this by arguing that in this area of change, there is much commonality.

READER ACTIVITY: THE MANAGER, THE ORGANIZATION AND DESIGN ISSUES

Before we go any further we would like you to undertake a short, relatively painless exercise to try to gauge your own assumptions about your organization and the people who work in it. Below are 10 sets of paired statements. We would like you to allocate 10 points per pair of statements. For example, if you agree more with the first statement then allocate more points to that one than the second.

Points

1　There are very few people in my organization who come up with good ideas.　A . . .

　Given the chance most people in my organization will come up with good ideas.　B . . .

2　The majority of people in my organization can and do exercise self-control and self-direction.　C . . .

　The majority of people in my organization prefer to be given direction.　D . . .

3　People in my organization do not have enough experience to offer practical ideas.　E . . .

　Getting people to contribute ideas leads to the development of useful suggestions.　F . . .

4　For the manager to admit that an employee is right and they are wrong weakens their status among other employees.　G . . .

　The manager's respect and reputation are enhanced by admitting to their mistakes.　H . . .

5　A job that is interesting and challenging can go a long way in eradicating complaints about pay and benefits.　J . . .

　Paying people enough for the job means that they are less bothered with responsibility and recognition.　K . . .

6　If employees are allowed to set their own objectives and standards of performance, they tend to set them higher than their manager would.　L . . .

　If employees set their own standards, they tend to be lower than those set by the manager.　M . . .

7 The more a person knows about the job and is free to make decisions about it, the more you have to keep an eye on them to keep them in line. N . . .

Knowledge of the job and freedom to make decisions means fewer controls are needed to ensure competent performance. P . . .

8 The restrictions imposed by the job limit the ability of people to show imagination and creativity. Q . . .

In the workplace, people do not use imagination and inventiveness because they do not have much of either. R . . .

9 When responsible for their own quality, people tend to raise their standards. T . . .

Quality tends to fall off when it is not supervised and imposed on people. V . . .

10 Truth is better than fiction and most people prefer the full story no matter whether bad or good. X . . .

When there is bad news about the organization employees prefer the manager to keep it to him/herself until it needs to be broken. Z . . .

Scoring

Add up the total points scored for each of the letters in the column below:

A   . . .
D   . . .
E   . . .
G   . . .
K   . . .
M   . . .
N   . . .
R   . . .
V   . . .
Z   . . .
_____

= your X score

100 − X score = your Y score

Score analysis

This simple exercise tells you something about the type of manager that you are. It is based on McGregor's theory X and theory Y classifications. If you have a high X score then the assumptions that you make about people and the design of work in organizations operate around a certain set of values. The framework you use is one that views the individual in the organization as someone who needs to be directed, avoids responsibility, must be controlled and coerced into effort, and has an inherent dislike of work. If you have a high Y score then your assumptions are that individual and organizational goals can be integrated and that the individual is a person that strives for better performance, has commitment to the organization for whom they work, and can contribute more than is currently being asked of them.

We would certainly hope that your Y score is higher than your X score as it will assist in your willingness to use some of the ideas and concepts within the ODM. Either way, you should reflect on the scoring that you have just achieved. That score is based on the assumptions you make about individuals in your organization, and hence influences how you go about managing change in organizations.

Where does organization development come from?

There are a number of broad definitions of the term *organization development*. However, there is a body of opinion from authors such as Beckhard, Bennis, Blake and Mouton, French and Bell, Lawler, Schein, Walton, Warner Burke and so on who regard OD as a process by which the members of an organization can influence change and help the organization achieve its goals. The ultimate aim is to achieve greater organizational effectiveness and this is accomplished by use of a number of different approaches. These set out to unlock issues that are currently hampering performance. The process of facilitation involves a change agent or agents who help members of the organization move forward towards an agreed set of goals and objectives that can then be implemented. This occurs at three levels – individual, group and organization.

The first level is that of the individual and what motivates individuals to higher standards of performance. This emphasizes two areas of thought: need and expectancy theories. Need theory concentrates analysis on issues associated with how jobs are designed for best effect, career development, and human relations training. Expectancy theory concerns itself with needs and rewards systems. The second level is that of the group and intergroup perspective. This emphasizes the importance of group behaviour, group belonging and their effect on the motivation of the individual. The group acts as the major leverage point for change. The third level is organizational. Emphasis is placed on management style and approach, organization structure and the environment.

To get a better understanding of organization development it is useful to understand its historical progression. Rather than chart the history of the subject from time immemorial, we shall examine the development of OD in a number of subject areas and include a number of authors. We divide these into two phases. The first phase concerns the work of Douglas McGregor leading to theory X and theory Y, and the work of Eric Trist and Ken Bamforth at the Tavistock Institute which led to the development of socio-technical systems design. The second phase looks at the growth of subject-specific work related to organization development techniques from the 1960s onwards.

McGregor and the human side of enterprise

One of the many starting points for OD comes from the work of Douglas McGregor, author of *The Human Side of Enterprise* (1960), which set the tone for management thought during the 1960s. McGregor worked at the Sloan School of Management at the Massachusetts Institute of Technology (MIT) and developed OD programmes for many organizations including Union Carbide and Esso. These training programmes usually took the form of team-building events. McGregor along with Beckhard also worked on changing organization structures to enhance teamwork and increase decision making at the shop floor level. They termed this work 'organization development'. The publication of *The Human Side of Enterprise* clarified the role of management and created the concept of theory X and theory Y. In this, McGregor classified managers' attitudes and perceptions about the worker and the design of organizations as falling into two categories:

McGregor's (1960) assumptions leading to theories X and Y

Theory X assumptions

1 The average human being has an inherent dislike of work and will avoid it if he can.
2 Because of this human characteristic of dislike of work, most people must be coerced, controlled, directed and threatened with punishment to get them to put forth adequate effort toward the achievement of organizational objectives.
3 The average human being prefers to be directed, wishes to avoid responsibility, has relatively little ambition, and wants security above all.

Theory Y assumptions

1 The expenditure of physical and mental effort in work is as natural as play or rest.
2 External control and the threat of punishment are not the only means for bringing about effort towards organizational objectives. People will exercise self-direction and self-control in the service of objectives to which they are committed.
3 Commitment to objectives is a function of the rewards associated with their achievement.
4 The average human being learns, under proper conditions, not only to accept but to seek responsibility.
5 The capacity to exercise a relatively high degree of imagination, ingenuity and creativity in the solution of organizational problems is widely, not narrowly, distributed in the population.
6 Under the conditions of modern industrial life, the intellectual potentialities of the average human being are only partially utilized.

The last reader activity you completed placed you in one of the two camps. By creating a form of extremism in terms of management perceptions of the workforce and the design of organizations, McGregor intentionally set out to accomplish a particular objective:

> It is not important that management accept the assumptions of Theory Y . . . It *is* important that management abandon limiting assumptions like those of Theory X, so that future inventions with respect to the human side of enterprise will be more than minor changes in already obsolescent conceptions of organized human effort. (1960: 245)

At this point it may be useful to refer back to the reader activity you completed and reflect again on which side of the fence you came down. We would suggest that if you came down heavily on the side of theory X then the use of organization development techniques and the ODM would be difficult for you, given its emphasis on participatory management techniques.

The Tavistock Institute and socio-technical systems

Not all theories and practices relevant to the OD model emanated from the United States. At around the same time that McGregor et al. were undertaking research analysis on issues such as sensitivity training, a second influential body of research work was being undertaken at the Tavistock Institute of Human Relations in London. At Tavistock, researchers such as Eric Trist, Ken Bamforth and A.K. Rice were developing the model of socio-technical systems design from their research work with Durham coalminers and textile workers at Ahmedabad, India.

The concept of socio-technical systems that resulted has had a great deal of influence on the field of OD as it relates to elements such as work design and autonomous/semi-autonomous work groups. The argument they put forward was that any organization exists as both a social and a technical subsystem and that both these subsystems need to be taken into consideration when organizations contemplate change. It is a powerful technique in terms of work design but lacks popularity. One of the reasons for this is that the approach itself directly challenges the status and responsibilities of managers at supervisory levels whose duties can be taken on by self-managing groups. During the 1980s and 1990s, as problems within organizations grew in significance, the concept received a new lease of life. Radical solutions that called for a redefinition of the management function as well as reorganization of work became more acceptable and gained management credence under these circumstances. However, applications of this particular type of work design model have mainly been the prerogative of large, multinational organizations (Buchanan and McCalman, 1989: 209–12). The Tavistock model is outlined in Figure 8.1.

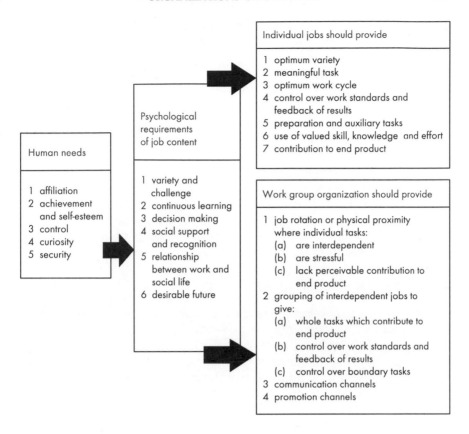

Figure 8.1   *The Tavistock work organization model*

In analysing the effectiveness of socio-technical systems and especially the concept of autonomous or semi-autonomous work groups in organizations, Hunt (1979) comments that:

> Probably more than any other method, this approach recognizes the common sense of individuals who for decades have been treated as morons by managers of large organizations.

Three important issues for organization development emerge from the Tavistock studies. We have not done the studies justice here and would suggest that the reader delve deeper into them. However, the three important issues are:

1   It is managers that make decisions about work organization, job allocations, the formation of groups and the amount of discretion allowed to workers.

2   Mass production techniques can be replaced by alternatives that maintain or even enhance performance whilst offering a better quality of working life.
3   Working in groups is the best form of work organization to meet both technical and social needs within the workplace.

If we relate this to change management and how the OD model can best be used, we argue that: *it is managers that make choices about change in organizations. There are also alternatives that they can consider when looking at work design. These alternatives can prove to be more effective.* Therefore, the organization development model is about management choice. When faced with changing situations within your own organization, you have the opportunity via the OD model to instigate change for the better. This is a choice that many firms in the past have made, and which has led to the use of organization development as we now know it.

Subject-specific development

The term *organization development* gained contemporary and pronounced usage in the 1960s when a number of researchers and authors dealt with the concepts of instigating change in organizations. They all fall within the area of organization development because of the interrelatedness of their work, the similarity in the use of the methodologies and techniques applied, and the acceptance by many of them of a need to define what was meant by the term:

> a number of us recognized that the rapidly growing field of 'OD' was not well understood or defined. We also recognized that there was no one OD philosophy, and hence one could not at that time write a textbook on the theory and practice of OD, but one could make clear what various practitioners were doing under this label. (Warner Burke, 1994: xvii)

This is precisely what we intend to do here. Because of the development of OD it is more appropriate to analyse this part of the historical progress via the subject material of some of its major proponents. In this instance, we have selected specific areas that we feel best represent what is meant by the OD model that we shall propose later on in this chapter. These areas are individual motivation at work, job and work design, interpersonal skills in groups, and participative management.

Motivation of the individual

One of the key areas of organization development is understanding human behaviour. The work of writers such as Victor Vroom (1969) and Edward Lawler (1969) was concerned with what motivated individuals to perform within their organization. Their research work led to the conclusion that motivation was dependent on situational and personality variables. In relation to this, Vroom comments that:

> The situational variables correspond to the amounts of different kinds of outcomes (e.g. pay, influence, variety) provided by the work roles, and the personality variables correspond to individual differences in the strength of their desire or aversion for these outcomes. (1969: 200–8)

Motivation was linked to three factors or assumptions concerning individual behaviour. The first pertained to what the individual saw as the expected outcome of their behaviour. For example, if an individual believes that the accomplishment of a certain task will lead to rewards then they will undertake that behaviour in the expectation that reward will be forthcoming. This belief is classified as performance–outcome expectancy. The second assumption was that the rewards associated with behaviour have a different value (valence) for different individuals. In this sense, what motivates some individuals may not motivate others to the same degree. One individual may place a greater emphasis on monetary gain than another would. Third, individuals had to have a certain degree of belief that their behaviour would have a reasonable chance of success. A manager may believe that he can finish a company report within 10 days but his expectation that he can finish it within seven days is very low, no matter how hard he works on it.

Research work on motivation led to the conclusion that the individual would be personally motivated when they perceived that rewards would accrue, where they valued those rewards, and where they believed they could perform at a level where attainment of the rewards was feasible. Vroom also included a fourth variable related to past performance. That is, the amount of reward that the individual expected to receive or had received in the past would also influence their behaviour within the organization (1969: 200–8).

Lawler's work also extended into analysis of job design and the importance of issues such as meaningful contribution and feedback in stimulating motivation in the individual. In relation to this, Lawler comments that:

> it has been argued that when jobs are structured in a way that makes intrinsic rewards appear to result from good performance then the jobs themselves can be very effective motivators. In addition the point was made that if job content is to be a source of motivation, the job must allow for meaningful feedback, test the individual's valued abilities and allow a great amount of self-control by the job holder. (1969: 426–35)

The work of writers such as Lawler and Vroom is important in an OD sense because of its emphasis on motivating the individual towards higher standards of performance. Their work is also crucial because its focus of attention is on job design and structure as well as the provision of feedback as mechanisms for enhancing organizational performance. Similarly, their work suggests that reward systems are an important variable in effective OD change processes. These are issues we will look at in greater depth later in this chapter.

Job and work design

Work design is an important part of OD models. The research work in this area, especially that of writers such as Hackman and Oldham (1975; 1980), looks at work design from a position of need and expectancy theories. The focus of attention, in this instance, is how work design leads to greater worker satisfaction. The variables associated with greater worker satisfaction are:

1 meaningfulness of the work
2 responsibility for the work and its outcomes
3 performance feedback.

Hackman and Oldham (1980) attempted to separate the main features of work as being:

- core job dimensions
- critical psychological states
- employee experience.

They did this to establish a causal link between job implementing concepts such as:

- natural work units
- feedback channels
- core job dimensions, such as task identity and autonomy
- critical psychological states, such as responsibility for the work and knowledge of the results
- personal and work outcomes resulting in high internal work motivation, high-quality work performance etc.

Figure 8.2 details the worker motivation and job satisfaction criteria associated with OD.

Interpersonal relations

The work of writers such as Chris Argyris is important to OD because of the emphasis they placed on issues related to developing the individual within the organization. Argyris's work falls into two main streams as far as OD is concerned: individual development towards maturity at work, and interpersonal relations within the group at work. Argyris

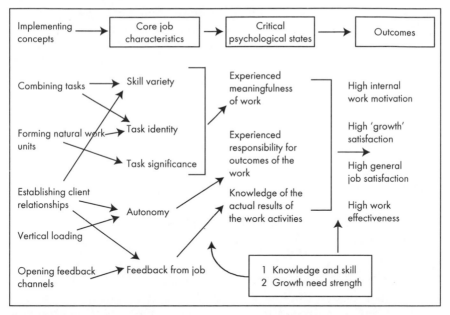

Figure 8.2   *The complete job characteristics model (adapted from Hackman and Oldham, 1980)*

argued that what prevents maturity in individuals in the workplace is the approach of management and the lack of interpersonal competence. Developing on from the work of McGregor, he argued that certain behavioural patterns of management emerge in organizations. A manager may espouse theory Y values but his pattern of behaviour (which Argyris referred to as pattern A) associates his managerial competence with that of theory X (Argyris, 1970). In this sense, management self-perpetuates its own need for control:

> The increased use of management controls deprives employees of any opportunity of participating in the important decisions which affect their working life, leading to feelings of psychological failure. It is not they themselves but the control systems (such as work study and cost accounting) which define, inspect and evaluate the quality and quantity of their performance. (Pugh and Hickson, 1989: 168–9)

In terms of change management, managers adopt a certain model of behaviour. Argyris and Schon (1978) argue that managers seek solutions in the form of a model of behaviour where they:

1 take action based on valid information that has been freely and openly obtained

2   take action after consultation with those competent and relevant to
    that action based on their informed and free choice
3   sustain commitment to the choice made and monitor the prepared-
    ness of the organization for change and implementation of change
    itself.

The appropriateness of this approach for the model of OD we are
proposing is clear. The solutions argued by Argyris and Schon assume
that the manager in this instance adopts and displays an open and
participatory approach to the process of change in organizations. There
is a need here to remove the defensiveness associated with control
orientation in order to obtain contributions from others likely to be
affected by change. To do so, Argyris and Schon argue that the organization needs to be able to call on the assistance of outside agents,
another characteristic of OD.

Participative management

Organization design is a key element of the development process. The
ability of any organization to design itself to effectively meet the performance criteria which it sets will determine the success or not of that
change effort. Likert (1967) described four models of organization design:

1   *Exploitive authoritative*   Management uses the techniques of fear and
    threat to control members of the organization. Communication chan-
    nels are downwards. Management and the workforce are physically
    and psychologically separate. Most of the decisions affecting the
    organization are taken at the top of the hierarchy and fed down.
2   *Benevolent authoritative*   Management uses the technique of reward
    as a control mechanism but the views and opinions of the workforce
    are subservient to those of management. Communication channels
    upwards are restricted to what is acceptable to managers. Decisions
    affecting the organization are taken at the top but may be delegated
    to lower levels for implementation.
3   *Consultative*   Management uses both rewards and occasional punish-
    ments whilst seeking some limited form of involvement. Com-
    munication channels are both upward and downward but upward
    communication is still limited to acceptability on the part of manage-
    ment. Policy is determined at the top with implementation and some
    limited form of workforce participation occurring at departmental
    level.
4   *Participative*   Management uses the technique of group rewards to
    attain participation and involvement of the workforce. High
    standards of performance, goal setting and improvement of work
    methods are all characteristic of the participative organization. Com-
    munication channels flow upwards, downwards and horizontally.

Decisions are made through group processes and integrated through-out the organization via 'linking pin' individuals who are members of more than one group.

Likert was also primarily responsible for one of the main techniques used in OD models, the survey feedback method. This will be looked at in greater depth when we examine the processes associated with OD.

The organization development model: how do organizations develop effectively?

We now wish to look at some effective mechanisms and techniques for using organization development. What we are interested in is the concept of organization development, what it can do, and what specifics it can deal with. Here we begin to get into the technicalities or substance of the OD model. For example, in terms of what OD expects to address, French (1969) identified seven objectives behind the use of organization development programmes. These objectives, it was argued,

reflect problems which are very common in organizations:

1 To increase the level of trust and support among organizational members.
2 To increase the incidence of confrontation of organizational problems, both within groups and among groups, in contrast to 'sweeping problems under the rug.'
3 To create an environment in which authority of assigned role is augmented by authority based on knowledge and skill.
4 To increase openness of communications laterally, vertically, and diagonally.
5 To increase the level of personal enthusiasm and satisfaction in the organ-ization.
6 To find synergistic solutions to problems with greater frequency.
7 To increase the level of self and group responsibility in planning and implementation. (1969: 23)

Organizational development is about changing the organization from one situation, which is regarded as unsatisfactory, to another by means of social science techniques for change. In terms of organizational change, it is important to remember the concept of anticipation. The manager has to be always thinking ahead. Pugh (1978) argues that the effective manager anticipates change, diagnoses the nature of the change, and then manages the change process. In this and the next chapter we argue that the manager is often too near to the problem to be able to anticipate, diagnose and manage the change him/herself. What is needed is the assistance of an outside agent, either internal to the organization or brought in speci-fically for that task.

In terms of managing change, the organization has to follow a five-step process of planned change that moves it through specific phases (Lippit et al., 1958):

1 *recognition* by senior management that there is a need for change in the organization
2 establishment of a change *relationship*
3 *movement* towards the desired change by the organization and its members
4 *stabilizing* the changes within the organization
5 allowing the change agent to *move on.*

When we look at change in organizations it is important to be able to understand why it is taking place. Pugh (1978) argues that there are four principal issues associated with the use of organization development, and that to understand the basis of OD one has to place it within the context of the organization itself.

Pugh's (1978) four principles for understanding organizational change

1 *Organizations as organisms* The organization is not a machine and change must be approached carefully and rationally. Do not make changes too frequently because they become dysfunctional or cosmetic.
2 *Organizations are occupational and political systems* The reaction to change relates to what is best for the firm, how it affects individuals and groups, and how it affects the power, prestige and status of individuals and groups.
3 *Members of an organization operate in occupational, political and rational systems at the same time* Arguments for and against change will be presented using rational argument as well as occupational and political considerations.
4 *Change occurs most effectively where success and tension combine* Two factors are important here: confidence and motivation to change. Successful individuals or groups will have the confidence to change aspects of their work which are creating problems. Unsuccessful members of the organization are difficult to change because to protect themselves they will use their rigidity.

Having established some basic principles related to the organization and how its members will react to, anticipate and deal with change, it is now useful to look at what attributes the model of organizational development has. Margulies and Raia (1978) identify 13 characteristics common to organization development:

1   It is a total organizational system approach.
2   It adopts a systems approach to the organization.
3   It is positively supported by top management.
4   It uses third-party change agents to develop the change process.
5   It involves a planned change effort.
6   It uses behavioural science knowledge to instigate change.
7   It sets out to increase organizational competence.
8   It is a long-term change process.
9   It is an ongoing process.
10 It relies on experiential learning techniques.
11 It uses action research as an intervention model.
12 It emphasizes goal setting and action planning.
13 It focuses on changing attitudes, behaviours and performance of
    groups or teams in the organization rather than individuals.

Combining these characteristics with those mentioned by Lippit et al.,
French and Pugh, we can put forward the following definition of organization development.

Definition

Organization development is an ongoing process of change aimed at
resolving issues through the effective diagnosis and management of the
organization's culture. This development process uses behavioural and
social science techniques and methodologies through a consultant facilitator and employs action research as one of the main mechanisms for
instigating change in organizational groups.

This means that we are dealing with a philosophy of managing change
that involves a number of skills and practices. It is hoped that you will be
stimulated to enhance your knowledge of the subject area further and to
that end we have recommended a number of OD publications in this
chapter.
    When considering using OD as a means of managing change in the
organization you need to be aware of its characteristics:

1   The focus is on interdependencies and not on the individual. There-
    fore, teamwork is encouraged.
2   A climate for change is sought rather than superimposed unilaterally.
3   Interpersonal relationships are built upon using behavioural science
    techniques, for example role playing and problem solving exercises.
4   Goals relate to communication, decision making and problem
    solving.
5   The value system is humanistic, aimed at maximizing development
    and encouraging open relationships in the organization.

The organizational development process is a tricky one to get hold of. It means sometimes having to re-evaluate how you manage people to get the best from them. It means looking at change with an open mind and setting aside preconceptions about change.

READER ACTIVITY

The following exercise is adapted from Huse (1975). Rule number one is to be honest with yourself. Do not try to second-guess the answers from what you think is wanted. Read carefully through the statements below and consider what your views on these are. As you read through each statement, you should allocate a mark to the statement depending on whether you agree with it or not. Mark your view in the column to the right using the following five-point scale:

5 strongly agree
4 agree
3 neutral
2 disagree
1 strongly disagree.

Statements

1   Personal growth is the engine that drives organization performance. This is best provided within an open and challenging environment.   . . .
2   The individual does not work in a vacuum and prefers to work within and is influenced by groups at the workplace.   . . .
3   The way organizations go about design leads to clashes of personality that are not of the individual's own making.   . . .
4   Work groups increase effectiveness by attaining individual needs and organizational requirements. Leadership in this instance is of a participatory nature.   . . .
5   Not considering people's feelings is likely to hinder leadership, communications and organizational effectiveness.   . . .
6   The formal organization forces people to conform. This prevents individual growth and innovation and wastes talent.   . . .
7   People are the most important asset an organization has; yet they are demotivated in formal organizations and do not take on more responsibility.   . . .
8   When problems arise in the organization the ability to be open and honest in discussion helps both the individual concerned and the organization as a whole.   . . .
9   To be effective, organizations have to enhance the level of interpersonal trust and cooperation amongst individuals at all levels.   . . .
10 The way we structure and design the organization can reflect the needs of the individual, the group, and the organization as a whole.   . . .

Scoring

Your rating of the items will give you an indication of your willingness to consider using OD techniques to manage change. First calculate your total score on the 10 statements. The range of total scores is from 10 to 50; the higher the score, the more you are in agreement with OD values. The following scoring ranges indicate where you, as a manager, lie in terms of willingness to use OD as a model for change:

Score	*Rating*
40–50	You are largely in agreement with the principles and practices associated with OD. The way you feel about managing the organization, the people within the organization and the concept of attaining effective change is in line with basic organization development principles. You may pass GO and collect £200.
26–39	You agree with most of the OD principles and are quite willing to experiment with the concept for overall development of your organization. Some doubts remain as to the efficacy of some of the ideas, but there is a willingness to experiment. Pass GO and collect your £200 next time round.
10–25	You have serious doubts about the basic concepts of organization development. You are willing to give some attention to the concepts but basically you want to see some evidence before being fully convinced. Do not pass GO. Do not collect £200.
<10	Go straight to JAIL, do not pass GO, do not even think of collecting £200! You probably know all the answers to 'Trivial Pursuit'!

Organizations that use the OD process can be seen as falling into one of two categories, 'black' and 'white'. The 'white' category relates to the organization that has a well-defined OD strategy. This is tied into its overall business strategy and is used continuously as a mechanism of stimulating change at all levels. As with many innovative management practices, OD has been used more often in the United States, and by larger corporations facing constant change. In the 'black' category we have the organization in such an internal mess that it needs to call on OD to address resistance to change. Resistance to change reflects bad management of the process of change. Where it does occur there are a number of factors that may help recover what is seen as a lost position.

The organization development process

Organization development, as it suggests, is about trying to progress change through more than one element within the firm. It is viewed very much as a long-term, strategic mechanism for initiating change that places emphasis on the process of attaining change.

The purpose of training people in OD techniques is to help increase organizational effectiveness by providing expertise and skilled resources. The amount of change that is undertaken is reflective of the environment of the firm. The type of work, the type and mix of skills, structures and systems, response times, performance measurement of operating units and people, and the way in which different parts of the organization are designed and operate are all factors which will have a bearing on organizational effectiveness. The main essence of organizational development is trying to maintain control over an organization that is in constant change.

A leading American electronics multinational's justification for a $300,000 OD training programme

Why organization development is so important

1   The volume of change in many organizations is massive.
2   The economic scene places demands on managers while they are reluctant to change from tried and tested methods.
3   The role of management is changing and new models are needed.
4   Change management takes time.
5   Some changes challenge basic assumptions – for example, the role of supervisory staff.
6   The need for control remains: the skill is remaining in control when so much change is going on.
7   More comprehensive strategic pictures are needed which integrate different changes in the organization and alleviate confusion.
8   Organization design and redesign are *as important and necessary as* product, process or system design and are the responsibility of management and people in organizations, not just specialists.

By this point you will have reached the stage where you understand that change in the organization requires both planning and management. It doesn't occur on an *ad hoc* basis. There is a role for the social sciences in instigating change in organizations, and organizational development is one of the key methods of instigating and attaining successful change. There are four situations where organizational development is needed:

1   The current nature of the organization is leading to a failure to achieve objectives.
2   Change is required to react faster to external alterations.
3   The introduction of factors such as new technology requires change in the organization itself.
4   The introduction of change allows a new approach to be adopted.

It was suggested earlier that you test your own values and assumptions concerning organizational development. Similarly, the importance of factors such as group work have been expressed as important elements of OD. The important point to note here is that change is a continuous process of confrontation, identification, evaluation and action. The key here is what is referred to in OD as an *action research model*. French (1969) argued that this model involved collaboration between the consultant (who could be an internal or external change agent, as we shall see in Chapter 9) and the client group towards data gathering, data discussion, action planning and action. Figure 8.3 details French's action research model for organization development.

The organization development matrix

One of the important aspects of change is developing an appropriate strategy. This involves creating a matrix of change diagnosis and initiation associated with behaviour, structure and context at four levels: the organization as a whole, intergroup, group and individual. The importance of this matrix concerns the two main factors that have to be identified in the organizational development process. These are:

• At what level do we focus our analysis?
• How much change has to take place?

Figure 8.4 details an organization development matrix conceptualized and developed by Pugh (1986). The matrix is one of the keys for organizations in developing their OD strategy. Go over the matrix slowly at first and be prepared to break it into its constituent parts. It will be useful to do so by writing it out several times in individual areas. For example, take a specific case from your own organization (you will probably be able to cite an example at the individual level fairly easily) and work through the matrix.

If we are to identify any one part as being crucial to your understanding of organizational development – this is it! Pugh's analysis of the most common strategies used in OD provides an excellent example of diagnosing and initiating change. These are strategies that apply to organizational development, which depend on the level within the organization at which change is contemplated, and the approaches taken which correspond to these levels. Action at the organizational level is likely to be different from that at the individual level, although there are areas where overlap exists. There are a number of aspects of the matrix that you may be unfamiliar with. For example, Table 8.1 details some of the methods of initiating change.

If there is one underlying theme of organizational development, then it is related to the need to be able to manage change. The process by which

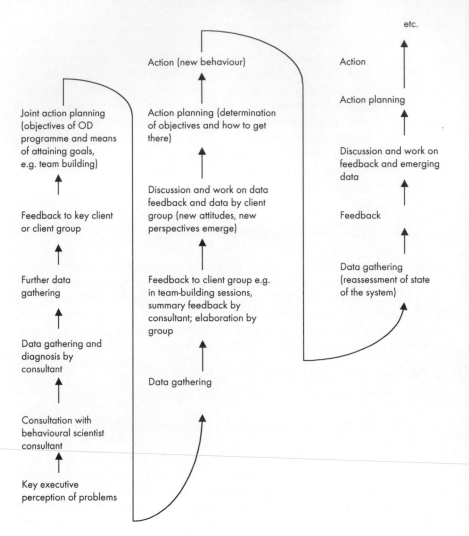

Figure 8.3   *The action research model for organizational development (copyright 1969 by the Regents of the University of California; reprinted from California Management Review, Vol. XII, No. 2, p. 26, Figure 1)*

an organization moves from an unsatisfactory state of affairs, through the recognition of this, identification of alternatives, communicating these and receiving feedback, educating on the changes required, reviewing development in the light of experience, and progressing the change process forward, is both lengthy and messy. Therefore, there is a need to manage this positively. Organizations go through what can best be described as interlocking layers of perpetual change management which reflect aspects such as the trigger layer where opportunity or threat triggers responses for change in the organization. This can sometimes

	Behaviour (What is happening now?)	**Structure** (What is the required system?)	**Context** (What is the setting?)
Organizational level	General climate of poor morale, pressure, anxiety, suspicion, lack of awareness of, or response to, environmental changes *Survey feedback, organizational monitoring*	Systems goals – poorly defined or inappropriate; strategy inappropriate and misunderstood; organizational structure inappropriate; centralization, divisionalization, standardization: inadequacy of environmental monitoring mechanisms *Change the structure*	Geographical setting, market pressures, labour market, physical conditions, basic technology *Change strategy, location, physical set-up, culture (by saturation OD)*
Intergroup level	Lack of effective cooperation between subunits, conflict, excessive competition, limited war, failure to confront differences in priorities, unresolved feelings *Intergroup confrontation (with a third party as consultant), role negotiation*	Lack of integrated task perspective; subunit optimization, required interaction difficult to achieve *Redefine responsibilities, change reporting relationships, improve coordination and liaison mechanisms*	Different subunit values, lifestyle, physical distance *Reduce psychological and physical distance, exchange roles, attachments, cross-functional social overlay*
Group level	Inappropriate working relationships, atmosphere, participation, poor understanding and acceptance of goals, avoidance, inappropriate leadership style, leader not trusted, respected leader in conflict with peers and superiors *Process consultation, team building*	Task requirements poorly defined; role relationships unclear or inappropriate; leader's role overloaded, inappropriate reporting procedures *Redesign work relationships (socio-technical systems), autonomous working groups*	Insufficient resources, poor group composition for cohesion, inadequate physical set-up, personality clashes *Change technology, layout, group composition*

continues overleaf

Figure 8.4   *The organization development matrix (Pugh, 1986)*

	Behaviour (What is happening now?)	**Structure** (What is the required system?)	**Context** (What is the setting?)
Individual level	Failure to fulfil individual's needs; frustration responses; unwillingness to consider change, little chance for learning and development *Counselling, role analysis, career planning*	Poor job definition, task too easy or too difficult *Job restructuring or modification, redesign, enrichment, MBO*	Poor match of individual with job, poor selection or promotion, inadequate preparation and training, recognition and remuneration at variance with objectives *Personnel changes, improved selection and promotion procedures, improved training and education, bring recognition and remuneration in line with objectives*

> There are two dimensions to the matrix which represent the two main factors that have to be identified during the diagnosis stage of the OD process: level of analytical focus and degree of required intervention.

Figure 8.4   (*continued*)

create a vision of where the organization might be able to go. This visionary state then has to be communicated to individuals and groups and their commitment gained. Having gone through this process of change, what can best be described as a maintenance and renewal layer closes up the loop. Revision of what the organization sets out to do, and whether this is appropriate at this point in time, leads to a further process of change analysis. This is related to the basic rules for managing a change process (adapted from Pugh, 1978):

1   Establish that there is a need.
2   Think it through thoroughly.
3   Discuss it informally with those likely to be affected.
4   Encourage the expression of all objections.
5   Make sure you are willing to undertake change yourself.
6   Monitor the changes and reinforce them at all points.

Phases of an OD Intervention

In terms of the process of OD, there are a number of phases that an organization will go through. Lewin (1958) describes these as unfreezing,

Table 8.1   *Methods of initiating change in organizations*

Method	Level	Explanation
Survey feedback	Organization	Organization-wide review of attitudes and morale used as basis for discussion of change
Intergroup confrontation (third party present)	Intergroup	Bringing together groups in the presence of an external consultant to discuss and attain change
Role negotiation	Intergroup/individual	Review process on the appropriate areas of concern for individuals and groups and levels of interaction between groups
Cross-functional social overlay	Intergroup	Attaining movement between groups which enhances cohesion through continuous interaction
Process consultation	Group/individual	Review of work patterns and relationships to develop effective organization forms
Redesign work relationships (socio-technical systems)	Group	Effective coordination of people and technology in organization for a 'best fit' solution
Autonomous work groups	Group	Self-managing team approach to job design

changing and refreezing the organization into its new state. Warner Burke (1994: 72) identifies seven phases which the organization experiences during a typical OD change process. These are described below with appropriate examples from our own experience.

Phase 1: entry

At this point an initial contact is made between the organization and the consultant to begin the entry phase. There may be many reasons for this initial contact, but largely this will be based on the organization's initiative, as it has perceived a need for change. Both the organization and the consultant will explore the issues and establish a rapport or capability for working on the OD intervention. From the organization's perspective it has to be sure that it has the right person for the job and whether they will be able to work with the consultant. The consultant also has a number of criteria that have to be satisfied. These relate to factors such as whether they can work with the organization, whether or not there is a readiness for change, the motivation and values of the individual(s) calling on the consultant, their position power within the organization as a leverage point for instigating change, and the amount of resources at hand for change (1994: 73).

It is also useful for both the consultant and the organization to check that there is a clear understanding of the roles to be adopted by each prior to the establishment of the contract stage. In our experience it is useful to have the first meeting and then provide the client with a copy of what we understand to be the salient points of the meeting and how both consultant and organization should proceed. This should be done as soon as possible after the first contact to maintain the flow and to check for any possible misinterpretations on the part of either party.

Phase 2: formalizing the contact

The second phase is the drafting of a contract that explains and clarifies what will be done. This is a two-way process in which the consultant lays out what they intend to do but which also explains what the organization is contracting to do. At this point, the client organization will internally discuss the consultant's proposal with its key people and may propose amendments before agreeing the terms. We would encourage organizations to view this phase as similar to any other negotiations that take place with any other type of supplier. Unless the consultant has a clear specification of what the client desires in terms of an OD intervention, then they are unsure of issues such as what each expects of the other, how much time will be involved, the associated costs and the ground rules which will operate. Most organizations treat the OD intervention by an external consultant in this way, even to the point of issuing a purchase order.

Phase 3: information gathering and analysis

Having successfully negotiated a contract, it is then up to the consultant in conjunction with the client to begin the diagnosis phase. There are two important elements here: getting the information required, and being able to make sense of it. However, the two do not necessarily follow on from one another. The consultant will have begun the diagnosis phase from the initial entry point based on the information gathered, on observations, on gut feelings about the state of play in the organization, and in many cases on previous experience with other similar issues. French and Bell comment that: 'organization development is at heart an action program based on valid information about the status quo, current problems and opportunities, and effects of actions as they relate to goal achievement. An OD program thus starts with diagnosis and continuously employs data collecting and data analysing throughout' (1990: 63).

Formal information gathering is therefore necessary and this usually comes in the form of interviews, staff surveys and organization records associated with the issue being analysed. Margerison argues that this is a crucial stage in terms of what could be considered the diplomacy and partiality displayed on the part of the consultant related to whom they gather information from:

> A former colleague once gave me a phrase which has stuck with me as an important principle in all my work. 'Selection implies rejection', he said. This is absolutely right. Make sure you don't offend people by ignoring their opinion. (1988: 64)

We would recommend that when gathering data, the consultant, whether internal or external, gleans information from all those likely to be affected by the OD change programme, from a political and/or content perspective.

Phase 4: feedback

Having gathered the data, it is then up to the consultant to analyse it, summarize the information, and organize it into a format which can be readily understood by the organization's members to enable action to take place based on that information. This is the point where the OD consultant will use their previous experience to draw conclusions from what they have observed, and to feed back data in a form which is both understandable and acceptable to the organization and gets the necessary messages across. We would recommend two mechanisms for accomplishing these tasks. The first is the preparation of a report of the work carried out and the consultant's conclusions from this, namely issues for the future and proposals for change. This is distributed to all who took part in the data gathering stage for their information and commentary, and acts as a further source of information or feedback. The second is a presentation to the management body initiating the OD change programme. This is likely to include those to be affected by any change proposals and the consultant needs to be prepared to enter into what one might consider a 'lion's den' on many occasions. The important point here is to facilitate discussion of the data being presented.

The feedback session must contain three basic elements: a summary of the data gathered and the consultant's initial analysis; a general discussion which clarifies points of confusion that may have arisen on the organization's side; and interpretation of what has taken place and how this will be carried forward. The consultant must also be flexible during this process, as changes to their analysis and interpretation will often be generated in light of the feedback session.

Phase 5: planning the change process

This is the second stage of the change programme – the action phase of the OD intervention. The basis of all OD programmes is to improve the organization's processes from what they are now to what they will be in the future – the unfreezing, change, refreezing process. There are two possibilities here. First, the planning for change stage may take place towards the end of the feedback session as the consultant and organization get a clearer picture of the steps that are likely to be needed. However, for more complex, larger organization development issues the planning process may be lengthened in time and incorporate those likely to be involved in the process itself. The whole point of the planning for change phase is to look at what alternative actions are open to the organization in terms of response to the feedback given by the consultant, and to consider the best way forward or plan of action to take.

We would recommend that the consultant move through this phase in collaboration with the organization in order to gain commitment to both the plans for change and its implementation. The consultant should act both as an idea generator, putting forward alternatives and getting the organization to consider the consequences of each proposal; and as a sounding board for the organization's proposals for the way forward, using his/her experiences of similar attempts at change. This is a crucial phase, but it is the organization, above all, that has to live with the consequences of decisions made during this phase. They need to fully agree with the proposals for the way forward.

Phase 6: implementing the changes

Once the organization has decided what action it will take, the implementation of change can take place. The consultant may or may not be involved at this stage depending on the actions to be taken, the degree of experience required within the organization to take these actions, and the consultant's own assessment of his/her role at this stage. We would suggest here that the consultant, even if not actively involved in the intervention phase, keep an eye on the development of this phase. It is difficult to force an organization to change; those most likely to be negatively impacted by change will resist the strongest. As Warner Burke noted, 'the OD practitioner continues to work with the client system to help make the intervention successful' (1994: 78). This is most effectively done with the consultant still involved, as most failures at the implementation stage result from unanticipated consequences of the change process and it is here that the consultant may be able to help anticipate likely outcomes.

Phase 7: assessment

The final phase of the OD process of change is to evaluate the results of what has taken place. Margerison (1988) argues that this should take the form of a review and that the principle of establishing a review stage would assist in preventing all the previous work going astray. The process of assessment also assists the change effort by focusing attention on what has taken place. In our introduction to this book we referred to the layers of transition management. The final layer was associated with maintenance and renewal. The assessment phase is useful here in looking at what has gone before, what the current state of play is, and what action steps need to be taken to move the organization forward.

Guiding values and philosophy

Before moving on to an analysis of the role of the consultant in the OD change process, it is worthwhile considering what we have looked at over this and the previous chapter. It is crucial here to summarize why we place such emphasis on people management and the OD process of change. This is a guiding value and belief that organizations should have as the cornerstone of their operating philosophy – all successful organizations do. Margulies and Raia argue that the values of a fully functioning organization could be stated as:

1 Providing opportunities for people to function as human beings rather than resources in the productive process.
2 Providing opportunities for each organizational member, as well as the organization itself, to develop to full potential.
3 Seeking to increase the effectiveness of the organization in terms of all its goals.
4 Attempting to create an environment in which it is possible to find exciting and challenging work.
5 Providing opportunities for people in organizations to influence the way in which they relate to work, the organization, and the environment.
6 Treating each human being as a person with a complex set of needs, all of which are important in work and in life. (1972: 3)

Individually, we each have our own set of values or personal philosophy for life. However, for the organization this is often lacking. The organization needs a philosophy, a description of basic principles guiding its behaviour. The values are the beliefs that flow from these basic principles. Philosophy and values apply to human behaviour in organizations. All organizations have their own philosophy and values about human behaviour, but these are seldom charted and used as a guide to organization design and development, as a guide to managerial and people policies, or as a checklist for daily practice.

We make no apologies for repeating Megson:

> They are based on a *philosophy* that I describe as follows. People are the most important asset we have. They want and need to grow. Without growth interest wanes and talents waste away. With growth interest flourishes and talents develop. People really do care, they do exquisite work – if it is designed to enable them to grow. *In other words, personal growth is the engine that drives organization performance.* (1988: 16)

Through the process of organization development it is possible to put expressions of values and philosophy such as these into practice at individual, group and organizational levels – to let the engine itself develop enough momentum that it drives effective performance.

Margulies and Raia sum this up as: 'the usefulness and effectiveness of OD is dependent upon the degree to which organizational values become consistent with the core values of organizational development' (1988: 9).

In the next chapter we describe the role of the consultant or change agent in the OD model. The consultant can be either internal or external to the organization depending on the level of experience with OD techniques, the strategy being adopted, and the level of change. What the consultant is, however, is the driver – the change agent. They drive the change process, and as such occupy a linchpin role.

9 The Objective Outsider

The use of organization development in stimulating and implementing change rests very much on the way it is handled. The successful use of the ODM is influenced by a number of factors, not least of which are the purpose and process of change itself. One of the key underpinnings of this process is the role of the consultant acting as a facilitator of change. More often than not, an outsider is needed to move the part of the organization contemplating change to its new position. However, this outsider may well come from another part of the organization and thus be an internal figure. To this end, we prefer the term 'change agent'. Whether internal or external, the change agent facilitates change in the particular area in which it is needed.

Why is an outsider needed? What does facilitation mean? Why bother when the manager of the department in question knows what they want and knows how to get there? Good questions! But again the underlying assumption is that of predestination: the manager, in his or her infinite wisdom, knows best. Schein (1988) argues that managers in organizations need assistance in managing the process of change in order that they learn how to do it more effectively the next time round. He cites seven reasons for using a change agent:

1 Clients/managers often do not know what is wrong and need special help in diagnosing what their problems actually are.
2 Clients/managers often do not know what kinds of help consultants can give to them; they need to be helped to know what kind of help to seek.
3 Most clients/managers have a constructive intent to improve things, but they need help in identifying what to improve, and how to improve it.
4 Most organizations can be more effective than they are if they learn to diagnose and manage their own strengths and weaknesses.
5 A consultant probably cannot, without exhaustive and time-consuming study or actual participation in the client organization, learn enough about the culture of the organization to suggest reliable new courses of action. Therefore, unless remedies are worked out jointly with members of the organization who *do* know what will and

will not work in their culture, such remedies are likely either to be wrong or to be resisted because they come from an outsider.

6   Unless the client/manager learns to see the problem for himself and thinks through the remedy, he will not be able to implement the solution and, more importantly, will not learn to fix such problems should they recur.

7   The essential function of process consultation is to pass on the skills of how to diagnose and fix organizational problems so that the client is more able to continue on his own to improve the organization.

When we look at who should be a change agent, we are concerned with the personality and style of the individual. Margulies and Raia (1972) note that there are three attributes that the individual needs to enable them to take on a consulting role in the area of organization development.

1   The change agent must have a particular *personality*. As a result of the need to establish, maintain and work on relationships with people within the organization, the change agent needs to show an aware-ness and sensitivity to social issues. This means more than it actually says. The change agent has to feel comfortable with people, that is, have an ability to get on well with people, and be able to understand and recognize their worries and fears as well as their hopes and aspirations. In particular, you must not pay scant or transient atten-tion to fears and aspirations as part of the process of accomplishing the change task. The change agent has to have an ability to listen to others and show empathy. This means that the change agent has to have numerous people-oriented skills. In essence, this is a flair or a natural empathy. The theory X manager, described in Chapter 8, has few of these skills.

2   The change agent requires both *analytical and diagnostic skills*. This enables them to identify and solve problems by using techniques that are available to them to facilitate the change process. However, the change agent has to be conscious that they are using these skills as part of the change process and not as an exploitative mechanism, as a means of going through the motions.

3   Finally, the change agent needs to have *client-related experience* – the 'been there, done that' school of experience related to expertise.

There is a degree of both expertise and facilitation associated with the change agent. The change agent has to come from outside the social system where change is being contemplated. The reasons for this are fairly straightforward. It allows the individual to have an unbiased view of the need for change, and also allows them to take a non-controversial line in considering actions for change. In addition, this is a mechanism that allows for all views within the change setting to be taken into consideration. The potential change agent has to be able to recognize and reconcile what type of person they intend being. The change agent, like most managers, is a person occupying a role for a particular period. To do so, they have to be able to determine what that role entails.

What type of change agent is required?

The first issue that needs to be clarified when looking at the role played by the change agent in the change process is how that role is defined and implemented. The type of role adopted has a significant bearing on the results that one can expect to achieve using the organization development model. The most widely used model by organization development practitioners is that of a collaborative approach which helps the client organization define, understand and act on process events which occur within their own environment (Schein, 1988). There are a number of characteristics associated with this model. Margulies and Raia argue that these are

> based upon the following assumptions and beliefs:
>
> 1 Managers often do not know what is wrong and need special help in diagnosing what their probelms actually are.
> 2 They do not know what kinds of help to seek. Consequently, they need help in this regard.
> 3 Organizations can be more effective if they learn how to diagnose their own strengths and weaknesses.
> 4 The consultant cannot hope to learn all he or she needs to know about the culture of an organization to suggest reliable solutions. Therefore, it is necessary to work jointly with organization members who *do* know.
> 5 Since the decision is the client's, it is important that the client learns to see the problem clearly, to share in the diagnosis, and to be actually involved in generating solutions.
> 6 The consultant is an expert on how to diagnose processes and how to establish effective helping relationships with clients. Effective process consultation involves passing on *both* of these skills to the client system. (1978: 111)

By contrast, the popular view of the consultant is that associated with the doctor–patient model of consultation. In this model, the organization brings in a consultant to find out what is wrong with it and the consultant then recommends change. This type of expert–client relationship has a number of problems when applied in an organization development setting. For one, it may hamper individuals' willingness to open up to the doctor. The patient is not totally involved in the diagnostic process and therefore feels left out of the solution. Finally, the patient may be unable to understand the proposed solution or the mechanisms of achieving it.

Lippit and Lippit (1975) argue that the behaviour of the change agent runs along a continuum of eight different roles depending on whether the change agent is being directive or non-directive. These roles are not mutually exclusive and may vary according to the stage the change project has reached. They range from advocate, technical specialist, trainer or educator on the directive side to collaborator in problem solving, alternative identifier, fact finder, process specialist and reflector on the non-directive side. What Lippit and Lippit emphasize is the multiple role nature of the change agent, the situational focus which determines these roles, and the need to work in close conjunction with the client organization no matter what role is being used.

The collaborative nature of the process model of organization development defines the role to be adopted by the change agent. When taking up this role the change agent needs to be fully aware of a number of key criteria. First, in defining the problem the change agent works with the client organization to verify this. Second, the relationship between change agent and client is crucial to developing the change process and needs to be nurtured and developed. Third, the change agent's focus of attention is in helping the client organization discover and implement solutions to the problem. Fourth, the change agent's expertise is in diagnosing and facilitating the process of change – steering the organization through. Fifth, the change agent helps the organization improve its own diagnostic and problem solving skills. Finally, the change agent assists the organization to a position where it can manage change itself (Margulies and Raia, 1978: 113).

The effective change agent takes on a number of roles:

1   to help the organization define the problem by asking for definition of what it is
2   to help the organization examine what causes the problem and diagnose how this can be overcome
3   to assist in getting the organization to offer alternative solutions
4   to provide direction in the implementation of alternative solutions
5   to transmit the learning process that allows the client to deal with change on an ongoing basis in the future.

Broadly speaking, the change agent will tread a line between expert and process facilitator depending on their individual approach to the process, the skills and competencies which they possess, the values and assumptions they make about change in the organization, and their own personal characteristics. However, the experience of the organization in terms of its past dealings with change, their willingness to change, and the size and complexity of the problem will also influence the change process. Early on in the process the role of the change agent is that of information seeker. As the process develops and solutions emerge, the role of the change agent becomes one of being more directive in terms of moving the organization through learning to the accomplishment of new procedures that solve the particular problem. In general, the change agent should try taking a position within the process that serves to assist the organization in every way possible. This involves assessment of problems, attempts at resolution and implementation issues.

Moving towards change

In Chapter 8 we noted that there were four situations where organization development is needed:

1 The current nature of the organization is leading to failure to meet objectives.
2 Change is required to react faster to external alterations.
3 The introduction of one form of change (for example, new technology) requires change in other parts of the organization (work organization, reward systems etc.).
4 The introduction of change acts as the trigger for consideration of other new approaches.

We would like to give you the opportunity here to look at a situation where a change process has to be managed, and ask you to work your way through it, in terms of how you, as a potential change agent, would approach this situation. This is to be treated as a non-threatening, simulated example. There isn't a right answer to it, but there are a number of different approaches, each with their own consequences. Read through the case described below, and think about how you would tackle this situation.

READER ACTIVITY: MAKING FRIENDS AT QUILTCO

Bob Smeaton, the Managing Director of Quiltco, a West Midlands textile manufacturer, was quite pleased with himself. It was Friday afternoon and his flight from Tokyo was just about to land at Heathrow. In conjunction with his Sales Director, Peter Wilson, he had just returned from Japan where he had managed to successfully complete negotiations on a £2.5 million order from the Japanese golfing equipment manufacturer, Kokuna. The order was for the manufacture of a new range of golf sweaters and accessories and was the biggest single order that the company had dealt with in their five-year history. They had come up against stiff competition from other sportswear manufacturers in the United Kingdom and Japan.

To secure the order, Quiltco had to promise delivery of the first batch of newly designed golf wear within six weeks and bulk order shipments of 10,000 pullovers every two months. This created a problem. At maximum production, Quiltco could only manufacture and meet these order require-ments by dropping 80 per cent of its ongoing business. It also meant that three new computer-controlled manufacturing machines and a new computer-aided design system would be put to work to come up with the new styles and design and to manufacture the sweaters. These had been recently purchased at great expense. The problem was who would operate the machinery and design systems to meet the order requirements, and what to do with Quiltco's current workload.

Still, it had been a good trip and Bob had the weekend to plan the future development of the company.

Patricia Kennedy, Production Director at Quiltco, was called into the board meeting on the Monday morning. 'It's like this, Pat,' said Bob Smeaton. 'We need the new designs in a matter of weeks and they have to be computer-generated to fit straight into our new machinery. Our people haven't been trained on them yet so we'll have to subcontract this to some freelance designers who specialize in this field. They'll do the designs for us and we should be able to meet the six-week deadline with some ease.'

Patricia paused. 'So who is going to actually make all these lovely new golf sweaters then, and who will tell Parks and Dencing that we can't provide them with any knitwear for the next nine months? You can't just tell the design shop that they are surplus to requirements for the next couple of weeks, and then tell P&D that we're sorry but they'll just have to wait. That's not how we do business, is it?'

Bob's reply was succinct and to the point. 'Pat, this is a new millennium. If this company is going to survive it has to become an international concern. Sure, P&D are a big contract for us but we'll deal with that problem when it arises. As for the designers, I'm going to have a meeting with all operating staff this afternoon and let them have the good news.'

Work stopped at Quiltco at 4.30 p.m. that day. Bob Smeaton, accompanied by Peter Wilson and Patricia Kennedy, addressed the staff in the company cafeteria. Bob started off in ebullient mood. 'Well, the situation facing us is one that I'm sure other companies would like to be in. I am sure you are aware by now that we have managed to win the biggest order in this company's short history, with the Japanese golfing company Kokuna. This assures our future and means that jobs are secure. However, it does put us all under a bit of pressure. To this end I have made arrangements for an outside design and production team to join us temporarily to design and manufacture the Kokuna sweaters on our new equipment. This should allow the rest of you to carry on your normal duties, allowing us to meet the tight deadlines Kokuna have set. The outside team will be independent but will gradually bring in our own staff on design and production matters when they feel that the time to pass on the contract is right. To me it's the best of both worlds, and with a little bit of a squeeze we can do the Kokuna work and still satisfy the needs of our other customers like P&D. There are some good times ahead, lots of hard work, but I'm sure you'll agree with me that it'll be worth the struggle in the end?'

Smeaton's comments were met initially with stunned silence. However, it did not take long for murmuring to begin. The first comment came from one of the designers: 'Are you saying that we aren't good enough to do the design for the new sweaters?' 'Yeah, and we can't handle the new machinery so we'll buy in some smart alecs from outside, is that it?' The meeting soon deteriorated into a slanging match from the floor, with comments such as, 'We're only good for the simple stuff', 'Who are these outsiders anyway?', and 'Don't you trust us to be able to deliver this for you?'

As the meeting finally began to get out of hand, Bob Smeaton turned to the assembled group and said, 'Who do you people think you are? We bring in the biggest order we've ever had and all you can think about is yourselves. Obviously we'll have to get this situation resolved before we go anywhere.' At that, he closed the meeting. However, on his way out of the cafeteria he turned to Patricia Kennedy. 'This bolshie lot need a good sorting out. Come and see me tomorrow morning first thing and we'll get to the bottom of this.'

Questions

- Was Bob Smeaton wrong? How should he have approached the situation?
- What advice would you give Patricia before the Tuesday morning meeting?
- How should Quiltco try to recover the situation?

Case analysis

Quiltco is a good example of managing the process of change and also dealing with the potential for resistance to change. The manner in which change is brought about is an important determinant of the level of success associated with it. Huse (1975) argues that there are eight factors associated with reducing the level of resistance to change. One of the more important factors is that associated with allowing those likely to be affected by change a participatory role. So when considering the Quiltco case above, or any change process, three options are available.

Option 1 is likely to be the most unsuccessful. This is where change is introduced in a top-down manner with *no consultation* with those about to be affected. In this sense, the effect of change is likely to be more negative in its orientation. It is logical that those about to be affected, for example by the introduction of new technology, should have their views and feelings taken into consideration prior to the change process taking place. Resistance to change is not resistance to the change itself; rather, it is a reaction to the way in which change is introduced and the levels of consultation and information provided related to that change.

Option 2 is likely to create the greatest chance of success, but is also likely to be time-consuming. This involves *full participation* by all likely to be affected by the forthcoming change. As Huse (1975) points out:

> The amount of opposition to change is reduced when those people who are to be changed and those who are to exert influence for a change have a strong sense of belonging to the same group. Change that comes from within is much less threatening and creates less opposition than change that is proposed from the outside. There are varying degrees of participation in this context.

The argument that Huse makes is relevant to the use of organization development as a model for instigating change in organizations because of its participatory nature, and the use of the change agent, especially one from within the organization. Full participation allows all to become involved and even enthused by change. However, it is a slow and time-consuming process and may not be appropriate where the need for change has been left too late, as in the Quiltco example.

Where change has to occur rapidly, for example to ensure company survival or growth, then option 3, *limited participation*, is a more effective strategy. This is accomplished by targeting, selecting and involving key members likely to be affected by change, and using them as a short-term project group to assess and implement the change process. This allows participation to occur as well as keeping to specific deadlines when these are crucial. The most obvious (but not the only route) is to involve depart-mental managers, trade union representatives and a number of key staff. So Patricia Kennedy might recommend the adoption of this type of solution.

The learning element for the change agent, in terms of moving the organization with which they are dealing towards change, is that of allowing and taking advantage of participation. The individual problem will determine whether options 2 or 3 are pursued. However, in an OD setting, option 1 is an anathema to successful change interventions. As Warner Burke (1994) notes:

> Thus the primary though not exclusive function of OD consultants is to help clients learn how to help themselves more effectively. Although consultants occasionally provide expert information and may sometimes prescribe a remedy, their more typical mode of operating is facilitation.

Dealing with change is one of the most crucial factors that a manager will have to experience within an organization. More often than not, it is resistance to change as a result of insufficient attention being paid to the process of change that causes problems. Huse (1975, adapted) suggests eight ways to reduce resistance to change:

1   Any change process needs to take into account the needs, attitudes and beliefs of the individual(s) involved as well as the forces of the organization. The individual must see some personal benefit to be gained from the change before he will be willing to participate in the change process.
2   The greater the prestige of the supervisor, the greater the influence he can exert for change. However, the official leader of a group and the actual (although informal) leader need not be the same individual. Frequently, an unofficial leader with high prestige and influence within the work group can be highly influential in the change process.
3   Strong pressure for change in behaviour can be established by providing specific information desired by the group about itself and

its behaviour. The more central, relevant and meaningful the information, the greater the possibility for change. For example, if properly used, data obtained through a survey questionnaire may be much more meaningful to a particular work group than data about attitudes in general.

4   Strong pressures for change can be established by creating shared perceptions by the group members of the need for change, thus making the pressure come from within the unit. In particular, the participation in analysis and interpretation helps to reduce or bypass resistance which comes from proceeding either too rapidly or too slowly.

5   The amount of opposition to change is reduced when those people who are to be changed and those who are to exert influence for a change have a strong sense of belonging to the same group. Change that comes from within is much less threatening and creates less opposition than change that is proposed from the outside.

6   Group cohesiveness or 'togetherness' may operate either to increase or to reduce resistance to change, depending on the issue and the way in which the group sees the change as being valuable or harmful.

7   A group that has a continuing psychological meaning to an individual has more influence than a group with only temporary membership. Therefore, a change process that involves bringing individuals together, off the job, in temporary groups, has less force for lasting change than those change processes that involve the individual in the immediate job situation.

8   All relevant people in the group must share information relating to the need for change, plans for change, and consequences of change. A change process ordinarily requires the specific and deliberate opening of communication channels. Blocking these channels usually leads to distrust and hostility. Change processes which provide specific knowledge on the progress to date, and specify the criteria against which improvement is to be measured, are more likely to be successful.

At this point it is important to be able to relate the concepts of what is involved in the change process to your own organization, as well as highlighting that change is messy, affects many, requires systematic diagnosis and needs an effective strategy. Before moving on to examine the rules and procedures to be adopted by the change agent during the lifetime of a project, it is worthwhile considering the implications of selecting a change agent from within the organization.

The internal change agent: pros and cons?

Many organizations have invested resources to establish their own internal organization development consultants as a means of instigating change. For example, staff at an American computer manufacturer prepared an organizational development training proposal. The purpose of this document was to secure internal company funding for the establishment of a training programme for internal OD consultants. Part of the introduction is reproduced in the display here. Why would a company wish to become so heavily resourced in the area of organization development? One reason is that it is an investment in getting ahead and being able to manage change. Similarly, the costs involved in external change agents getting up to speed with the culture and values of an organization are expensive in time and money. There are several organizations willing to invest heavily in this field as a means of forgoing external costs via change consultants.

Purpose of training

The purpose of the Organization Development Training is to help increase the effectiveness of manufacturing by providing expertise and skilled resources to help manage the massive changes now taking place in our manufacturing operations in Europe.

The amount of change going on in manufacturing – the type of work, the type and mix of skills, structures and systems, response times, performance measurement of operating units and people, and the way the manufacturing operations are designed and operate – is already high and is increasing. Manufacturing must change the way it operates in order to correspond with changes going on in customers, vendors, marketing and sales, and engineering. Products and processes are changing rapidly. Manufacturing also needs to influence the operations and style of these other organizations.

Training internal consultants drawn from existing, experienced employees is preferred. This has the great advantage of providing resources who know how our company works and who can actively redesign and make changes in the organization rather than just consult. The learning and the experience become embedded in the organization.

Source: Organization Development Training: proposal for Skills Council funding (an in-house proposal for training managers in OD techniques and capabilities)

The benefits of using an internal change agent are linked directly to two key issues: cost factors and access to information. By comparison, the costs associated with training an employee in the techniques and practices of OD are minimal when the alternative is the use of an outside consultancy firm over a lengthy period of time. External consultants charge by the day and, more often than not, the cost of one change project can run into tens of thousands of pounds. The external consultancy firm has to build in overhead costs, which runs up the bill.

The internal change agent may also have the benefit of having access to information that the external agent cannot hope to get to, no matter how long the project runs. However, as Margulies and Raia (1978) point out, to be effective the internal consultant is required to maintain a marginal status between being internal and being objective. The value of the internal change agent rests with being inside the organization and able to have information at hand whilst remaining objective with regard to the problem and the client organization. This is a particularly difficult situation for an employee of an organization to be in. There are a number of factors which may hinder the internal change agent's objectivity:

- being too close to see what the problem is
- being part of the problem
- being willing to confront issues when promotion and pay issues are forthcoming
- being part of the power system being examined
- being aware of the needs and demands of superiors.

The use of internal change agents, who have been effectively trained in the techniques of managing change, will obviously benefit the organization. However, there are a number of issues that the change agent should be aware of that may inhibit their ability to influence change within the organization. Two of these relate to the method of entry into projects and the nature of the voluntary relationship.

In terms of entry into a change management process as a facilitator, the internal change agent has to convince management and employees within a particular part of the organization of their expertise in this area. There is also a need to display the willingness to help. These issues are no different from those experienced by the external change agent, and confidence and trust will come from successful change management projects within the organization over time. However, the internal change agent needs to use these successful interventions as an open education process for the organization far more than the external agent ever has to.

The voluntary nature of the relationship between the change agent and the client is one of the golden rules outlined below. The internal change agent may not be given the opportunity to pick and choose clients from within the organization. Nor can they always expect to be free in their choice of the manner and mode of facilitation employed. The internal change agent is constrained by his/her involvement and participation in the organization and by their specified role which others may seek to exploit to their advantage.

The internal change agent must not and cannot become involved in change within his/her own area. For most internal change agents this rules out the development of projects for change in the personnel area, but leaves them free to deal with issues related to sales and marketing, manufacturing etc. Ideally, any organization training internal change agents would select a number of them from different departments to be able to deal with this difficulty.

In assessing the need for internal and external change agents, Margulies and Raia argue that:

> organizations must learn to use external and internal consultants in more effective ways. Perhaps the best approach consists in the use of both. External consultants can bring objectivity, expertise and fresh approaches to organization problem solving. Internal consultants provide knowledge and understanding of organizational processes, information about current issues, and continuity of effort . . . a collaborative relationship provides an opportunity to transfer the external consultant's skills to the client system . . . since the capacity for organization development must ultimately emerge from the organization itself. (1972: 477)

The golden rules of the change agent

The issues related to participation become apparent when we look in closer detail at the role and positioning of the change agent in the process of change itself. In essence, there are four 'golden rules' (Lippit, 1959) that the change agent has to observe.

Rule 1: the nature of the relationship

This has to be seen as a voluntary one between the professional helper (the change agent) and the part of the business classified as the system needing help. The most clear-cut example is that of a consultant from one of the large consultancy organizations who is brought in to assist the process of change in an organization.

In our work with organizations we make a point at the start of the process of stressing that it is a voluntary link between two parties which can be severed, at any time, by either party. We make the point of continually reiterating this at stages in the relationship and to all concerned in the change process. The reasons for this are that it allows those who feel uncomfortable with the relationship to express their discomfort openly, allows both parties to begin to address this, if possible, and maintains an open and honest atmosphere. It also has the benefit of allowing the change agent to withdraw if they feel that the assistance being provided is not what is needed, or wanted.

Rule 2: to action an organization development process within any organization, the change agent has to help solve a current or potential problem

This is obvious but important. There are two issues here. First, the organization itself must recognize that a problem exists. This should come from senior management, as the instigation of change stands a greater chance of success with top management support. Recognition of a need for change can take several forms. For example, an increase in employee absence figures should be recognized as an issue for concern that needs to be addressed. Absenteeism over a period of time costs money. Similarly, major changes in organization structure, the introduction of new technology being one example, are also situations where problems may occur and some form of OD analysis may be required.

The second issue relates to the help the change agent can provide. To help solve a problem, the change agent has to be able to offer some form of expertise. Traditionally, this is based on knowledge of the subject. However, for the organization development agent, the knowledge, more often than not, is in dealing with people and helping the organization find its own solutions to structuring, absenteeism etc. This is a skill that few have, and fewer still use effectively.

Rule 3: the relationship is a temporary one and the change agent and the organization must accept the temporary nature of the assistance being provided

In effect this means recognition of withdrawal from the system as a fact of life. One of the main criticisms of consultants is that they get others to solve their own problems, and charge them for the privilege, leaving the organization to manage the mess. Any change agent worth his salt cannot expect to stay in business long using this approach. The old adage that if you ask a consultant the time, he'll ask if he can borrow your watch, may have a grain of truth to it and can be applied in this context to the change agent. The important point is that the change agent has to be temporary but needs to see the project through to satisfactory completion. They are not employed full-time by the organization, and in the case of internal change agents they may have a day job! Both parties must recognize the need to sever the relationship at some point. This does not prevent the change agent from returning periodically to see how the organization is coping with the changes introduced, and some form of neutral or objective audit of change helps the process. However, this should occur after the initial change process has been completed and the change agent has withdrawn to allow the organization to manage its own affairs.

Rule 4: the change agent must be an outsider who is not part of the hierarchical power system in which the client organization is located

Why? Three main reasons immediately spring to mind. The first concerns the nature of being an objective outsider. Again, the obvious choice here is an external change agent. There is no particular axe to grind and therefore the nature of the assistance provided is that of being truly impartial. Change agents from within the confines of the organization, but from another department, may also be able to remain impartial, although the obstacles are greater. Second, as the change agent is from outside the immediate hierarchy, they are less likely to be influenced by the machinations of power, and therefore more likely to remain fair-minded. Third, to be truly effective in helping the client organization, the change agent has to be *seen* to be non-partisan by those within the client system.

In our dealings with client organizations we make a point of stressing to all we come into contact with that we will remain objective, open-minded and, above all, free from influence. This is a difficult situation to maintain balance from. At the end of the day, the change process often involves payment to the change agent, and there is an argument that one has to be aware of whom one is working for. This would also be true for the internal change agent in terms of the intrinsic or extrinsic rewards associated with a successful change project.

These, then, are the rules which the change agent must accept as guiding the change process. Remember that it is a voluntary relationship in which you, as the change agent, are attempting to solve a current or potential problem on a temporary contract with the client organization.

The change agent's approach to change

In Chapter 8 we set out the process the change agent has to go through from the beginning to the end of a project in terms of negotiating access, undertaking the intervention etc. In this section we outline, in more detail, the issues that the change agent will have to deal with in terms of each stage of the process. Where possible, we have tried to use examples from our own experience to highlight some of the issues that one can expect to encounter. We have also tried to relate these to some of the difficulties that an internal change agent can expect to meet with under similar circumstances.

The first problem facing the change agent is one of definition. They have to ask the following.

What is causing the problem?

This should be in terms of trying to define:

- What is going wrong?
- What/who is causing the problem?
- Why does it continue to be a problem?

At this point, it is essential to be able to describe to oneself what the current situation is, why it exists, what is going on etc. This ability to be able to apply a descriptive-analytical capability combines with the skill of diagnosis to enable the change agent to focus on the symptoms of the problem before drawing attention to the causes.

In our experience, this is where the change agent can make their first and perhaps fatal mistake. Under the doctor–patient scheme of system intervention, you tell me the symptoms and I prescribe the remedy. However, diagnosis via expertise may not be the most appropriate form of action in an organization development sense. This is related to why and how the change agent becomes involved in the process. At this point the change agent should ask the next question.

Why do I want to enter into this relationship?

If the answer is to provide the solution via analysis, diagnosis and application of a cure by a fairly standard and mechanized means, then the damage inflicted may be greater than that which the actual problem warrants. The change agent has to be clear about their own goals and the reasons for motivating and influencing others. This is related to who sets the goals for the change process. The client organization and the change agent should define these together. In an organization development mode it has to be both parties because of the nature of what is being changed. More often than not, this is people within a particular setting within the organization, and the change agent has to assist in helping people change themselves. Therefore, description of what the problem is, what is causing it, and how it can be remedied has to come from both parties to this process. The doctor–patient relationship denies mutual exchange.

In one of our first projects as external change agents, one of us was set the task of determining ways of making a customer services department 'work smarter'. The definition of the problem was set by the client organization as a simple one of finding out how the people resources of that department could be better utilized. In the naivety of youth, the description of the problem and its analysis were accepted as straight-forward. The answer simply meant talking to the department's main internal customers to find out what better service they could provide. This ignored the fact that the customer services department could find its own way of working smarter, and that these ideas could and should be taken into consideration. The fundamental flaw was the process by which diagnosis was sought. This was externally driven and discounted the importance of getting those within the department involved in defining the problem and looking for solutions to it.

Having begun the process of defining what the problem is, in alliance with the client organization, the change agent should also look at what potential there is for change. The change agent needs to be sure that there is, within the organization, a motivation towards change. Otherwise, all attempts at instigating change with the client system may be hampered. The motivation can come from two main sources – ambition or dissatisfaction. Lippit noted that, in terms of the motivation for change among individuals,

> pain and dissatisfaction with the present situation are most frequently the dominating driving forces for change, but with groups very often one of the most important motivations is a desire to improve group efficiency . . . even though there may be no critical problems in the present situation. (1959: 8)

Often the motivation for change by one part of the client system may be hampered by other parts of the organization. The change agent has to be aware of the potential for resistance from other areas, has to be aware that they may be viewed as 'on the side' of the immediate client organization, and has to be aware of the impact that both factors may have on the change process. The change agents should at the outset ask themselves the next question.

Who is likely to be affected by change in this client system, and how are they likely to react?

Answers to these questions may go a long way in determining how successful change is likely to be, who is likely to be impacted by it, and how motivated the organization as a whole is to change.

Another important issue that the change agents need to look at, and be honest about, is their own capabilities to manage the change process. In this sense, the change agent needs to ask the following question.

What can I do to help this organization change?

This brings us back to the temporary nature of the change process and the full role of the change agent. The change agent in their role of facilitator is more often than not seen as being an individual who diagnoses problems and offers recommendations for improvement. However, the role is a temporary one and the change agent must also be seen to offer continuity in interpreting the consequences for change made in their recommendations. The logic behind this is fairly straightforward. Having assisted the organization to define its current problem, and helped it consider alternative solutions, the change agent should also assist in the process of working out the meaning of change for the organization in terms of practices, procedures and resultant design.

Change can create a level of disruption within the organization which, if not handled adequately, can lead to demoralization. Having gone through the diagnostic process and outlined the changes needed, the organization may also feel that it has insufficient capabilities to cope with the implications for change without the assistance of the change agent.

It is therefore necessary, as a change agent, to be able to offer both diagnostic and application skills. Lippit (1959: 9) recommends that a consultative team is best placed to offer such solutions. Either way, walking away from the process halfway through would appear to be an inadequate means of dealing with change.

In our dealings with organizations we have often called on the resources of our own outside observer for a neutral standpoint. In this sense, what we get is the viewpoint from someone that has not been closely involved with the organization and may be able to look at the implications of change from a fresher viewpoint. More often than not, this confirms our diagnosis and assessment of the implications of change. It would assist the change agent greatly if they have a 'sounding board' to bounce ideas off. What we recommend here is that organizations invest their resources in more than one individual as change agent, to provide the security and efficiency associated with a team.

There are two other important issues that the change agent needs to take into careful consideration during the course of managing a change project. The first relates to their role during the different phases of the project. The second is linked to establishing change as the norm within organizations.

In terms of the developing role of the change agent, the important question here is the following.

Who should I be at certain points in time?

In essence this involves movement from information gatherer towards a more active training role. Lippit et al. (1958) identified seven stages of change within what they term the consultant/client relationship:

1   development of the need for change
2   establishment of the consultancy relationship
3   clarification of the client problem
4   examination of alternative solutions
5   transformation of intentions to actual change
6   generalization and stabilization of a new level of functioning or group structure
7   achieving a terminal relationship with the consultant and the continuity of the ability to change.

The first crucial area is the move from change agent as information and opinion seeker towards that of facilitator and adviser/trainer. This occurs between stages 4 and 5 and involves taking on a more directive role with the client organization. This prevents the organization regressing backwards by allowing individuals to focus on the application of the alternatives they helped develop. In this way the client organization will see what happens during the change process and will be able to learn from it, and hopefully apply the techniques the next time.

In our experience, it is better for the change agent to deliberately separate the information gathering from the diagnosis and recommendation stages. In our dealings with organizations we make a point of using the summary session at the end of the information gathering stages 1 through 4 to get commitment that we can move forward in a different mode. This involves a form of contract renewal where we either seek permission to lead the transformation of intentions into actual change, or offer to act as observers of how the organization is managing this stage itself. The latter is preferable in terms of gaining the commitment from those being affected by change. It also assists in the termination of the relationship for the organization to be seen to be taking a greater participatory role. However, the change agent still has a part in terms of helping the organization learn new procedures and skills associated with the alternative solutions they have helped to establish. You must be acutely aware of the change in role. Do not hide behind the information-seeker phase. Be prepared to move on to the training and guidance role with the ultimate aim of removing the need for the change agent.

The second issue directly concerns the question of learning in the organization. The change agent should, during the change process, ask the following question.

How do I get constant change in this organization?

The process of working through the definition of the problem and possible solutions helps the organization learn to cope with the problems that initiated the need for change. It now knows what the causes were and is hopefully in a position to remedy them on its own should they occur again. However, if the change process has been successful, the organization will also have learned how to go about defining problems and clarifying them as they emerge. In this sense, they are learning directly from the change agent about the mechanisms they used to clarify problems as they emerged: the types of questions asked, the way in which meetings were run, the way the change agent communicated and got the involvement of all concerned. The organization learns in this way when it has reached its own limits in dealing with problems, and hopefully learns about making decisions about when it needs to seek outside help.

We were asked by the VLSI (integrated circuit manufacture) business of Digital Equipment in Ayr, Scotland to undertake a short review of the development of semi-autonomous work teams. This was a fairly straightforward process that involved the design of an opinion survey questionnaire, the running of a number of workshops on issues of concern and critical success factors with operating staff, and conversations with managers within the business. We worked through the process of information gathering and analysis and provided feedback on how the teams were operating, what were the critical success factors and a number of issues that gave cause for concern. However, one of the unexpected success criteria from our perspective was that having used the teams to help design and run the questionnaire and the workshops, the organization decided that this method of data collection and analysis could be successfully adopted inside the business and used as a mechanism for assessing where they were, what changes were likely to affect them, and what issues staff felt were likely to be problematic. The change agents, ourselves, had left the relationship, but the mechanisms for making change ongoing remained and had been built into the business.

Conclusion: OD and the effective change agent

We pointed out earlier on that experience suggests that creating a sense of involvement with those likely to be affected by change encourages their commitment to change, and higher levels or standards of performance result. The mechanisms used during the process of change, and the efforts of the change agent to ensure participation and involvement in the changes being contemplated, can increase the likelihood of a successful change intervention.

Many organizations now involve people through consultation, participation and communication. However, this still creates a degree of controversy related to timing, effectiveness and applicability. Schein (1988) comments that:

> As long as organizations are networks of people engaged in achieving some common goals, there will be various kinds of processes occurring between them. Therefore, the more we understand about how to diagnose and improve such processes, the greater will be our chances of finding solutions to the more technical problems and of ensuring that such solutions will be accepted and used by members of the organization.

The effective change agent has to be able to manage the bridge between the managers' desire to solve the problem immediately and the time it takes the organization to solve its own problems via the change agent and their facilitation process. The effective change agent also has to remain on an unstable borderline, or what Margulies and Raia (1978) term 'marginality', between being in the organization and remaining aloof. Similarly, the change agent has to strike a balance between being the 'technical' expert – the person assumed to have the answers – and the process facilitator – the person with the techniques to allow the organization to find its own answers. Most effective change agents need to find a balance. This lies between what they know is the correct solution, having done it before and thus knowing what types of answers and solutions are likely to emerge, and the processes by which they get the organization's members to find their own answers to their own problems – a tricky task!

In our experience, many managers will readily accept the overall argument for a need to change organization structures and management styles for more effective performance. However, they feel that there is a lack of adequate guidance on how this transformation takes place. This reverts back to the desire for instantly applicable, off-the-shelf solutions to their problems. The real world, even from an OD perspective, is less clear-cut. The concept of perpetual transition management, as an approach to implementing and sustaining organizational change, is an example of dealing with change as it is lived. To this end, it is the job of the effective change agent to get those involved with the change process to pay attention to how it is lived. It is only in this respect that the experience of change can be learned from, and applied effectively at a later date. The change agent, to be effective, needs to constantly work on the basis that they are doing themselves out of a job, and that the client is big enough to be able to handle their own problems – another tricky task!

How do organizations learn these OD processes? In Chapter 10 we look at the development of learning organizations.

10 The Learning Organization

It would be erroneous to chart the development of OD without giving some consideration to the learning organization. This terminology, perhaps coined by Peter Senge, became increasingly popular with both management gurus and CEOs during the 1990s. Learning organizations have joined the litany of corporate buzzwords and terms such as knowledge working, business solutions and creative workforces that, many pundits would argue, are the prerequisites to corporate survival and success. Before continuing with an exploration of the concepts and practices that underlie the learning organization it is perhaps appropriate to give some consideration to whether they are the invention of the corporate marketing world, or whether indeed there is some substance and justification to support such a claim. It is important to make a distinction between fads and trends. Fads exist to respond to short-term changes in demand such as business process re-engineering or outsourcing. Trends by contrast are the consequence of long-term patterns of change which are indicative of the changing nature of society, such as increased health consciousness and the need for increased flexibility of organizational resources.

To what extent then might learning organizations be considered as a fad, as a response to some wider corporate trend, or indeed as a trend in themselves? There is little doubt that the term itself is widely used both as an external marketing vehicle, and internally as a means of developing staff consciousness and awareness of the need to be more receptive to opportunities for service or product improvement. There is however a general trend, not only at the organizational level but also at the level of society at large, to realize the full potential of the working community. From a human resource perspective, one might argue that there is nothing new in such a notion; however, the realization of such an ideal in practice requires nothing less than a cultural revolution.

Management theorists constantly portray the external environment as 'turbulent'. Rapidly evolving technology, dynamic markets and increasingly sophisticated customers and competitors combine forces to challenge the traditional notions of successful businesses. It is a widely accepted belief that successful organizations of the future will be those who are sufficiently flexible to respond to these constantly changing demands and have the ability to redirect, focus and resource effectively, appropriately and more quickly than their competitors. Argyris and Schon (1996) describe the conventional wisdom that suggests all organizations need to draw lessons from the past, detect and correct errors, anticipate and respond to impending threats, engage in continuing innovation and build and realize images of a desirable future. They suggest that a virtual consensus exists and that we are all subject to a learning imperative. Clearly, it is not enough merely to *respond* to the changes; we must develop the capability to *predict* what they may be, to develop a corporate understanding of a range of possible futures and position the organization appropriately to meet any of these potential demands.

Developments in the field of strategy, where strategic thinking may be rethought in terms of organizational change, has also triggered the interest in how organizations learn. Reflecting the growing agreement that development of strategy is an active, iterative process involving whole organizations, it strongly suggests a requirement to understand the processes of institutional learning and what creates a learning organization (Argyris and Schon, 1996).

Drucker (1998) suggests that the development of information technology will have a significant effect on the internal appearance of organizations of the future. He argues for a reduced hierarchy as fewer managers are required to act as conduits for information, but also describes the enhanced dissemination of information that he predicts will shift the responsibility for decision making further down the organization. This movement creates the need to develop the skills of those who use data, convert it into information and then use that information to acquire knowledge which guides the organizational response to the external environment. It is not only the terminology he uses but also the process he describes that suggests learning. This is further supported by his advocacy of executives and specialists, who 'need to think through what data they need – first to know what they are doing, then to be able to decide what they should be doing and finally to appraise how well they are doing' (Drucker, 1998).

Despite its recent rise in appeal, the concept of a learning organization is not new. A number of initiatives and models have been developed to guide organizations to an enhanced level of effectiveness that can be translated into competitive advantage. Such programmes include continuous improvement (CI), business process re-engineering (BPR), and total quality management (TQM), all of which suggest a consideration of what organizations need to do differently to maintain their competitiveness.

Garratt (1994) suggests that the major ideas underlying the concept of a learning organization have been in place since the 1940s. He cites the pioneering work of Revans, the proponent of action learning, the economist Fritz Schumaker and the cybernetic research of Norbert Weiner,

Ross Ashby and Jacob Bronowski. He argues that through their work developed the notion that the sole source of organizational learning is people, that learning has an intrinsic (personal development) value and an extrinsic (organizational asset creating) value, and that multiple feedback loops of learning are required for developing continuous organizational learning. He argues that the recent acceptance of the concept of a learning organization is a result of economic recession in the West and fierce competition from Asia.

The learning organization concept has been suggested as a way of moving an organization towards improved performance on the understanding that improvement depends on learning something new, on seeing things with a different perspective, and that to *continuously improve* requires a commitment to learning. The risk of not learning is that old practices will be repeated and any changes will be merely cosmetic. If it can be said to have a central theme, the notion of the learning organization is one that relates to formally acknowledging and providing feedback as a basis for change.

There are many definitions of what constitutes a learning organization, and much of the literature emphasizes 'aspirational' theory, with little focus on the practical aspects which organizations need to consider. As Garvin (1993) describes, academics are partly responsible for the plethora of definitions, and he criticizes them for their 'reverential and utopian . . . near mystical terminology'. He argues that the recommendations of leading theorists such as Senge and Nonaka are often too abstract and too many questions remain unanswered, such as:

- How will managers know when their organizations have achieved the lofty heights of the learning organization?
- What concrete changes in behaviour are required?
- What policies and programmes must be in place?
- How do you get from here to there?

Defining the nature of the beast

There is an abundance of literature surrounding the concept of the learning organization, and it can be divided into two distinct categories. The first addresses the conceptual aspects of the theory of organizational learning, relates to opinions on the types of learning and the process of learning, and seeks to differentiate between individual and organizational learning. The second category of work has developed as a result of the experiences of practitioners who have attempted to introduce these concepts into organizations.

It has long been argued that there are two types of learning: single-loop and double-loop learning. *Single-loop*, or *instrumental learning* is described by Senge (1990a) as *adaptive learning*, which changes the 'theory of action' and response to a problem but not the 'theory-in-use' (Argyris and Schon, 1996). It pertains to the detection and correction of the error within the boundaries of current thinking that, potentially, allows the problem to re-emerge in the future. Within an organization, this is a process by which an entity learns to do better what it is currently doing; adaptive learning is about *coping*. This basic form of learning is restrictive and non-challenging. The problems of the day are solved without taking time to understand their root cause and taking action to ensure that they will not be repeated. The term 'learning organization' has been used by some as implying a transformational approach to change that comes from double-loop learning. Incremental change or adaptation via such processes as TQM is the outcome of single-loop learning. This narrow frame of reference can, over time, transform the perceived core capabilities of an organization to 'core rigidities' as members consistently fail to challenge existing patterns of thinking and behaviour, resulting in an inflexible, reactive company, characterized by short-termism (Slater and Narver, 1995). This perpetual cycle, whilst it exists, can be a source of comfort to organizations who enjoy a sense of security in their ability to repeatedly solve familiar day-to-day issues. The potentially different outcomes for organization change from single- and double-loop learning are really the essential implication of Argyris and Schon's work.

Double-loop learning or *generative learning* (Senge, 1990b) occurs when there is a willingness to challenge long-held assumptions and create new ways of looking at the world. Generative learning is about *creating* knowledge. The two feedback loops connect the observed effects of action with strategies and the values served by those strategies and may be carried out by either individuals or organizations. This 'frame breaking' approach within organizations is most likely to lead to competitive advantage because it focuses on reviewing and changing business systems rather than functional efficiency (Slater and Narver, 1995). It is more challenging to organizations because it forces them to consider that their accepted ways of thinking and behaving may no longer be appropriate, and this process of review can be painful. Nevertheless, if organizations are to develop the capability to renew themselves to meet the demands of the emerging environment then they will need the capacity for generative learning.

Carr (1997: 224-31), in reviewing the work of Argyris and Schon, argues that 'single-loop learning has had the practical effect of diverting attention away from the possibility of double-loop learning'. This is an interesting point, for in recent years some of the literature has actually made a distinction between the terms 'learning organization' and 'organizational learning' on the basis of the conservatism implied in single-loop learning for organization change.

Fulmer (1996) argues an alternative but complementary approach to the understanding of types of learning. His theory of *maintenance learning*

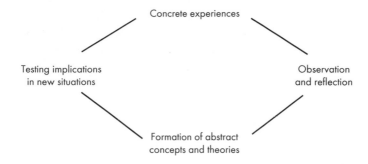

Figure 10.1 *The Kolb learning cycle*

relates to single-loop learning, as does his theory of *shock learning*, a response to crisis, both of which are short-term, reactive learning systems involving little creativity or challenge to developed thinking. Conversely, *anticipatory learning* is more akin to generative/double-loop learning in that it is participatory, future oriented and long term in its outlook.

Argyris and Schon (1996) present a schema for learning:

- informational content – *the learning product*
- *the learning process* – acquiring, processing and storing of information
- *a learner* to whom the process is attributed.

The learning cycle developed by David Kolb (1976) is often used to describe the second phase of this schema: the 'natural process of learning'. A four-phase process based on concrete experience, reflection and observation and the development of theories and concepts which are tested for their relevance and validity (Figure 10.1), it is closely aligned to the Deming cycle of plan–do–check–act and the model presented by Buckler (1996), which prescribes the identification of problems, experimentation to discover solutions, development of new theory, change in behaviour and application to new situations (Figure 10.2).

All models emphasize learning from experience, reflecting on that experience and forming new ideas that are then tested in a reiterative process.

The Kolb cycle was initially developed to represent the process of individual learning. However, he describes how this can be adapted for organizational learning. Building upon the notion that individuals have diverse learning styles and will therefore have unique capabilities that lend themselves more closely to specific phases, he recommends the development of teams that incorporate the specific skills required at each phase.

Kolb's argument suggests that organizational learning be differentiated from individual learning by the nature of *collective experience*. This

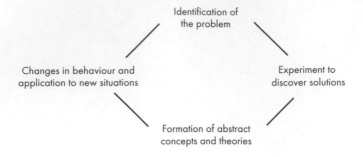

Figure 10.2   *The Buckler model*

is accepted by Argyris and Schon (1996) who argue that for action and inquiry to be truly 'organizational', it must be within previously agreed boundaries and parameters of policy that turn a group of individuals into an organization. Van der Heijden and Eden (1994) extend this by distinguishing individual and organizational learning by an *alignment of thinking*. Supporting the idea of learning from experience, they suggest that learning from uncoordinated activity will remain an individual affair. They argue that Kolb's model emphasizes the proactive approach required for organizational learning – the need to consciously *create* experiences from which to learn – but stress that an alignment of thinking will direct the creation of experience and encourage joint reflection and testing of theory, developing common understanding and consensus as to the required response to the problem. This argument echoes Senge (1990b) who presents shared vision and mental models as prerequisites for organizational learning.

It has been argued that the distinguishing factor between individual and organizational learning is *information dissemination* (Slater and Narver, 1995). Initially this seems a simplistic theory, but on closer examination it supports the previously presented arguments. They argue that information is shared with the objective of increasing its value via the process of feedback, providing a broader context from which to view the world and providing new insights into potential solutions to problems. It is only by disseminating information that a shared interpretation can be achieved and a consensus reached as to the meaning and implication for the business that will shape future activity.

Organizational enquiry

Van der Heijden and Eden (1994) and Argyris and Schon (1996) suggest that learning will only occur when the results of organizational inquiry are *different to expectation*, which triggers further thought and reflection and challenges the current 'theory-in-use'. To become organizational, learning must be embedded in the images of the organization held in the minds of its members or the physical artefacts embedded in the environment. The challenge may trigger changes in organizational activity in order to realign with the new system of beliefs. This element of change is the learning product and, interestingly, Argyris and Schon argue that it is not always positive. Individuals can learn collectively to respond to error by scapegoating, using systematic patterns of deception, camouflage of intention and maintenance of taboos. They argue that *productive learning* takes place when organizational inquiry is pursued for the improvement of business performance and when values and criteria that define 'improvement' shape that inquiry. Finally, productive learning enhances the capabilities for future learning as individuals practise the process of inquiry and development of commonly held definitions.

Conversation and shared language

For an organization to take effective advantage of learning opportunities, members must identify and break down the barriers that inhibit productive learning. There is a need for meaningful, open conversations, however developing the *capabilities for conversation* is not easy (Senge, 1990b). Van der Heijden and Eden (1994) expand upon this by arguing the need for a shared language, developed through collective experience, to facilitate productive verbal exchange. They describe the existence of labels and jargon as manifestations of the process of language building and they refer to the way concepts of strategy have been codified in management textbooks to aid effective conversation. Nevertheless, they argue that language can only represent yesterday's problems and will evolve as organizations seek for new responses to the new reality.

Arguing from the context of strategy development, they contend that via institutional action, the alignment of mental models and the facilitation by shared language, planning becomes a joint activity and learning experience. Stata (1989) develops the concept of a collective experience and introduces *organizational memory*. This depends on the mechanisms used to retain knowledge: policies, strategies and explicit models of documentation, information systems etc. Reliance on individual memory clearly constitutes a major risk as personnel change roles or leave the business.

To sum up these ideas on organization and learning:

- Learning takes place as a result of experience. The key differentiators between individual and organizational learning are the collective nature of experience, and the joint testing of potential responses to that experience to develop a shared view of what constitutes appropriate action.

- Organizational learning does not occur when individual members of the organization learn; there is a major emphasis on the sharing of information and establishing a shared interpretation.
- Change is blocked unless all the major decision makers learn together and are committed to the actions necessary for change.
- Learning only happens if the results of experience are different to expectation and it is facilitated by a shared language and enhanced capability for meaningful conversation.
- Meaningful conversation takes place when there is a willingness to challenge assumptions that trigger change in behaviour. It is this environment that is most conducive to double-loop/generative learning.

The relevance of a learning organization

Stata (1989) is often quoted:

> I would argue that the rate at which individuals and organizations learn may become the only sustainable competitive advantage, especially in knowledge-intensive industries.

Competitive advantage can appear under different guises. Senge (1995) argues that it is generated within organizations committed to marrying individual development with superior economic performance to improve quality, to delight customers, to energize and motivate employees and to manage change. It is further argued that learning provides a buffer between the organization and its environment to stop a reactive response to every event (Slater and Narver, 1995). Despite being built from a platform of past experience, a company committed to learning is inherently forward looking, which reduces the frequency of major shocks and fosters an enhanced level of flexibility with which to respond to, and predict, emergent opportunities. This develops the rationale for a learning organization by presenting the view that learning is a natural human process, and that to encourage it will unleash previously unharnessed individual and thus organizational energy. It suggests that it stems naturally from previous thinking in organizational development, and that it is reflected in the modern Japanese management approach. Because of these influences, development of learning is essential to create superior performance and sustain competitive advantage.

Senge builds upon the belief that 'human beings are designed for learning' and that the major institutions and their processes are designed to control, which stifles that natural learning process. He comments that by focusing on performance for someone else's approval, corporations create the conditions that lead to mediocre performance. He quotes W. Edwards Deming, leader of the quality movement:

Our prevailing system of management has destroyed our people. People are born with intrinsic motivation, self-esteem, dignity, curiosity to learn, joy in learning. The forces of destruction begin with toddlers – the prizes for the best Halloween costume, grades in school, gold stars, and on up through university. On the job, people, teams, divisions are ranked – reward for the one at the top, punished at the bottom. Management by objectives, quotas, incentive pay, business plans, put together separately, division by division cause further loss, unknown and unknowable.

Senge (1990b) contends that a young child entering school soon discovers that the name of the game is getting the right answer and not making mistakes. This manifests itself in organizations of individuals who also understand the game and avoid making mistakes or, at least, avoid admitting to them. This prohibits the superior learning that Senge believes is required for superior performance. He also challenges the role of the leader who 'learned for the organization', arguing that it is no longer feasible to 'figure it out at the top' and that a dynamic, interdependent and unpredictable world requires integration of learning and acting at all levels. Senge attributes the rise of the Japanese manufacturing companies to a recognition of the need to integrate. Recognizing that the key to reducing cost was the elimination of process delays, they worked extensively to build networks with trusted suppliers and to reduce delays in materials procurement, production set-up and in-process inventory. The attitude of continuous improvement and total quality management is essentially a generative learning process geared towards understanding the latent needs of customers – what they really value but have never experienced and would never think to demand.

The evolution of learning organizations: impact on training and development

Pedler et al. (1991) offer a different perspective to the contemporary relevance of a learning organization which is seen as an evolutionary process, combining the phases of organizational development with significant impact on training and development. This supports the view of Garratt (1994). They describe the movement from the *primal* to the *rational* phase, where the organization develops from the entrepreneurial form, characterized by charismatic leadership, flat structures and limited specialization, to a more complex organization with hierarchical structures, increasing levels of specialization and a commitment to the profession which outweighs that to the organization. Energy becomes focused on building systems and structures to cope with the increasing requirements for analysis and recording.

This leads to a bureaucratic crisis and increasing alienation from both customers and fellow members of the organization. One potential response is the matrix organization where horizontal, temporary project teams supplement the original vertical authority relationships in an attempt to break down the barriers. Team building, conflict resolution and customer care programmes are the norm. This is followed by the *differentiated* phase of organizational development and the integrated organization – one that has been described as a shamrock by Handy (1989) and a cloverleaf by others. The key factor is that throughout the organization, at all levels and in all directions, there is increasing integration between people, functions and ideas. An example of practice in this type of organization is the increasing collaboration with external suppliers and customers, which is mirrored internally. Similarly, there is an emphasis on aligning the espoused values of the organization with its business processes.

Movement in training and development mirrors these changes in organization design. The rational phase is complemented by a *systematic approach* to training illustrated by establishing best practice, job descriptions, job analysis, behavioural objectives and systematic evaluation. As alienation and frustration become more pronounced, the response is geared towards *organizational development*, *self-development*, and *the pursuit of excellence* (Peters and Waterman, 1982), which has manifested itself in a plethora of initiatives (TQM, CI, BPR). Many organizations facing this evolutionary phase have found their training and development programmes unfocused, individualistic and without longevity. There has been an increasing sense of the organization not actually getting anywhere despite the level of activity. The evolutionary response to this, argue Pedler et al., is *organizational transformation*: the response to self-development and action learning is the concept of the learning organization.

Organizational transformation (OT) has been described as 'the extension to organization development that seeks to create massive changes in an organization's structures, processes, culture and orientation to its environment' (French et al., 1994). It is the application of behavioural science theory and practice to effect large-scale paradigm-shifting organizational change and usually results in totally new paradigms or models for organizing and performing work.

In trying to develop a relationship between the learning organization, OD and the management of change one can identify three key linkages:

- The concept of a *learning organization* is increasingly relevant as businesses seek to deal with complex environments.
- It is a natural evolution from earlier forms of training and development as organizations evolve new behaviours and structures.
- It harnesses the belief that humans are designed for learning.

The emerging challenge is how to accelerate organizational learning, build consensus for change and facilitate the change process. The concept of a learning organization seems to fit comfortably with this challenge, but there are many models, definitions and characteristics which are used to illustrate what a learning organization might look like, and how to achieve one. The next section presents some of the more influential ideas.

Building a learning organization

The body of work relating to definitions, characteristics and models for creating a learning organization seems to fall naturally into three categories:

1   the application of the academic theory of systemic learning to business
2   the presentation of definitions followed by prescriptive, practical solutions
3   the work of practitioners who decry a prescriptive approach but offer guidelines and practical hints as to how organizations can develop a bespoke approach.

Academic theories of systemic learning

Peter Senge and colleagues at the Massachusetts Institute of Technology are at the forefront of those efforts to apply the academic theory of the learning organization to business. Senge has been described as the 'intellectual and spiritual champion' of the learning organization by *Fortune* magazine and his philosophy is based on a humanist view of organizational change: that businesses should pay more attention to the conditions that motivate people to do great things for themselves and for their companies.

> Our organizations work the way they work, ultimately, because of how we think and how we interact. Only by changing how we think can we change deeply embedded policies and practices. Only by changing how we interact can shared visions, shared understandings and new capacities for co-ordinated action be established. (Senge, 1990b)

This involves a commitment to lifelong learning. Senge's work has led to the development of the *five disciplines*, which he describes as artistic rather than traditional management disciplines, aimed at enhancing an organization's creative capability.

- *Personal mastery* (1990b: 139–73)   This is the ability to clarify what one most desires in life and work and to apply the principles and values most important to achieving those goals. Essential to the process is building self-awareness and understanding personal strengths and weaknesses. He also argues that managing the creative tension between the vision and the current reality is a critical dimension.

- *Mental models* (1990b: 174–204)   These are the assumptions that shape one's view of the world, developed from past experience, and feed the judgements and perceptions that influence what one hears and says and how one reacts to others. Senge argues that it is not easy to articulate these models because people naturally seek evidence consistent with prior beliefs and this blindness provides a resistance to change. In organizations, mental models shape the views of the market and influence the development of strategies. In an organization it has been established that success is more likely to stem from an alignment of thinking; therefore it is not necessarily important in the first instance to judge whether they are right or wrong, but rather it is necessary to understand what they are and how they influence thinking.

- *Building a shared vision* (1990b: 205–32)   Senge argues that whether a vision is created by an entire company or a team of two is not important. The key factor is that it is created collectively because the collective capability to realize the vision is more powerful than that of a single individual. Nevertheless it follows that, in an organization, the more members that have been actively involved in the process of developing a shared vision, the higher the degree of ownership and the greater the commitment to achieving it. Furthermore, it is less open to misinterpretation as it is communicated to members of the business.

- *Team learning* (1990b: 233–72)   This is based on the acceptance that people who work well together can learn more and accomplish more than is possible individually. It builds from the previous three disciplines. Senge suggests that effective group learning involves listening to others without confirmation bias, being receptive to new ideas and being comfortable with not knowing the answers to every question.

- *Systems thinking* (1990b: 6–7)   This refers to a conceptual framework that defines a system as a set of interrelated parts. The key is to understand how all the parts connect and interrelate. Naturally a business organization is a complex system with many subsystems, and applying systems thinking means viewing each function as part of the larger system rather than as a collection of isolated tasks. It is the nature of the relationship between these subsystems that influences the performance of the whole. This is clearly seen in Chapter 4 where we discussed the intervention strategy model. This was based on a detailed and proactive review of organizational systems and their interrelated parts.

These disciplines have emerged from the belief that, for sustainable success, contemporary leaders need to adopt new roles and develop new skills that signal a movement away from the authoritarian decision maker. Senge argues that complex environments require leaders to become designers, teachers and stewards.

As *teachers* they are required to act as coach, guide and facilitator, encouraging members of the organization to gain more insightful views of the current reality – to bring to the surface those assumptions which influence thinking and behaviour but which usually remain tacit. He argues it signals a movement away from a short-term response to events (single-loop learning) to an investigation of the systemic structure of long-term trends which reveal the underlying causes and pave the way for successful change.

As *stewards*, he argues, leaders are responsible for establishing the attitude towards members of the organization and towards the essential mission of the business. They need to act as role models, displaying commitment to the espoused values and behaviour they expect to witness in others.

It is in his description of leaders as *designers* that the most interesting perspectives are given. Leaders are responsible for designing the governing ideas of purpose, vision and core values. Furthermore, they are responsible for designing the policies, tasks and structures that translate those ideas into business decisions. It is this process, he argues, that can stimulate effective learning. We can relate this directly back to Chapter 7 where we discussed the need for organizations to develop purpose, vision and guiding values and beliefs.

Senge notes that the process of strategy development is changing and can be seen as an iterative process, and therefore attention should be given to developing the process of strategic thinking rather than the publication of a carefully developed document. This is supported by de Geus (1988) and his experience at Royal–Dutch Shell where corporate planners, after failing to convince the decision makers that the stable world of rising demand for oil was changing, adapted their role to one of fostering learning rather than devising plans. The rise of scenario analysis engaged the key decision makers in the process of understanding the business implications of a range of possible futures. In doing so, they leveraged institutional learning processes as 'management teams shared their mental models of their company, their markets and their competitors'.

Senge's work is popular because it draws on a range of disciplines – psychology, physics, education and systems dynamics – in a powerful form. It is aligned to much of the theory espoused by Argyris and Schon and by Van der Heijden and Eden and builds upon the values of a collective, participative approach, the alignment of thinking and shared interpretation, and quite clearly espouses double-loop or generative learning. But he offers little in the way of guidance as to how to master these disciplines in a business environment or how to recognize the achievement. To a considerable extent this criticism is answered in his *Fieldbook* – a collection of essays, case studies, personal insights and practical suggestions to guide the business leader towards a successful learning environment (Senge, 1995). It is not designed to be prescriptive; it is rather an encyclopaedia or reference work from which to develop an appropriate approach for individual organizations.

In general, Senge's work reinforces the core message of this book. People – in particular the way in which they are organized – determine, through shared and forward looking strategies, the degree to which an organization will succeed in a rapidly changing environment.

The Nonaka and Takeuchi (1991) model distinguishes between organizational learning and knowledge creation, insisting that the former is an assimilation of existing knowledge and the latter constitutes 'breakthrough thinking' which leads to new knowledge and innovation. Breakthrough thinking is dependent on the interplay between tacit and explicit knowledge, i.e. the relationship between unarticulated, intuitive knowledge and the knowledge that is captured in written documents and computerized data banks.

They attribute the success of Japanese companies to the mechanisms and culture developed to harness tacit knowledge: on-the-job training, employee autonomy, long-term employment and a cultural tendency to internalize experience. When tacit knowledge is made explicit it can be used in product or process innovation. This new knowledge is internalized which becomes part of the tacit knowledge base of the company. They argue that the Western practice of rendering work practices explicit in manuals and detailed analyses generates little room for creativity.

Their model depicts five requirements for knowledge creation.

- *Organizational intention* Identified in the organization's strategic vision, which should be sufficiently broad to allow room for interpretation, but provide a cohesive direction.
- *Autonomy* All employees should be trusted to act independently; teams can share ideas generated by individuals. Teams should be encouraged to pursue innovation even when they challenge conventional wisdom.
- *Fluctuation and creative chaos* Fluctuation describes the concept of challenging mental models or behaviours. Creative chaos refers to the sense of urgency to stimulate efforts to generate breakthrough thinking and is the result of leaders intentionally disturbing the environment via new goals or missions.
- *Redundancy* This refers to the intentional overlapping of information and management responsibilities based on a theory that duplication spreads information more widely and accelerates the

knowledge creation process. In Japan this is demonstrated by com-
petitions between different development teams working on the same
project. Another example would be functional rotation to broaden
employees' understanding of the business system and improving
cross-functional communication.

- *Requisite variety*   The creation of environments which facilitate the
  sharing of diverse perspectives and a variety of information. This is
  most readily witnessed in the creation of multi-functional project
  teams, to pool varied skills and to minimize the number of surprises
  as the product is handed from design to production and marketing.

Nonaka and Takeuchi share Senge's commitment to human dynamics
and build upon the theory of organizational learning and the notions of
team effort, shared vision, the balance between individual freedom and
organizational discipline, and the continuous testing of assumptions
about how things get done. It may be argued that their definition of
knowledge creation is akin to Senge's generative learning: both constitute a proactive approach in order to dramatically change the status
quo. Nevertheless, the model gives little guidance on how to bridge the
gap between theory and practice, and does little to address the inherent
difficulties of national cultural differences.

Once again these themes seem similar to the early work on OD and the
development of models of motivation such as autonomous teamwork.

Definitions and prescriptive, practical approaches

The Garvin (1993) model attempts to address this shortfall. Garvin's five-
component model is designed to create an organization 'that is skilled at
creating, acquiring and transferring knowledge, and at modifying its
behaviour to reflect new knowledge and insights'.

- *Systematic problem solving*   This is a scientific method rather than
  guesswork, building on data not assumptions and using statistical
  tools to organize data and draw inferences. He recommends specific
  training in small-group activities and problem solving techniques
  designed to generate ideas, analyse and display data and plan action.
  Furthermore, he recommends that these tools be imposed at all
  meetings.
- *Experimentation*   This requires the systematic searching for and
  testing of new knowledge – a scientific method akin to the problem
  solving techniques. The key to success is that opportunity and the
  desire to expand horizons, should motivate this activity. Experimentation can be witnessed in continuous programmes of small
  experiments to ensure a steady flow of new ideas, and needs to be
  supported by commitment to developing the skills necessary for

experiment design, process analysis and creativity techniques. Furthermore, programmes need to be tightly focused and tailored to employees' needs, so one would not necessarily expect the same development programme to be offered to manufacturing engineers and development personnel alike. Experimentation can also be encouraged via demonstration projects that involve holistic, system-wide approaches and are designed to transform superficial knowledge into deep understanding. They have the benefit of embodying the principles and approaches that will be adopted in the future; they establish policy guidelines and decision-making criteria and test the commitment of senior members of the organization. They are usually developed by multi-functional teams, but have little impact if they are not accompanied by a strategy for transferring the learning.

- *Learning from past experience*   Garvin insists that companies must review their successes and failures, assess them systematically and record them in a form that employees find open and accessible. He cites the Post-Project Appraisal Unit at British Petroleum, responsible for writing case studies following major projects, as an example of learning from the past and recognizing the value of productive failure when contrasted with unproductive success. Other, less costly, methods to capture learning include enlisting the help of universities and business schools to bring a fresh perspective.
- *Learning from others*   Powerful insights can be gained from looking outside one's immediate environment. Businesses in different industries can be a fertile source of ideas and catalysts for creative thinking. Benchmarking, a disciplined process and search for best practices via site visits and interviews, concludes with the analysis of results and a series of recommendations and implementation plans. Structured customer contact also invariably stimulates learning.
- *Transferring knowledge*   Ideas carry maximum impact when they are shared. Garvin recommends written, oral and visual reports, site visits, personnel rotation programmes and education, but stresses that each medium should be tailored to meet the needs of the audience. Reports are popular but cumbersome; he acknowledges that it is difficult to become knowledgeable in a passive way and emphasizes the benefit of transferring personnel with expertise to other areas and education programmes linked to live problems.

Unlike the previous models, Garvin discusses how to measure a learning organization and suggests learning audits via questionnaires, surveys and interviews to assess attitudes and depth of understanding. This should be supplemented where possible with direct observation to assess behavioural changes, and the development of performance measures such as the half-life curve (a method of measuring the time it takes to achieve a 50 per cent improvement in a specified performance indicator) to test how cognitive and behavioural changes have produced results. Without this, he argues, organizations will lack a rationale for investing in learning and the assurance that learning is serving the organization's ends.

He continues to recommend first steps:

1 Foster an environment conducive to learning; free up time for reflection and analysis, and for training in the required skill base.
2 Open the boundaries to stimulate the exchange of ideas; establish project teams and conferences that cross organizational levels or link the company with its external environment (customers, suppliers, industry associations).
3 Create learning forums – programmes or events designed with specific learning goals in mind. Strategic reviews, systems audits, internal benchmarking and study missions are examples.

The first two steps can be seen within the total project management model outlined in Chapter 6, where emphasis is placed on ensuring analytical approaches are employed by project teams in managing complex problems. As we discussed earlier, the use of external change agents, the objective outsiders, can assist in learning from others and transferring knowledge. In addition, by ensuring that the external agents bring with them the ability to disseminate and transfer previous knowledge and understanding, the organization fosters a creative learning environment.

Garvin's model does not ignore the theory of organizational learning. It incorporates the concepts of learning from experience, working through teams, and supports the belief implicit in the works of both Senge and Nonaka that productive learning is dependent on the development of a distinctive mindset and pattern of behaviour. It differs in its argument that the creation of learning organizations will only be truly successful if these elements are supported by systems and processes integrated into the fabric of daily life. They serve to both create and sustain a learning culture. His contention that commitment to learning will be maintained only by demonstrating its value to the organization is a realistic, if cynical, viewpoint. Importantly, he promotes the value of an external focus to developing learning opportunities, which is missing in the earlier models.

Guidelines and practical hints

Garvin's work is essentially prescriptive but this style has been criticized by practitioners such as Pedler et al. (1991) and Pearn et al. (1995). These works suggest that a definition of the learning organization cannot exist. Pearn et al. suggest that learning is a process not a state and that the possession of a number of characteristics does not necessarily entitle an organization to be called *the* learning organization. Pedler et al. prefer to use the term 'company' rather than organization, insisting that the latter is a mechanical word sounding abstract and lifeless. They suggest that the learning company is a *vision* of what might be possible, and have developed a list of 11 features of that vision:

- *The learning approach to strategy* The formation of policy, implementation, evaluation and improvement are structured as learning processes, with conscious experiments and feedback loops.
- *Participative policy making* This encourages debate and fosters the airing of differences as a way of reaching business decisions that all members are likely to support.
- *Informating* This is the state of affairs in which information technology is used to inform and empower people rather than just measure performance.
- *Formative accounting and control* These ensure that the systems of accounting, budgeting and reporting are structured to assist learning.
- *Internal exchange* This involves all departments recognizing themselves as customers and suppliers with the aim of 'delighting the customer'. This encourages constant dialogue regarding expectations and feedback on performance. It fosters the spirit of collaboration, a systemic view and an overall optimization of performance.
- *Reward flexibility* This relates to the examination of the reward system, to understanding the values and assumptions about the basis of pay and ensuring they are consistent with the characteristics of a learning company, where, perhaps, there has been a redistribution of power from the 'top pyramid' to the wider company.
- *Enabling structures* Flexible departmental boundaries can adapt in response to change, and loosely structured roles can meet the needs of internal customers and suppliers and also encourage personal development.
- *Boundary workers as environmental scanners* This is the external version of informating, and although there may be specialized departments it is the accepted role of all members of the organization.
- *Intercompany learning* This would be demonstrated by joint training, shared investment in research and development, job exchanges and benchmarking.
- *A learning climate* Managers will see their primary task as facilitating experimentation and learning from experience. Mistakes are allowed and there is no such thing as a failed experiment. Senior managers lead by example and openly question their own ideas, attitudes and behaviours.

- *Self-development opportunities for all* A range of resources and facilities is available to all members who are encouraged to take responsibility for their own learning and self-development.

As a vision it is aspirational, but unlike the models of Senge and Nonaka, Pedlar et al.'s model is designed to illustrate its relevance and value to an organization. Again, although not explicitly, their model builds upon the theory of organizational learning, and their recommended approach to strategy and policy making is closely aligned to the thinking of Senge, de Geus and Van der Heijden and Eden. Nevertheless, through a natural desire to avoid a prescriptive approach, some of their descriptions of features are nebulous. 'Temporary structures that can flex in response to changes' are eminently desirable but perhaps difficult to design.

Importantly, they introduce the process of self-development missing in Garvin's model but share his commitment to business processes and systems that facilitate and sustain learning. They balance an internal perspective with an external orientation and support Garvin and Nonaka in their attitude towards continuous experimentation to generate innovation. Like Senge, they recognize that the role of the leader is changing. Furthermore, like Senge and Nonaka, they recognize the power of diversity and its potential value to creativity.

A similar approach is suggested by Pearn et al. (1995) who provide a framework and range of tools to guide thinking as to what a learning organization might look like. Rather than provide a vision, definition or list of characteristics, their approach facilitates the process by which an organization can develop its own view. They suggest 10 building blocks for use to develop a tailored working approach:

1 Examine the concept at top management level.
2 Analyse the current state of learning.
3 Devise an implementation plan.
4 Examine the role of training and trainers.
5 Equip managers to encourage learning.
6 Support learning.
7 Develop group and team learning.
8 Upgrade the learning skills of all employees.
9 Promote open learning.
10 Analyse jobs in terms of learning needs.

Although their recommendations are built from their combined experience and knowledge, their underlying philosophy is to create commitment through shared understanding and participation which they believe has a greater impact and longevity than imposing the views of an external 'expert'. This would match well with the participative role of the external change agent, by not imposing solutions but helping the organization develop its own.

Conclusion

The models and visions of learning organizations presented here have common themes. They emphasize a collaborative, participative approach centred on team processes. They demonstrate a commitment to the creation of a shared vision of the future direction of the company and the necessary steps, structural and behavioural, to achieve that vision. They stress a proactive approach to learning, creating new experiences with which to challenge the status quo and a culture that encourages continuous experimentation and risk-taking. Finally, they each emphasize the role of leaders to facilitate the change process and to foster a commitment to learning, primarily by leading by example.

Interestingly, in each case the concept of creating a learning environment, however it is expressed, is seen as a holistic process and not the preserve of HR specialists or limited to training and development.

Emerging from the most recent thinking is the value attributed to developing an external orientation, in scanning the environment for emerging opportunities, in cultivating productive relationships with customers, suppliers and other appropriate businesses, and in establishing sophisticated benchmarking processes.

There is growing recognition that the humanist approach to organizational learning needs supporting with appropriate business systems – IT networks, communication strategies and organization structures. Appropriate changes in mindset and behaviour, although most critical, form only part of the answer.

It is apparent that there is no 'one best way' to approach the development of superior learning in organizations. This is supported by the Economist Intelligence Unit who in 1996 conducted research which suggested that, for success organizations need to establish an approach that is best suited to their culture, their orientation and their perception of performance requirements.

The learning organization assumes managers will work in a learning partnership with other members of the organization. This involves trust and open dialogue as a climate that can engender a greater sense of development and empowerment for the workforce. This has significant implications for the nature of management within organizations. As was seen in Chapters 7 and 8, much of our thinking related to management is control oriented with an emphasis on job design, performance appraisal and supervisory activity, and on the merit of hierarchy in organization design and function. New forms of organization structure, processes and workplace relationships will need to be developed which are more in keeping with the different values and beliefs. These need to stress a more collaborative, learning framework. The skill base of managers needs to be enhanced in such a setting.

The question related to the impact of the learning organization is similar to managing OD in general. How do organizations and their management unlearn the old ways, challenge the past and in doing so minimize resistance to change? In seeking to transform the culture of the organization, transformations need to take managers along too. It would be impossible to shift cultural norms without first changing the management mindset. Similarly, in creating an environment of learning where problems are openly declared, managers need the skill of being able to do so in a manner that will encourage the workforce to embrace the learning mode and feel comfortable with change.

Much of the literature on the learning organization assumes that the only area that organizations work within is that of rationality. Neglecting the political and emotional aspects of change in a learning context is a major oversight in the sense that change may be met with resistance if it does not appear logical. We all have comfort zones which when challenged lead to an emotional response. It may well be that the development of strategies to address such factors is beyond the scope of individual managers and traditional human resource departments and may require the more expert assistance of the change agent. Here the change agent would call on their social and behavioural skills.

PART 4

Practical Cases in Change Management

11 Cases in Systems Intervention

We have tried, throughout the previous chapters, to illustrate models, techniques and concepts by the use of mini cases, reader activities and examples. It is hoped that you, whether a practising manager or not, have found them of some use. They have been selected from a wide variety of change management projects covering a range of issues, sectors and situations. The cases and examples introduced and developed in Chapters 4 and 5 illustrated various different features and attributes associated with the intervention strategy model (ISM). In this chapter we will return to a number of the ISM-related examples and cases with a view to developing them more fully, the aim being to enable the reader to sample ISM cycles in their entirety. However, as always, the best way to learn and evaluate is by doing and experiencing: we strongly suggest that you try out for yourself the techniques, models and approaches covered within this book.

Three cases taken from a range of diverse organizations have been selected. The first comes from the National Health Service and illustrates the use of the ISM on an externally imposed change. Caledonian Airmotive Ltd provides the second case, which involves a considerable reorganization of a manufacturing system; this organizational change was tackled successfully by employing a systems interventionist approach. This case exhibits many features associated with the total project management model (TPMM). The final case involves an externally imposed change, with organizational implications, within the Scottish operations of British Gas. They have been selected not for their topicality, as has been the case with many of the more tactical and strategic examples previously encountered, but rather to illustrate ISM in action.

Each case will be told as far as possible as it happened: the reader will follow the change management route taken by each problem owner and their associated team of change agents. At the end of each case there will be a brief review of the key points to be noted and the lessons learned. Previous chapters have highlighted casework by using mini cases; here, however, as the cases form the core of this chapter they will be fully integrated within the text.

Case study 1: the Argyll and Clyde Health Board

The Scottish Health Boards were required to submit their morbidity records, the Scottish morbidity records (SMRs), to the Common Services Agency (CSA) of the National Health Service. Under the old system the performance target was rather relaxed: the SMRs had only to be submitted on an annual basis, with returns being required by the following summer of any given year. In response to the government's White Paper entitled *Working for Patients*, the SMR returns were required to be submitted, and completed, within two months of the end of any particular month.

SMRs were much more than statistical returns; they detailed the case histories of each patient treated within an NHS hospital. They detailed individual treatments; in effect, SMRs provided an audit trail. With an audit trail the management, at hospital, board or national level, can compare and contrast performance across facilities and regions. More importantly, when treatments are aligned with costs then SMRs provide a means of measuring planned against actual budgetary expenditure. The importance of these documents to each Health Board cannot be overstated. The CSA collates the data for all the Health Boards in Scotland and funding is then allocated according to the numbers, costs and categories of patient treated.

Background information specific to the change

An admission to an NHS hospital initiated an SMR document, one for each patient, with a member of medical records staff performing the task. At this point the document contains basic patient information and demographic details. On discharge, clinical codes detailing diagnoses and any operating procedures carried out are assigned and recorded by coding staff of the Medical Records Department. The information required to complete this final section of the SMR is taken from the discharge letter, which must be completed for patients by their medical consultant.

In the case of the Argyll and Clyde Health Board the use of a fully computerized patient administration system, by each of the major hospitals, obviated the need for hard copy SMR documentation. Completed SMRs were stored, having been categorized, on magnetic tape. (Please note that the case described occurred in the early 1990s. Operating units, Health Boards and national centres were only beginning to move towards electronic data transfer and/or communication.) The tapes from each hospital were submitted to a central computer centre at which the tapes were input to the SMR standard system. After a cyclical process, involving the production of error and query reports followed by data resubmission, the standard system produced aggregated and validated data for the Board. This output was then forwarded to the CSA to await further analysis, which may have involved further communication to fully validate the statistics. When the analysis of the national SMR returns had been completed, various comparisons were made and informed discussions took place, after which funding allocations were decided and granted.

The problem owner and the definition phase

The problem, which as far as this case is concerned relates to the need to accelerate SMR processing speed while maintaining data integrity, was assigned to a member of the Board's Information Services Division (ISD). ISD was ultimately responsible for centralized data processing and provided an information and internal consulting service to the Board. The change situation had, on the appointment of the problem owner, been effectively entered. The problem owner then set about clarifying the change environment. They developed a number of diagrams to define the systems processes and environment under review.

It was at this point of systems specification that the Argyll and Clyde case was first visited. Figure 3.6 deals with the activity sequences associated with SMR production. and Figure 3.7 describes the inputs and outputs from the SMR standard system.

READER ACTIVITY

Please return to Chapter 3. Consult and carefully review Figures 3.6 and 3.7 and then return to this case.

In addition to the diagrams illustrated in Chapter 3 the problem owner also produced an input/output diagram drawn from a geographical perspective. Figure 11.1 summarizes the situation as seen from the position of the problem owner.

When the definition of the systems information flow had been completed, the next step was to consider the relationships that existed between system components. In the old system, magnetic tapes were produced at hospital locations and ISD staff arranged collection by any member of staff who happened to be on site. Alternatively, tapes were entrusted to the internal transport system. The outputs of the SMR standard system were similarly treated. ISD's role was one of facilitation and coordination. Figure 11.2 depicts the relationship map used to identify all those who might, to a greater or lesser extent, be involved in the existing SMR system. They therefore would likely play a significant role in determining the success of the proposed change.

The information flows and staff involved were well defined. As the objective, namely 'to have the SMR data for month n validated, processed

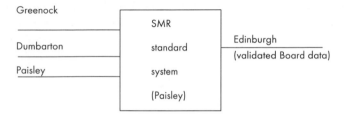

Figure 11.1   *Geographic sources (computerized hospitals only)*

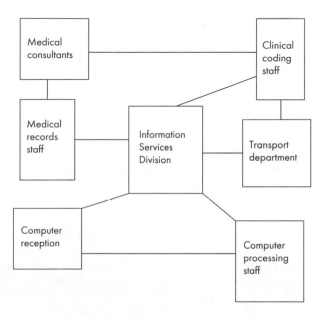

Figure 11.2   *Relationship map for SMR problem*

and submitted to the CSA, Edinburgh, by the end of month $n+2'$, had come from government and as such was not negotiable, attention was turned to the factors which influence the achievement of this objective. The new performance criteria affected the whole of the country. The problem owner, along with other senior management, was involved in discussions at a national level. All agreed that there were three key factors that had to be addressed:

1 the length of time after discharge before diagnostic details were available
2 the travel time of the magnetic tapes and associated follow-up error and/or query reports

3   the number of resubmissions of data before finalizing validated SMR
     returns.

The third factor was to be addressed by a separate study, undertaken at a
national level, which dealt with the quality assurance issues associated
with the integration of a new computerized coding system with the
existing patient administration systems. The problem owner was therefore left with factors 1 and 2 to deal with in relation to the overall
objective. Both studies knew of each other's existence and were working
towards the same overall goal.

The problem owner was fortunate that clear and, at least at a senior
management level, uncontroversial objectives existed. In addition, the
objectives relating to both factors had associated quantifiable time
measures, which would provide a means of assessing potential options.
All concerned, at a local senior management level, agreed that any
systems changes must be achieved at a minimal cost.

Evaluation phase

Up to this point the problem owner had essentially been working alone.
Systems investigations had really only been informed by the problem
owner's and senior management's knowledge and understanding of
the situation. On entering the design phase it was decided to involve
representatives from those departments highlighted within the relationships map. A meeting was organized and structured around the two
factors previously identified. After a brainstorming session and protracted discussions, a number of options were generated which addressed
the issues surrounding both factors. Options were then evaluated, once
again by the key players led by the problem owner. Table 11.1 details both
the options generated and the group's evaluation of them.

It was eventually decided, by all concerned, that option B, the interim
discharge form, would be selected to influence factor 1, and that option F
would be selected for factor 2.

Implementation

The problem owner tackled the implementation strategy as follows:

- *Factor 1*   An interim discharge form was designed by medical
  records staff and inserted in the patient's case notes. Consultants
  were requested to complete this at the time of discharge and return it
  to the clinical coding staff via the internal mail. The target was to
  have coding performed within three to five days of discharge.
- *Factor 2*   A meeting was held with the transport manager and it was
  agreed that a system known as 'data in transit' would be attempted.
  This involved making use of the existing transport runs but with the
  addition of the following three features:

Table 11.1   *Option generation and evaluation*

	Option A Consultants code diagnoses and enter them	Option B Consultants write diagnoses on interim discharge form	Option C Consultants write diagnosis letter immediately upon discharge	
Factor 1 To minimize time from discharge to diagnostic coding (coding time)	Lack of training and no access to the system	Additional work for consultants	Operationally difficult to achieve	

	Option D Networking of hospital system to SMR standard system	Option E Special van driver hired by ISD	Option F Negotiate with Board transport department	Option G Improve data quality
Factor 2 Speed up SMR processing (travel time)	Technically difficult at present, plus costs	Extra recurring cost, leave cover, maintenance	Special arrangements needed	Ongoing subject of another study

1   specifically designed multiple part forms to allow tracking of tapes and error and query reports
2   specially purchased colour-coded transport bags for ease of identification
3   special arrangements for pick-up and delivery directly to and from the clinical coders at each hospital.

The necessary items were then ordered and forms designed. The new scheme was explained and communicated to all staff likely to be affected by the change. All communications stressed that the amended system had been designed and evaluated by a multi-disciplinary team drawn from across all operating units. There was no visible opposition to the proposed changes. A consolidation period followed. ISD staff monitored the new system, lending support and encouragement when necessary.

Epilogue

The transport system as envisaged within option F, designed to tackle factor 2, was fully implemented. There were no unforeseen difficulties and it significantly reduced SMR travel time. Performance levels associated with factor 1, and tackled by option B, only slightly improved. The coding target of three to five days after discharge was not being met at all sites. Once again the problem owner consulted those directly involved, detailing the problem, explaining the rationale, recruiting appropriate senior management support, and involving those at the 'coalface' in providing a solution. The medical consultants seemed to be the problem. They simply were not following procedures. It should be noted that as a group they had been represented on the change management team and were not being asked to do anything that they did not already do. But they were being asked to perform a task at a different time using amended documentation.

Case analysis

On the surface this case appears to be well suited to a systems investigation. The success of the new transport system bears testimony to the appropriateness of ISM. A well-structured and systematic solution was developed to answer a particularly hard problem.

Throughout the case the problem owner followed the ISM approach, except in the definition phase, in which the need to formally address the issue of constraints appears to have been ignored. The financial constraint was an obvious one to those concerned and could be taken for granted, in so far that all knew a minimum spend was required; what appears to have been less obvious was the constraint placed on the solution by the medical consultants. This was an organizational constraint and should have been dealt with accordingly. The implementation strategy for factor 1 did not fully address it. Involving a representative of the medical consultants in the design process did not guarantee acceptance of the implementation strategy. This factor had to be revisited as detailed in the above 'Epilogue'.

In effect the 'Epilogue' describes an iteration. It was required to address the failure to fully involve, persuade and stimulate the medics. The consultants probably did not recognize their important role within the process that ultimately decides their budgets. They had to be tactfully educated and cajoled into acceptance of the change. Change creates multi-disciplinary problems, which often require a blend of the systems and organizational approaches to be applied, especially within the implementation phase.

The key lesson that should be drawn from this case relates to how one should deal with powerful stakeholders. One tries to address such issues by involving them in the change; however, very often those who volunteer are simply viewed as management puppets, or fail to make meaningful contributions. There are no easy answers to such problems. Employing effective change agents who possess the necessary skills and attributes, from both a process and an interpersonal perspective, can assist in identifying, managing and ultimately winning the support of powerful stakeholder groups.

Case study 2: Caledonian Airmotive Ltd

The core business of Caledonian Airmotive Ltd (CAL) is the overhaul and maintenance of aero-engines. It is a highly competitive market and CAL competes as a worldwide player. The principal production facility is based within the precincts of Prestwick Airport. The company is well established and has developed a reputation for excellence. An extremely dynamic operational and organizational environment was developed in response to ever increasing customer expectations and requirements. CAL's customers compete in an extremely competitive and volatile marketplace, one in which time is indeed money. An under-utilized piece of expensive resource, an aircraft, cannot earn optimal revenue. Similarly, revenue is lost when an aeroplane's downtime interferes with service performance.

The ability to readily adapt to customer requirements, and to manage any associated changes or disruptions, is seen by the company and their marketplace as a distinct competitive advantage. Responding to externally driven change, in an effective manner, has become over the years a way of life for the company. CAL's main customer grouping, the airlines, require two main classes of engineering support:

1 provision of serviceable engines after a repair or overhaul in as short a time as possible
2 provision of a repair service with respect to line replaceable units (LRUs), which are removed at the operator's base and sent for repair independently of the engine.

This case deals, in the main, with the second class of engineering service, namely the LRUs. There are a variety of engine components that can be classed as LRUs. Such a diversity of potential components requires that a flexible production response be adopted. Management is therefore faced with the problem of maintaining mainstream engine overhaul and repair production whilst dealing with the varied disturbances caused to the operating system by processing LRUs. In the competitive environment of aero-engine overhaul and repair, in which the minimization of engine turnaround time is crucial, the production system must favour the mainstream flow- and process-oriented work. Any disruption to this system results in downtime and thus extended engine turnaround cycles; value is therefore lost not added. Although lucrative, and a necessary business service within the aero-engine market, servicing LRUs necessitates disrupting the production line. For this reason CAL were always willing to consider production or business systems changes which could potentially minimize disruptions and maximize mainstream productivity.

The accessory shop that was ultimately responsible for LRU repair was also an integral part of the mainstream production process. It was dependent on such services as the machine shop, general provisioning, non-destructive testing (NDT) inspection and new part stores. As one would expect, priority status always went to mainstream engine overhaul and repair activities. The net result was that LRUs suffered delays and clients responded accordingly. The situation may be seen as a mismatch between customer requirements, namely quick turnaround on both engine and LRU repairs, and the company's norms which seek efficient production flows and a minimization of costs. Over time clients could become dissatisfied and either LRU business would be lost or the company could somehow try to maintain a balancing act between its two principal services. The company aims to be more capable than their competitors at identifying and correcting such mismatches and by so doing maintain a competitive edge. The LRU problem was therefore treated seriously and formed the basis of an extensive change management exercise.

The change objective, or project brief, was clear: to successfully intervene in the working process of the current accessory shop system with the aim of effectively changing that system from being one of dependency to one of self-sufficiency, and to create a stable new environment which could support both shop engine and single-item LRU requirements.

The problem owner and the definition phase

Senior management decided to commission an analysis of system relationships and workflow patterns. In particular they were interested in determining the precise causes of turnaround time delays. They appointed a project manager, in effect the problem owner and principal change agent, with direct knowledge of the problem and the necessary skills and position to facilitate the change. In Figures 3.10 and 3.15 the accessory shop relationship and influence maps were introduced.

READER ACTIVITY

Please return to Chapter 3 prior to continuing. Review Figures 3.10 and 3.15 carefully and then return to the case.

In addition to these figures the project manager also produced a multiple cause diagram relating to LRU delays. A summary of this is illustrated in Figure 11.3.

The project manager's initial reaction was that there was one obvious solution: a truly autonomous accessory shop, operating as a satellite plant.

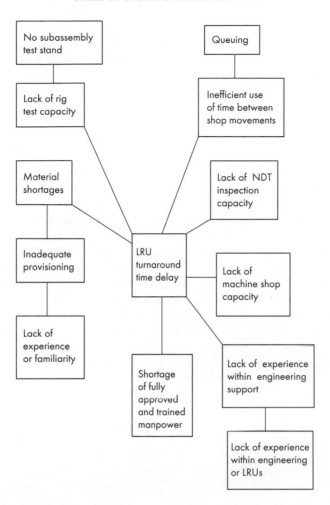

Figure 11.3   *Multiple cause diagram for LRU delays*

This conclusion was based not only on the diagrams so far covered but also on highly detailed flow diagrams detailing virtually every activity and link associated with the existing accessory shop system. The detailed, technical and, most importantly, commercially sensitive nature of these diagrams precluded their publication. The investigations relating to the proposed systems intervention were conducted in an open and collaborative manner. In addition to the systems studies the project manager also spoke informally to the existing client base. The market expressed both interest and enthusiasm for the proposed provision of a dedicated LRU service.

Indulging in a *forward iteration* the project manager decided to evaluate what appeared to be the one and only obvious solution. Representatives of finance, marketing, production and engineering were called upon to form an investigative team. Their brief was to evaluate the costs and general viability associated with the formation of a dedicated LRU facility. After careful study it was decided that this was not a viable option owing to both logistical and cost constraints. Essentially the detailed cost–benefit analysis came out against an autonomous LRU facility.

The assembled group then turned their attention, having seen the potential production and service benefits of the proposed change, to a derivative of the original proposal. A semi-autonomous system could be created within the existing plant, with the control of critical areas passing over from mainstream production to the new LRU accessory shop. The only services to be shared with mainstream production would be of an administrative and functional nature, such as systems, personnel and quality. Analysis and evaluation of this option proved more favourable. Proposed expenditure could be justified against the anticipated increase in orders for both LRUs and engines, which would be gained through a reduction in turnaround time. In addition, less downtime and the rationalization of services and responsibilities would also lead to reduced operating costs. Market research was commissioned to ensure that orders would be forthcoming and detailed financial analysis was conducted which confirmed the cost savings. In terms of the 'bottom line' the proposed change had been justified.

Evaluation phase

In reality the project team had entered the evaluation phase. They had decided what they wanted to do and justified their decision. Armed with a validated solution the project manager set about the actual task of detailing the practical activity requirements associated with the solution. Several factors associated with the successful implementation of the change still had to be addressed and evaluated:

1 shop layout
2 equipment requirements
3 organizational structure
4 training requirements
5 disruption effects of change to the current production cycle.

The company and the project manager knew that the success of the change would depend on the willing support of all those concerned. Diagrammatic representations detailing the old and new systems, along with updated organizational charts, were produced in consultation with the key stakeholders and players. This material was then used to communicate the change to the rest of the organization. The project manager actively sold the concept first to senior management and then with their support to the other management levels and functions. Having gained widespread support additional change agents were named and charged with addressing the factors raised above.

Implementation phase

An incremental and logical implementation plan was initiated. It proposed that both the old and the new system should run in parallel, with the phased handover from old to new occurring in a planned sequence over a specified time period. The actual work groups, who would form the new semi-autonomous accessory shop, would be involved throughout the process. Not only would they be trained, if required, but they would also play a major role in defining the working environment. The CAL implementation plan was used in Chapter 5 to illustrate the generic issues associated with the implementation of change within the ISM.

READER ACTIVITY

You should now return to the section on the implementation phase in Chapter 5. Review the CAL example carefully (Mini Case 5.4) and then return to this case.

The implementation phase has since been completed and the project has been consolidated. The semi-autonomous LRU approach is now an established feature of the CAL operating strategy and did indeed provide the expected benefits.

Case analysis

The CAL project represented a major change management exercise. The sheer scale of the project cannot be done justice to within an illustrative case study framework. Operating, organizational and business systems and cultures were impinged upon, old ideas were challenged and a multi-faceted competitive edge was developed. The change was successfully managed by adopting an approach that successfully combined both systems intervention strategies and more traditional project management methodologies. However, within this systems-oriented management approach the problem owner and the project team ensured that when appropriate the wider stakeholder body was involved. The rationale, proposals and consequences of the change were effectively communicated. Active participation and support were sought and integrated into the change process. Senior management were brought on board at an early stage and their support was fully exploited.

The project manager did not follow the ISM in a logical manner. The approach taken was in many ways more along the lines advocated by the TPMM. The definition phase concentrated on developing an understanding of the systems environment and bringing on board the appropriate expertise to solve the problem. As the project had to be validated prior to commencing change activities there was no choice but to corrupt the ISM approach to facilitate the early generation and evaluation of a solution. The TPMM stresses that in project management the solution to the problem generally has to be agreed prior to engaging in detailed planning. The CAL case was no exception to the general rule. However, it may have been possible to avoid the initial evaluation of the totally autonomous solution had the constraints associated with the project been more fully defined. Given that the desired solution had been both found and validated prior to the formulation phase there was no need for evaluation of options. Instead the project team set about analysing and planning for the key factors associated with the project solution. Again this process reflects the second phase of the TPMM. Implementation involved the development of a logical, integrated and sequential plan that lent itself to the adoption of network-based activity scheduling.

The major lessons for the practitioner that may be drawn from this case concern the actual application of intervention strategies. Firstly, an optimal solution can still be achieved even when the format of the model has been corrupted to reflect both practical and commercial environmental considerations. Secondly, care should be taken that the modifications to the format do not result in the complete omission of key process steps. Intervention strategy models are designed to reflect best practice as defined by both researchers and practitioners. Finally, when dealing with projects which are likely to gain the support of key stakeholders, it may be better to adopt the TPMM derivative of the ISM model, always of course remembering the need to identify and address relevant softer organizational issues.

Case study 3: British Gas PLC

This case concerns the Scottish operations of British Gas PLC and in particular the Scottish Region's central purchasing department. Each region serves a customer base that has its own unique appliance population. Regions held local stocks of frequently ordered parts and could therefore offer their customers what may be termed an 'off-the-shelf' service. All other spare parts for which local stockholding could not be justified, owing to irregular demand, were known as 'one-time buys' or OTBs for short. OTBs had to be ordered directly from the suppliers, who were usually the appliance manufacturers. This process, depending on the supplier and their location, could take on average about 15 days from order placement to delivery to the customer.

Background information specific to the case

As part of a drive to improve standards of customer service, British Gas, at corporate level, decided to set up their own stockholding facilities for OTBs. Two national stockholding centres, one at Manchester, the other in London, opened for business in March 1991 and provided the regions with approximately 80 per cent of their currently ordered OTBs. By centralizing the purchasing and holding of such stocks, economies of scale would be available to British Gas as a whole, and there would be no cost disadvantage for the regions trading with the new central resource. Central stockholding costs would be off-set by lower initial purchasing costs brought about by volume buying. Regions were instructed that on the opening of the new facilities they should all be in a position to commence ordering immediately. Lead times for OTBs were expected to drop from 15 days to a few days, probably three or four, thus improving customer service and securing associated benefits.

The problem owner and the definition phase

The problem owner within the Scottish Region was the purchasing manager, who was given the following change brief: 'to change (or intervene in) the current system of ordering OTBs to enable the purchasing department to make optimal use of the new national stockholding facility, thereby improving customer service levels'.

Following the problem initialization the problem owner quickly involved the other key players, namely the departmental systems development officer and the spares buyer. The steps taken by this group of change agents when defining the systems environment were detailed within the ISM definition phase, which may be found in Chapter 5.

READER ACTIVITY

The reader should now return to the definition phase of Chapter 5. Review the British Gas example carefully (Mini Case 5.1) and then return to this case.

A number of diagrams are referred to within the British Gas example in Chapter 5 (Mini Case 5.1). The figures illustrated here represent the change agents' total investigative diagrammatic output. The first diagram, Figure 11.4, deals with the OTB flow chart. It was produced to further the management group's understanding of the present system.

From the flow chart the group moved on to develop an activity sequence diagram, Figure 11.5, depicting the situation before and after the change. This was a useful analysis exercise and provided a means of communicating the exact nature of the proposed change to the ordering

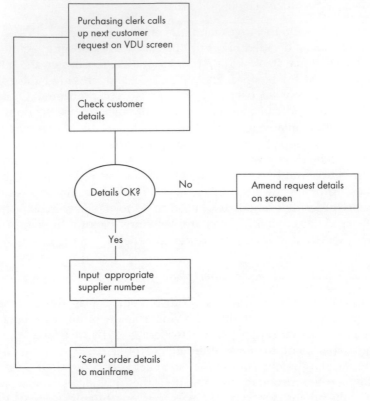

Figure 11.4   OTB flow chart

clerks. It would be the clerks who would be most directly affected. It was possible at this stage to define the process elements of the new system owing to the detailed information that was provided by corporate headquarters. In addition, the process activities were unlikely to alter drastically as the change essentially involved altering only the source of supplies.

The activity sequence diagram highlighted the need to consider all the parties involved as there were going to be additional external links after the change. Again, 'before' and 'after' relationship maps were produced and these are shown in Figure 11.6.

The systems definition stage was completed by the construction of two systems maps as shown in Figure 11.7.

With the actual systems definitions completed to everyone's satisfaction, the problem owner then turned the managing group's attention to the change forces at work within the operations environment. A number of force field analysis diagrams, as depicted in Figure 11.8, were produced which assisted in describing and evaluating the forces acting upon those involved.

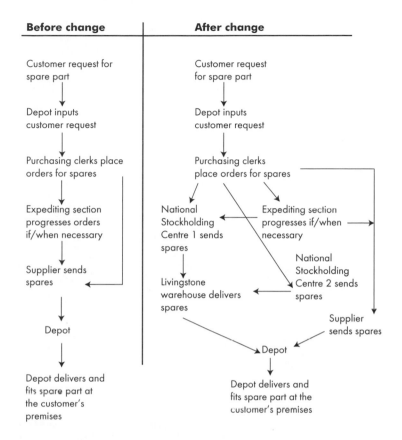

Figure 11.5 *Activity sequence diagram for OTB change*

It was evident from a number of the diagrams produced that the workload of the expediting section would be reduced by the proposed systems changes. They were consulted and the changes were explained and the likely impact was described. All staff concerned, both the ordering clerks and the expediters, were given assurances that no one would lose their jobs as a result of the changes. Redeployments to related disciplines were sensitively managed. These were used to overcome the problem of reduced workloads and operative resistance. The staff accepted both the assurances and the potential redeployments. Full cooperation and support were gained.

The problem owner, confident of staff support, now turned his attention to the constraints acting upon the change situation. To this end an objectives tree was produced, as illustrated in Figure 11.9, into which priorities were included as indicated by the numbers in parentheses.

The performance indicators were identified from the objectives tree. They fell into two categories associated with the financial and human

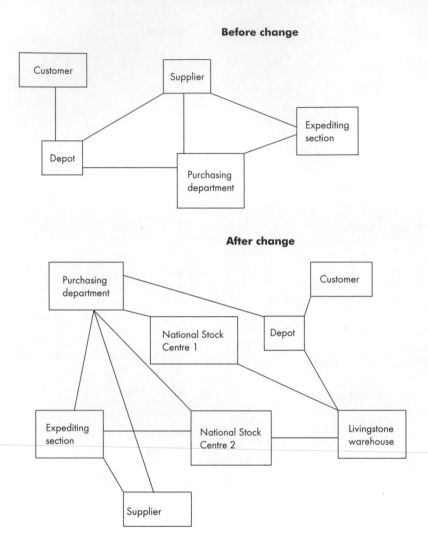

Figure 11.6   *Relationship maps for OTB change*

resources. Firstly, with regard to finance, budgetary constraints would produce financial measures for training, systems programming and equipment. Secondly, relating to the human resource, information systems staff were in high demand and therefore their services were difficult to secure. In addition, there were performance targets associated directly with the change itself. A target date of March 1991 had been set, by which time 80 per cent of all OTBs had to be ordered from the new facilities. There was also an imposed delivery target of three to four days from receipt of the customer's order.

Before change

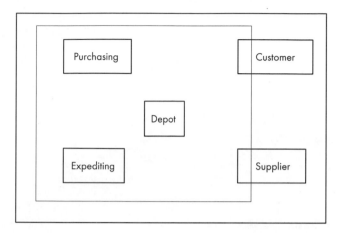

After change

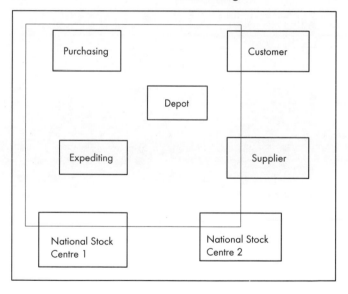

Figure 11.7   *Systems maps for OTB change*

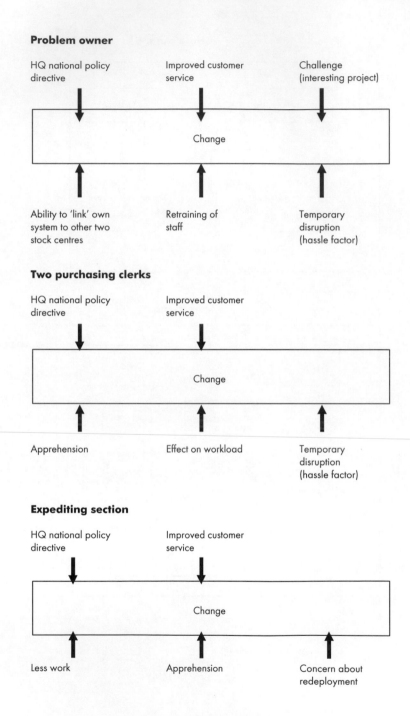

Figure 11.8   *Force field analysis for OTB change*

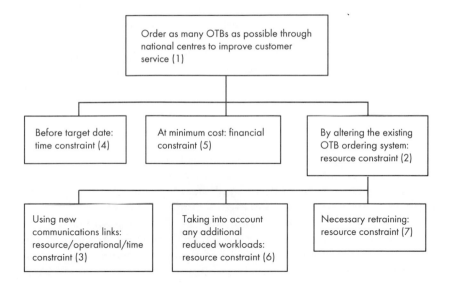

Figure 11.9   *Prioritized objectives tree for OTB change*

Evaluation phase

The actual process activities required for the new system had been previously detailed in the definition phase. The management team, along with the ordering clerks, now set about generating options for actually achieving the physical operations. This involved a detailed study of the existing computerized system. After much deliberation only one feasible solution could be identified. Each ordering clerk would require an additional VDU and a PC linked into the stockholding centre. Existing processing kit could not deal with the additional load and still maintain an effective service. It would therefore remain dedicated to the Region's existing ordering systems. Such a solution satisfied the main objectives and constraints. The problem owner, wary of implementation difficulties, contacted the systems people and confirmed that their resources were indeed stretched, but they would do all they could to help.

Implementation phase

The implementation strategy comprised three stages. The first involved the acquisition and installation of equipment, which was immediately followed by the setting up of external communications links to the central stockholding facilities. During this time the operatives entered the second stage. They were given access to dummy screens to allow them to become familiar with screen layout and input requirements. The third stage, once the new system was operational, involved the running of 10 pilot ordering runs. These tested the system, as well as the operatives, and also satisfied the management team of the benefits associated with the new system and the efficiency of the central warehousing resource.

A number of minor iterations were made as a result of the operator training phase and the pilot runs. These resulted in useful screen layout changes. Consolidation was never an internal issue and the national OTB ordering system achieved its objectives.

Case analysis

The British Gas case is a textbook example of how to successfully apply a systems intervention strategy. Certain details were omitted within the evaluation phase owing to their highly technical nature, but they were dealt with according to the ISM methodology.

The lessons to be learned from this case are all positive. The first concerns the initial selection of a solution methodology. This was a 'hard' systems problem which, although it had significant people implications, was best tackled by a systems-based approach. The human resource implications were dealt with at an early stage in the change cycle. Involvement was sought and participation gained. Redundancy fears were dispensed with effectively and systems training was provided well in advance of final commissioning. Time spent defining the old and new operating systems is generally never wasted. In this case the clear objectives, quantifiable performance measures, fixed target dates and well-bounded nature of the change environment all pointed in the direction of an ISM solution methodology.

The second lesson concerns the forward loop from the formulation to the implementation phase. The need to be aware of the pressures facing the systems resource was built into the implementation strategy. Parallel implementation was achieved by ensuring that the operatives had access to dummy screens while the installation was going ahead. This both avoided potential implementation delays and allowed minor systems updates to be incorporated while the systems people were on site.

12 Organizational Development Cases

This chapter introduces a number of OD case studies. The sixth of these, a group performance review, is aimed at getting you to reflect on how you would go about tackling a particular form of organization development with the information provided.

These case studies have been designed both to satisfy the needs of the individual reader, and to act as group exercises in a more formalized setting. To the extent that they try to satisfy two needs at the same time, there is a degree of compromise. In the organization development case studies, we have compromised in favour of the group learning approach rather than the individual. In our teaching on the management of change, we have found that a greater degree of thought and discussion is generated through group analysis of situations. Therefore, if you are reading these cases as an individual, it may be worthwhile thinking about working out a situation where they can be used in groups. Within your own organization, this could form part of an exercise prior to discussion of an actual change event that is likely to take place. You may also be considering some of the changes described in the cases. In this sense, they will act as a form of organization analysis. Look at what others did before considering how you wish to proceed.

Case study 1: Experience at SmithKline Beecham

The merger between Beecham Pharmaceuticals of the UK and Smith Kline French of the USA in 1989 created at that time what was claimed to be the first truly transnational pharmaceutical and health care company, SmithKline Beecham (SKB). The new executive committee obviously saw the need and opportunity to focus on creating a new company culture based on defined values and leadership practices. The term 'simply better' was generated as the way in which things should be done on a day-to-day basis.

Further communications exercises at one of SKB's sites in Irvine, Scotland detailed a number of key initiatives that fell under the so-called 'simply better' umbrella. They fell into three main categories in a triangle as in Figure 12.1.

Figure 12.1   *SKB initiatives*

Some of the initiatives had already been under way, some in fact even before the merger. Nevertheless this certainly was the first time that they had been grouped together and indeed set in the overall context of organizational change.

The opportunity was taken by the plant management at Irvine to intimate that employees would be expected to become more involved in the change process, and they were assured that the implementation would not result in any compulsory redundancies. A commitment was also given to train the employees in any new skills required. Although there were sceptics and dissenters amongst the workforce, generally the rollout sessions were well received owing to the job security factor. There were some genuine fears of a 'slash and burn' approach being possible owing to the newly acquired American influences within the organization.

This participative management approach within the company was developed further in 1994 as the focus switched from corporate level restructuring to reorganization specifically at the Irvine site. On this occasion senior site managers were initially taken out of their job roles for a period of several months to concentrate entirely on the transformation to a cellular structure. External change agents were employed extensively during this initial period and in due course the results were communicated to the plant staff. The change from traditional departments to more autonomous cells was announced along with the appointments of new cell leaders. It was explained that this was only the first step in the process which would take a further one to two years. This time employees were invited to volunteer for 'design team activities' to help the cell leaders reorganize within each cell.

Again the company had adopted an OD approach to organizational change by involving employees in the process. At the same time the talk was very much of radical changes within the cells, perhaps employing some of the attributes of business process re-engineering (BPR). A significant amount of training was carried out for those involved in the design team activities. Another output of 'simply better' was the promotion of teamwork and the identification and development of internal facilitators. New areas of training included process mapping, problem solving, analytical tools and so on.

The year that followed was a very busy one for people on the site, as many struggled with the issues of design teams while others were burdened with additional responsibilities to ensure production levels were maintained. Overall, the morale on site actually fell during this period as the workforce showed a significant reluctance to accept the changes that were being proposed. In the production areas in particular, the unions suspiciously viewed the design teams as a vehicle to reduce manning levels as 'facts and data' were being generated on existing processes. Non-value-added activities were closely scrutinized and attempts were made to design them out.

In terms of results, the prescribed changes from design team activities remained largely unfulfilled as insufficient resources for implementation were made available.

Questions

1 What was the main management lesson in introducing change at SKB?
2 What were some of the key OD lessons at the Irvine plant?

Analysis

Change has become a feature of organizational life and, although individuals have a natural tendency to feel uncomfortable and to resist change, further exposure leads to a degree of acclimatization. This would appear to be the experience at SKB Irvine where the rate of introduction of change had accelerated since the merger. The workforce and management appeared to be more relaxed about tackling change as a result of a no-redundancy policy and the widespread communications process.

There is a learning curve that the individual and the organization have to pass through, not only on acceptance of change but also on the process of change. The tried and tested activity-driven processes which had been the main experience at SKB had been found wanting in respect of the resource requirements to complete implementation. Frustration and disillusionment can be the order of the day as limited progress is achieved inside the design team, whilst outside others struggle to maintain the status quo. On the other hand, a BPR approach would have been completely inappropriate if the needs of the workforce were bypassed to deliver reduced costs with fewer but less motivated and more highly stressed employees. There can be a balance where both individual and organizational effectiveness are increased within a well-managed and resourced programme. The time frames for results must be controlled and this can be related to the work of Schaffer and Thomson (1992): 'By marrying long-term strategic objectives with short-term improvement projects, management can translate strategic direction into reality.'

Crucial to delivering the required change process is the change agent, who must be suitably equipped with the appropriate skills and the necessary charisma to tackle the complex issues head-on. SKB like many others started off with external change agents and then developed, with limited success, its own team of internal facilitators. They can be called upon to offer their expertise at any time. However, in SKB's experience there have been problems in change agent accessibility owing to their normal work activities.

Case study 2: Ethicon Ltd

An example of a company that appears to have successfully implemented a change is Ethicon Ltd, a medical device company that manufactures sutures for medical applications. They had been undergoing restructuring for some years; at the time, the most recent announcement was that the research and development function was to move to Germany and the new focus of the UK site was to be manufacturing.

In managing change, Ethicon set up new in-house systems to refocus people's ideas on three main goals:

- to improve process cycle times
- to decrease costs
- to improve quality.

Throughout the change process the company communicated well with employees and made them aware of the intentions and the benefits. A number of project managers were put in place to drive through change. Ethicon also introduced cross-functional teams that have broken down interdepartmental barriers and encouraged open forum discussions. They managed to involve the workers in the project and made them believe that there were gains to be made by changing the way they worked. This initiated change across the whole company. They also set in play a system of measurements against objectives in order to translate them into tangible business benefits. It is believed that one of the greatest achievements gained from this redesign project was the true sense of teamworking. The end result was a measured increase in productivity levels. The new ways of working were being implemented throughout the company and the hope was that they would produce positive results and cost savings to the company to ensure that Ethicon remained competitive.

Questions

1   How did management at Ethicon 'get it right'?
2   What particular aspects have encouraged the successful change?

Analysis

The change implementation process proved successful at Ethicon because of the following factors:

* The management team shared their vision and how it was going to be implemented.
* They employed project managers as change agents who were responsible for the initiation and implementation of the transformation process and monitored these changes.
* The progress of the implementation was communicated to the employees both directly and through newsletters that highlighted improvements made as a result of the changes.
* They encouraged the formation of coalitions, to work together in teams towards a set of common goals.

This is a textbook example of how to manage a complex change situation. Vision was shared, communicated and implemented in a holistic manner. The OD changes may also be seen to be further evidence of the value of integrative, participative and iterative planning as detailed in the TPM model introduced in Chapter 6.

Case study 3: United Kingdom Atomic Energy Authority, (UKAEA) Dounreay

After the closure of the Fast Breeder Reactor Programme, there had been considerable redundancies at the UKAEA's Dounreay facility. These were largely voluntary, and accompanied by well-funded civil service redundancy packages. This was followed by the contracting out of certain elements of the site organization to the private sector. The UKAEA had successfully implemented a Managing Agency system for the decommissioning work for Windscale Pile no. 1. In order to improve efficiency and to bring in commercial management practices, they had decided to install a similar system at Dounreay.

The approach taken by the incoming Managing Agency team (for which key members were transferred from Windscale) was autocratic. When problems were encountered, decisions were often made rapidly as to how they were to be resolved. Initiative was not encouraged, and it seemed that a decision did not stand for long before being reversed or modified.

One example of this best illustrates the confusion caused by the change. Project managers had initially been expected to produce quarterly progress reports. These were usually fairly detailed, and supported by financial information. They were also supported by 'short-form' monthly progress reports, which included exception reporting where appropriate. The difficulty was caused by the fact that the 'short-form' reports were not supported by the financial information system or by any of the project management tools available on the site. They relied on manual tracking of contracts and projects by spreadsheet.

The Managing Agency staff issued new formats and content requirements for the quarterly financial and earned value reports, requiring an additional level of detail (partly in order to support their own claims for incentive payments). This involved a considerable amount of extra effort. Although the declared aim was to reduce the amount of effort which went into reporting there was little evidence that this was being achieved.

The local management team did not have the power to make their own changes. The Managing Agency staff made matters worse by requiring further changes to these reporting formats and requested that they be submitted monthly. Moreover, they then changed the requirements each month for several months. The rearrangement of spreadsheets to meet these new requirements became far and away more time-consuming than the production of the reports themselves. 'What's the new monthly format for the monthly reports?' became a frequent query. The required changes were achieved but at a cost of diverting significant amounts of effort from productive operations and reducing the credibility of the Managing Agency. Project team leaders at Dounreay were fast becoming experts on accommodating changes in reporting requirements rather than on project management.

Another instance of a non-participative attempt at change concerned the implementation of the 1994 Construction (Design and Management) Regulations. The CDM Regulations required the appointment of a Principal Contractor to be legally responsible for the management of safety on relevant worksites. The Managing Agency's view was that the UKAEA could not legally delegate responsibility for safety on a nuclear licensed site. Therefore, UKAEA would have to retain the position of Principal Contractor, rather than contracting out as any other client might do. There were already individuals appointed to take full control and responsibility for safety within specific site areas. The holders of what was termed ATO (authority to operate) had absolute authority. The logical organizational stance was that the ATO holder should also be appointed Principal Contractor. This quite sensible approach was rejected by the ATO holders, who felt that:

- The new change was being foisted upon them with virtually no discussion.

- Their workload was already excessive: it was inappropriate to add a further legal and mandatory duty to their task list.
- They had insufficient training in the requirements of the CDM Regulations, and had very little idea as to what the Principal Contractor's duties were.

Whilst it should be stressed that there was never any safety problem, or contravention of any legal requirement, there was no attempt to win the hearts and minds of powerful stakeholders in the organization. The objections stated above could have been resolved very simply, by education, discussion, training, jointly establishing a strategy for implementation, and provision of a marginal quantity of staffing resource. The ATO holders were highly qualified and experienced personnel. They already had the vast majority of the skills and training needed for the role, which need not have added excessively to their duties. The lack of consultation simply served as another illustration of a management style which they did not appreciate, and built up resentment and resistance to change in a key segment of the site management.

Analysis

The Dounreay Managing Agency was employed to achieve cost savings in the public sector. The trigger for Managing Agency implementation was simply that 'it worked at Windscale, so it should work here'. There was no evidence that a detailed study of the required change processes was undertaken. Certainly there was no clarity as to how cost savings were to be achieved. The UKAEA appeared to think that the Managing Agency would achieve the cost savings for them. Few of the employees saw it as being in their interest to support the change process where decommissioning work was involved. Clearly, it was important to identify and communicate the reasons for change if support was to be generated for it.

The treatment of the ATO holders is a classic illustration of change management being introduced through lack of consultation or effective communication. This resulted in resistance to change and could have been more effectively handled. ATO holders already had responsibilities in this area and the formalization of this through a consultative process would have made the introduction of increased role responsibilities more straightforward.

The method of change management used by the Managing Agency was clearly of the project management genre (the change agent's expertise lay in dealing with contractors rather than change management). This approach had worked at Windscale where fewer stakeholders had been involved, but at Dounreay there was a considerable resistance to change in powerful segments of middle management, and the Managing

Agency did not have the power to simply drive through the changes in the way it had planned.

Not only had the process of change taken control of the strategy and rationale originally envisaged, the Holy Trinity discussed in Chapter 2 had clearly broken down. Roles, focus and goals had become confused and lacked purpose.

Case study 4: the National Health Service

The following case recounts changes that have taken place in the NHS both at primary and secondary care level. After nearly 50 years of a very rigid bureaucratic regime the NHS has been finding itself having to adapt very quickly to internal and external pressures.

The case is a cultural change which occurred after the appointment of a new general manager at Grampian Health Board. Grampian provided health care to half a million people living within 3360 square miles. The population was not evenly distributed, however: 43 per cent of inhabitants lived in or around Aberdeen. As a result, major acute, obstetric and psychiatric services were based in the city with Elgin providing a secondary centre. Peripheral hospitals and clinics provided additional services. Grampian employed 13,500 staff and received a budget of about £170 million per annum.

When Grampian first approached the issue of changing its culture the General Manager employed an external change agent to assist in a review of the organization's current position. The review concluded that there were a number of issues to be addressed. On the positive side, 'people in the organization are devoted, capable, and enthusiastic, but they have been bound up in a bureaucratic system of indecision'. There were a number of recommendations related to the need to adopt problem solving approaches capable of dealing with issues associated with costs, responsiveness to customers, expectations and strategic direction.

The review highlighted a number of motivators for change:

1 the external pressures of new government legislation – contracting for services, devolution of responsibility, and an emphasis on competitiveness
2 internal pressures from staff in the form of complaints about poor communication, lack of creativity, low motivation, unclear strategy, unclear structure, systems not understood, lack of teamwork
3 new standards of delivering services
4 a new General Manager.

The style they decided to adopt in instigating change was OD. This involved utilizing a toolkit of intervention methods including:

- process consultation
- survey feedback
- changing the structure
- team building
- intergroup development.

Price Waterhouse were used as process consultants. One of the first steps was to answer the question, 'Where are we now?' This involved an attitude survey of over 1000 members of the staff. From this, the following issues came to light:

- *Communication* Information was not disseminated throughout the organization in a way that allowed it to be understood and accepted.
- *Creativity* Ideas for improving the way in which the organization worked were not being put to good use and this led to stagnation.
- *Motivation* People did not feel greatly concerned about the organization and were not willing to expend much effort to further common goals.
- *Strategy* The reasons for doing things were unclear and/or poorly communicated. The systems to support management were inadequate and/or not understood.
- *Teamwork* People who should have been contributing to common tasks did not wish to work together or found too many obstacles to doing so.
- *Training* People were not learning to do things that would materially affect their performance.

This feedback showed that Grampian was a monolithic bureaucracy which was unable to cope with rapid and unpredictable change; the increasing complexity of modern organization; the diversity of specialist expertise; and participative management styles.

Further workshops and meetings followed to look at 'Where do we need to be?', after which the senior management produced three documents: a vision, a mission and a management approach, which stated the desired future culture at Grampian. A programme was then developed to address these issues as follows:

- A 10-year strategy for health care was developed through a highly participative process.
- Each of the units produced a five-year plan.
- Many team-building workshops were held throughout the organization but particularly at senior management level.
- The board structure was changed towards one more firmly based on consumer groupings.
- A team process was introduced and the in-house magazine was revamped.

- A comprehensive quality programme was devised, including patient surveys, quality standards and customer care training.
- A rigorous review of overhead costs was conducted which enabled over 15 per cent to be saved and reallocated.
- Personal objectives, appraisal and performance-related pay were cascaded throughout the management hierarchy.
- New training programmes were introduced, covering areas such as problem solving, planning and leadership.
- The whole senior management team went through a development process designed to identify personal potential.
- Twenty-one line managers were seconded for up to 70 per cent of their time to undertake the role of in-house consultants.

Analysis

Two years after this process was initiated, the original questionnaire was again sent out to see if the people in the organization felt that the objective of cultural change had been achieved. The results showed that at senior and middle management levels there was a definite view that cultural change had taken place, but supervisory and basic grades had a negative and neutral attitude respectively. This was justified by the management team as 'a matter of timing', and they stated that 'Cultural change takes a long time: it seeps down and permeates management structure from above.' Looking at this it could be suggested that the participative techniques used had focused mainly on senior and middle management. As this change took place over a long period of time there were a number of issues that could possibly have been addressed to avoid this negativity and neutrality.

Dunphy and Stace (1990) looked at the scale of change and the leadership styles required to facilitate this. The scale of change in this example lends itself to their description of corporate transformation. They described this as 'involving radical shifts in strategy, revolutionary changes throughout the organization, to structure, systems and procedures, to mission and the core values and to the distribution of power'. They argue that with this scale of change the required leadership style would be one of 'charismatic transformation' and as part of this the organization would require support for the radical change. It is unclear whether Grampian truly had this commitment from the supervisory and lower grades. Perhaps this left them lacking in trust and not fully understanding the purpose of the change. The vision in this case was clearly stated to the organization, but from the outcome the middle and senior management grades appeared to be the only ones who had taken it on board. The impact was concentrated at that level, gaining their trust but leaving the lower grades with a neutral feeling.

Change of this magnitude does take time to diffuse throughout the whole organization. However, one would have expected a greater degree of commitment to the change process from all grades. The emphasis of the management levels appears to have been at the expense of the total organization buying into the change process and may have created or exacerbated an 'us and them' syndrome. Too much stress may have been placed on developing management skills rather than enhancing Grampian's management processes.

Case study 5: MTC Ltd

Change is a continuous process of confrontation, identification, evaluation and action. The overlap between systems thinking and OD emerges in Pugh (1978) and in Rickards (1985). Both approaches have a great deal in common and it appears the theories are converging, with both emphasizing the importance of the process of intervention and the need for any change strategy to have self-regulating loops.

In this particular case the problems are basically people oriented and therefore tend towards the 'soft' end of the change continuum, resulting from changes made necessary through the rapid growth the company has experienced.

In applying the OD model this case study has used, by way of illustration, the changes that were necessary as a result of the company expanding into another sector of the market, namely, the provision of a national training programme for accountants, the success of which was in part responsible for the significant growth experienced by the company.

Political behaviour often emerges before and during organizational change efforts owing to the fact that any reorganization is usually feared because it means disturbance of the status quo. This case study is no exception to this and, owing to very rapid growth, displayed all the classic symptoms.

MTC Ltd were a substantial diverse and financially sound organization operating throughout Scotland from 20 locations and employing around 150 people. They were primarily involved in providing a wide range of training programmes. MTC identified a market opportunity for a 'technician' level of accountant. The firm commissioned consultants to conduct a market research survey to determine the likely level of demand throughout Scotland for such a training programme. Their findings indicated that there was a very significant level of demand and that none of the company's main competitors were currently involved.

In order to capture the lion's share of the potential market the company had to move swiftly:

1 To establish links with the Association of Accounting Technicians (AAT) who were the London-based body responsible for the award of the professional qualification, which was recognized and indeed sponsored by all five major accountancy bodies in the UK.

2   Similarly, to establish links with the Scottish sponsoring body, namely The Institute of Chartered Accountants of Scotland (ICAS).
3   To negotiate a contract for the provision of a government sponsored training scheme.
4   Based on market research, to quantify the resources that would be required in terms of additional premises, location of premises, equipment, timing, funding and manning.
5   To deal with the scale of the operations meant that the company's administrative and personnel procedures had to be reviewed and upgraded, with more formalized procedures being introduced.
6   To deal with the organizational changes meant reorganization was required, which with the anticipated increase in manning levels etc. meant that certain roles had to be changed.

It is a paradox of organizational life that situations and problems that cry out most strongly for change are often the very ones that resist change most stubbornly, and it was this resistance to change that was the major problem to overcome.

The OD process

The philosophy of organizational development is one of long-term change, and organizational change efforts that are based on inconsistent strategies tend to run into predictable problems. An effective manager is one who anticipates, diagnoses and manages the change process over a period of time to ensure it is effective, and in this case perhaps the use of a change facilitator or consultant would have been helpful in giving an unbiased 'helicopter' view of the organization. However, the organizational change was approached in the following way.

First, at the planning stage, consideration was given to the four principles and six rules given by Pugh (1978) as a guide to understanding organizational change together with the OD loop which emphasizes the recurrent nature of change. In order to adequately explain the process that was employed, a series of questions and prompts were formulated as a guide (see Figure 6.2).

Second, if the proposer or problem owner has sufficient power, the change can be pushed through but at the cost of conflict, resentment and reduced motivation. It was always anticipated that resistance to the change would be a major obstacle; the problem was to predict what form the resistance might take. The four most common reasons why people resist change are:

1   a desire not to lose something of value
2   a misunderstanding of the change and its implications
3   a belief that the change does not make sense for the organization
4   a low tolerance of change.

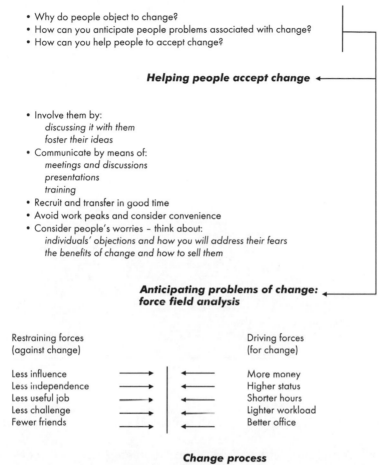

- Why do people object to change?
- How can you anticipate people problems associated with change?
- How can you help people to accept change?

Helping people accept change

- Involve them by:
    discussing it with them
    foster their ideas
- Communicate by means of:
    meetings and discussions
    presentations
    training
- Recruit and transfer in good time
- Avoid work peaks and consider convenience
- Consider people's worries – think about:
    individuals' objections and how you will address their fears
    the benefits of change and how to sell them

**Anticipating problems of change:
force field analysis**

Restraining forces   Driving forces
(against change)   (for change)

Less influence   More money
Less independence   Higher status
Less useful job   Shorter hours
Less challenge   Lighter workload
Fewer friends   Better office

Change process

- Identify and remove restraining forces
- Carry out the change
- Freeze the situation by reinforcing the new behaviour

Figure 12.2   *Management of change: people problems*

Managers who initiate changes often assume that they have all the relevant information required to conduct an adequate organization analysis, and that those who will be affected by the change have the same facts. Neither assumption is correct, and again because of the messy nature of the problem it was decided to diagram the 'people problems' in order to better understand the fears and objections of the individuals involved. The people problems and objections are detailed in Figure 12.2 and Table 12.1.

On organizational grounds, resistance to change can be understood when it is realized that from the behavioural viewpoint, organizations

Table 12.1 *People's objections to change*

Change threatens: their present position; their prospects

Change requires: physical work; mental work

How can change benefit their job?	How can change appear threatening?	What do people require from their jobs which change can threaten?
Enriching	Deskilling	Interest in their job:
Broadening	Impoverishing	using a skill
Given discretion	Removing discretion	having mental challenges
		using their discretion
Upgrading	Blocking promotion	Growth in their job:
Increased responsibility	Removing jobs	to more important work
Change of scene	Revising jobs	to harder work
Improved reward	Rejecting earlier work	to different work
Improved status	Rejecting ideas	
		A worthwhile job:
		recognized by self
		recognized by others
Training for the job	Increased apparent difficulty	A secure job:
Easier job	Appearing stupid	ability to handle the job
Permanence of job	Redundancy	fear of losing face
Better conditions	Degrading	fear of losing job
		fear of losing possessions

are coalitions of interest groups in tension. There is an interesting parallel here with the Cyert and March (1963) behavioural theory of the firm.

In overcoming individuals' resistance to having their job redesigned there is a motivational opportunity to be gained. Internalized motivation is implicit in McGregor's theory Y and is reinforced by Herzberg (1966) with his motivational factors which concentrate on the 'satisfiers'. These aspects were given considerable emphasis in order to overcome resistance.

In summary, the actual OD process model used was as follows:

1   *Confrontation with environmental changes, problems, opportunities*   The decision to diversify into accountancy training meant that a considerable upheaval would be required, as there was a high level of influencing factors both internal and external to the organization. Some of these factors are detailed as follows:

External	*Internal*
AAT	Environment
ICAS	Resources
Training Commission	Training

Sponsor companies   Communication
Competition   Motivation
Geographical spread   Funding
Ethnocentrism

2 *Identification of implications for organization*   The implications of these changes were far reaching, but the most important element by far was how to overcome people's resistance to change. The process described in Figure 12.2 dealt with this.

3 *Education to obtain understanding of implications for organization*   It was evident that attention had to be focused at the individual level and certain actions would have to be taken for those directly affected:

- training
- communication/involving
- career planning
- job enrichment
- re-establishment of a degree of loyalty.

The fact that this process was interactive was recognized, especially when at the implementation stage other factors were identified and the 'loop' would therefore continue.

4 *Obtaining involvement in project*   It was felt that involving people in carefully planning the change and considering how it would affect them was the best way of overcoming resistance and help develop a change philosophy.

5 *Change and development activities*   The process of change was accomplished by unfreezing, changing and refreezing. These terms can be explained as follows:

- *unfreezing*: developing an awareness of the need for change and establishing the relationships needed for successful change
- *changing*: defining problems, identifying solutions and implementing solutions
- *refreezing*: stabilizing the situation and building relationships.

6 *Evaluation of project and programme in current environment and reinforcement*   The evaluation was carried out by determining both what the benefits were and what had been learnt from the process. Some of these were as follows:

- increased profitability
- more accurate forecasting
- increased motivation
- increased propensity for change
- clearer role perceptions
- reduced intergroup confrontation.

READER ACTIVITY

Using an example from your own organization, comment on the applicability of Figure 12.2 to the resolution of people problems during the
management of change.

Analysis

Few organizational change efforts are complete failures, but few are
entirely successful either. This was stated by Kotter and Schlesinger
(1979) and reinforced by Pritchard (1984): 'There is no right strategy,
different combinations are likely to suit different company needs.'

In this particular case, whilst the changes had been successful, it was
too early to evaluate precisely the 'bottom line' effect – although there
was ample objective evidence of significant success and the people who
were directly affected felt that this style of management approach had
been worthwhile.

In reality, if you operate in an aggressive expanding environment,
change is continuous, leaving little time for formal planning. Management of change has become a fashionable topic but in essence the
processes described are merely the application of a logical and common-
sense approach when addressing a change situation, and this has always
been done by reasonably competent managers.

This approach to the organizational development process as illustrated
was constructed using a 'logical' approach and yet it contains all aspects
of the OD model.

In conclusion, it is important to look both conceptually and practically
at managing change and particularly the interdependence of political,
cultural and technical aspects of diagnosing, planning, implementing
and evaluating strategic changes.

Case study 6: group performance review

There is no correct answer to this particular example. The number of
ways of undertaking a group performance review are numerous and so
are the likely approaches. The difficulty that this case study provides you
with is in your own approach to the OD process of change from entry to
exit. Read through the case study problem, as it is set, and design your
own strategy.

During 1999, OILCo, a major oil company, established a number of
empowerment work groups (EWGs) throughout the organization. Six
of these EWGs attended a training event during the latter part of 1999 on

basic teamwork skills. EWGs have now been operating for some time and it would appear appropriate to undertake some form of review of their operation. Within OILCo, experience of EWGs had led to questions being asked about their widespread adoption throughout the organization over the next few years.

As the internal change agent responsible for the initial training of the EWGs, you have been asked to outline a proposal based on examining the impact of EWGs, staff and management attitudes related to EWGs, a performance review of EWGs to look at more detailed issues, and an analysis of the likely implications of the move towards wider application.

The remit

The basic remit for this proposal is to establish what stage of development EWGs have reached within OILCo. There are four issues associated with this analysis.

First, there is a need to determine whether the EWGs that are already in existence have resulted in accomplishments that benefit the individual member, the EWGs themselves, and the organization as a whole. It is the intention here to characterize the EWG at work by showing levels of success and/or failure, and relating these to greater employee involvement within OILCo.

Second, there is also a need to examine where EWGs are developing to, and the levels of surety within the groups that they have the capability to develop. This issue is related to whether the EWGs are a temporary or a permanent phenomenon within the organization, and whether those within the EWGs believe that they are worthwhile enough to be taken forward.

Third, what levels of skills and competencies do the EWGs contain? This issue relates to whether the groups feel confident amongst themselves that they have the necessary skills to be able to function as a coherent group and sustain accomplishments. A related issue here is the level of support that OILCo itself can offer EWGs to optimize their effectiveness, and what form this should take.

Fourth, physical indicators of the value of the work groups are needed by OILCo. This issue is linked to the overall benefit of EWGs to the organization as a whole by improvements in the way work is undertaken.

Questions

1 How do you intend approaching this problem? Draft a proposal outlining the way you intend carrying out the remit.
2 Using the ODM, what are likely to be the major benefits that OILCo can expect to gain from undertaking the proposal you put forward?

Analysis

Although there are no correct solutions to this case study, a proposal and a project were carried out by the authors in conjunction with staff at OILCo. These can be seen as indicators of the ODM approach to managing change in organizations. The important learning points are associated with three specific criteria:

- designing the process for involvement
- being able to acquire the necessary information to complete the project
- being able to provide both hard and soft data on the performance of EWGs.

A short summary of the proposal presented and accepted by the organization is outlined below.

The proposal

It is envisaged that the project will contain three stages.

STAGE 1: EWG WORKSHOPS AND OPINION SURVEY   The starting point for the project will be an opinion survey distributed among EWG members. The survey will be conducted with EWG members through an informal workshop session to obtain feedback on their views related to development of the EWGs. Some form of formal data gathering will take place via the opinion survey but it is envisaged that more relevant information may be obtained by an informal discussion session held immediately after the survey has been completed.

The mechanism for data gathering will be to visit each of the EWGs and managers that took part in the training events at their workplace. This would then be followed by a workshop to look at how the EWGs feel they are progressing. It is envisaged that each workshop will take a half-day to complete. The focus of the latter part of the workshop will be on evidence of the success that EWGs can identify as benefiting OILCo. Each EWG will be asked to make a short presentation on where they have been able to make a greater level of contribution to OILCo as an EWG, situations where the EWG has generated greater profits or cost savings than would otherwise have occurred, and projected plans for the future with an indication of the costs and benefits linked to these plans.

This stage will provide a good source of both quantitative and qualitative feedback on how well EWGs are currently working. It will also highlight problem areas that need to be addressed. The survey data will be analysed by the author with feedback provided at stage 3.

STAGE 2: MANAGERIAL ISSUES   Stage 2 involves a number of informal discussions with managers working within OILCo who have EWGs within their own organization. It is envisaged that these interviews will act as a managerial perspective on EWGs and will provide ideas and guidelines on their effectiveness and the best way to move forward. This would involve a number of visits to the EWG workplaces and dis- cussions with the relevant managers in these areas. This would be done on a confidential basis and selected (unattributed) commentary from these discussions will be incorporated into stage 3.

STAGE 3: PRODUCT DELIVERY   Stage 3 is the production of a short (25–30 page) analysis of EWGs at OILCo that will include:

- a one-page management summary
- the results from the opinion surveys
- workshop feedback on critical performance measurements
- managerial commentary
- a concluding assessment on overall group performance.

Opinion surveys are one of the key elements in OD. They provide information on factors likely to influence the OD change effort. They also have the benefit of allowing greater levels of contribution by those likely to be affected by change. However, a word of warning. Many organiz-ations use the opinion survey as window dressing. That is, a large number of surveys take place but very little is done to action the results. Feedback of results from the opinion survey is an obvious mechanism for encouraging greater participation in the change effort. Participants have to be able to see, however, that the organization is taking their views seriously, is paying attention to the trends, and more importantly, is taking action based on these. Otherwise, the gathering of data in this way becomes an exercise in public relations that the public, those within the organization, view as phoney and ultimately worthless.

Epilogue

Burdett (1998: 28–9) argues that organizations are approaching a new era and that that era requires a new response. In particular, he argues that organizations need insightful thinking and that there are three potential means to better respond to change:

1 'a belief that at the centre of every storm there needs to be an area of calm' – a need to define and manage with a set of well-stated organizational values
2 'at all times keep it simple' – complex theories and solutions take time and lose context
3 'the need for and the benefits of systems thinking' – a holistic perspective on change.

This would seem to sum up what we have been attempting in this book – a synergy between two different modes of managing change.

Dealing with the future

Managers, organizations and the societies they serve would be foolish, fatalistic, if they failed to realize the necessity of planning for the future. Planning for planning's sake must be avoided. The ultimate failure of centralist planning initiatives, as employed by economies such as the former Soviet Union and Maoist China, as well as many American corporations in the 1960s and early 1970s, illustrates the need to be realistic, proactive, responsive and flexible. Plans must be flexible and in tune with the environment in which they are to be implemented. Operating environments, in the broadest sense of the term, must be understood and managerial actions must reflect their complexities and intentions.

There is no evidence to suggest that the rate and the nature of change are likely to alter dramatically in the near future. Technologies, industries and societies will continue to converge. Organizations will continue to seek strategic alliances and maximize the benefits associated with an integrated and well-managed supply chain. Managers and employees in general will be judged, as they are now, on their ability to cope with and implement change. Adaptability, continuous improvement, lifelong learning and sustaining competitive advantage are and will remain crucial.

Corporate winners, whether public or private enterprises, will have fostered and maintained a desire to succeed through progressive, dynamic and challenging initiatives. Strategies and cultures that welcome, address and imaginatively manage change will continue to triumph. Once again, for it is worth repeating, in the words of John Cotter, from the book entitled *The 20% Solution* (1995):

> The first law of the jungle is that the most adaptable species are always the most successful. In the struggle for survival, the winners are those who are most sensitive to important changes in their environment and quickest to reshape their behaviour to meet each new environmental challenge.

Part of the adaptability equation is recognition that the environmental factors will be monitored not only by you, but by your competitors. It is not enough to simply evolve; successful organizations need to evolve at the speed of light. Organizations are reshaping to respond to their environment. Successful organizations are the ones that identify not only the need for change but also the requirement to steal a march on their competitors. They achieve this by:

- innovative responses to triggers
- holistic solutions
- visionary leadership
- committed support.

From this we can begin to identify some of the aspects of change that management in the future will have to confront.

First, all organizations have to be able to effectively identify the triggers of change. Management is a multi-disciplinary subject. You may recall, from Chapter 7, that Megson (1988) criticized the analytical and mechanistic approaches managers use to solve problems in organizations: such approaches tended to reflect current or past thinking styles – cognitive baggage. His recommendation was the development of systemic thinking, an ability to see the whole picture rather than its functional parts. This stresses more innovative responses to triggers. These must reflect the future not the past. As Sir James Goldsmith put it, 'If you see a bandwagon, it's too late.'

Being alert to the potential triggers is the first step an enterprise can take on the road to effectively managing change. Early identification and classification permit the creative, or at least proactive, management of subsequent events. According to Kanter (1983) effective organizations, or at least the masters of change within them, are adept at handling 'the triggers of change', namely:

- *Departures from tradition*   The Royal Bank of Scotland recognized that a 'transaction' was merely an exchange of information, and as such technology could handle it, so they launched a direct banking service.
- *The crisis of a galvanizing event*   The City intervention in the ailing Stakis group in the early 1990s led to the appointment of a new senior management team, the success of which has been well documented.
- *Strategic choice*   For example, the Virgin Group's move into the pension, PEP and banking sectors, and Tesco's proposed move into car sales. Ford and Mazda, Volvo and Jaguar, Chrysler and Daimler, and General Motors and SAAB represent alliances designed to provide strategic advantage and further economies of scale.
- *Prime movers*   Rupert Murdoch's single-minded, almost unique, approach to corporate empire building leaves many competitors stranded on the sidelines. For example, BSkyB's proposed purchase of Manchester United not only threatened a monopoly situation in terms of football coverage but opened up a synergy of interest in terms of global branding. Steve Jobs's return to the troubled Apple Corporation is another example.
- *Action vehicles*   3M's quality quest linked to their 'lifetime' guarantee promotion for videotapes, or British Telecom's 'for a better life' programme (Mason, 1998). British Airways' new corporate headquarters, the Waterside development, in many ways is a physical manifestation of an action vehicle. The intelligent state of the art building embodies BA's strategic and organizational aspirations and has been used to stimulate change.

These responses need not be revolutionary, they can be evolutionary. Doing something just slightly better is an innovative response to change. Organizations need to develop and stimulate creative thought. In a strategic sense, the identification of triggers must focus on multiple scenarios of the future. Pascale (1994) classifies this as managing the present from the future. Organizations have responded to this need for enlightened, but realistic, responses to change by developing structures, processes and cultures that encourage employees to question past assumptions and promote innovatory thought.

Second, once one has developed responses to change triggers, or indeed enacted proactive vision, the subsequent solutions have to be holistically managed. In Chapters 3 and 4, we stressed the need to view the change situation in terms of systems linkages and the environmental impact. The triggers and the consequences have knock-on effects for all. Kanter (1983) regards this as a need to develop an integrative approach to solving problems:

> To see problems integratively is to see them as wholes, related to larger wholes, and thus challenging established practices – rather than walling off a

piece of experience and preventing it from being touched or affected by any new experiences. . . . Companies where segmentalist approaches dominate find it difficult to innovate or to handle change.

Third, to be effective, change management needs to be supported from the top and to be characterized by 'full-blown' participation. Senior management needs to be seen to be making the time to be fully involved. There is also a need for this involvement to permeate throughout the organization, to gain commitment to the changes being made. For example, when Delta airlines were faced with significant redundancies in 1994 they took positive steps to control and manage the situation. A communications centre, with freephone numbers, was set up to provide immediate responses to employee questions. Open forums were organized and vice-presidents were dispatched to allay fears. In addition, the senior management team visited all Delta sites within two days of the announcement.

Strategic, tactical or operational change must be supported by those ultimately responsible for the wellbeing of the corporation, division or operating unit. Most travel agencies derive a healthy profit from their currency-related operations. However, what happens as Britain enters the Euro? A single currency, combined with a massive rise in credit and electronic currency transactions, will threaten profits, jobs and ultimately the enterprise. Thomas Cook are not waiting to see what will happen, but rather have attempted to anticipate and shape the future. The changes that face the travel industry are being faced head-on and staff at Thomas Cook's know what is expected of them and what they can expect by way of support and guidance.

Ten key factors in effective change management

We have expanded the three discussed above, namely innovative responses to triggers, holistic solutions, visionary leadership and committed support, into 10 factors which must be addressed and actioned if change is to be effectively managed. By ensuring that these factors have been considered, prior to initializing change, the problem owner and associated change agents will be in a position to confidently manage the process of transition from that which is inadequate to that which is desired.

1 CHANGE IS ALL-PERVASIVE

Any process of change is likely to have an impact greater than the sum of its parts. A holistic view must be taken to ensure that the full environmental impact is understood. When you consider making change in your organization, from buying a new coffee machine to gaining Investors In People (IIP) certification, look at change in terms of its impact on the organization as a whole. Forget the parts; look at the whole picture.

2 EFFECTIVE CHANGE NEEDS ACTIVE SENIOR MANAGEMENT SUPPORT

Whether you believe in a top-down or a bottom-up approach to change in organizations, one thing is vital: there is a need and desire for senior management to be seen to support the change process. This is self-evident. Without senior management support, three things will be missing. First, the change will lack vision. Those that can look forward supply vision. In most organizations, it is senior managers' responsibility to look forward, examine changes in the environment, and determine the future state of the business. There are numerous examples of senior management vision from Branson at Virgin, Gates at Microsoft, Souter at Stagecoach to Murdoch everywhere!

Second, you'll need effective allies. Senior management backing for the change process is crucial in recruiting the desired level of support to instigate change at all levels. Coming from a production department, with a desire to change levels of customer satisfaction and awareness, you will need help from marketing. Senior management support for the change process will assist in gaining this help. It will allow you and/or the change project to cross the functional boundaries that often impede change.

Third, you'll lack power. When the visible problem owner or change agent talks, it is senior management that is really speaking out. Senior management support guarantees that the problem owner 'speaks quietly but carries a big stick'.

Work on achieving senior management support from the outset. Talk out the ideas you have for change with your boss, or his or her boss. The sooner there is senior management awareness of the need and desirability, the sooner things will begin to change.

3 CHANGE IS A MULTI-DISCIPLINARY ACTIVITY

Most successful change projects accomplish their objectives via the project team. No one person is a change island. Recognition of the multi-disciplinary nature of change goes a long way in beginning the sequence of realizing the transformation. Problem owners are identified because of their association with the change. Change agents are recruited because of their expertise in facilitating change through its various stages. Their expertise may be based on people skills, technological know-how, or their experience of systems analysis.

When placed in charge of a change project, or when contemplating change in organizations, get yourself a team. The successful management of change, which is all-pervasive, will require a multi-disciplinary approach. None of us has the ability to deal with all the aspects of change management that are likely to occur over the lifetime of a project.

4 CHANGE IS ABOUT PEOPLE, PURE AND SIMPLE

In Chapter 7, we focused attention on the need to design organizations in a way that created effective performance. The key ingredient in this design was the human element. Remember that people are the most important asset: people want and need to grow, and personal growth is the engine that drives organization performance. Therefore, when contemplating change, involve the people in the process from the outset. Through active participation you accomplish two things. You gain commitment and ownership of the change process by all; and those experiencing the change will not need to be pushed but will begin to drive change themselves.

Change management is about people management. When managing change, you manage people. Remember the basics:

- openness
- communication
- involvement.

5 CHANGE IS ABOUT SUCCESS

Faced with competitive environments, which are growing in terms of both magnitude and ferocity, organizations must be flexible enough to rise to the challenges of today and tomorrow. Creating an organizational culture which is receptive to change should provide a competitive edge that will last the test of time. Stand still and be complacent if you wish, but you can be sure that your competitors, both current and future, will be striving towards greater efficiency and effectiveness.

Make your change project a mission, a way of life. However, watch how you do it. Going boldly forth where no organization has gone before, discovering new planets, and seeking out new life forms is all very well, but you need focus. The challenges created by looking too far ahead may be beyond the organization's current capabilities. On the other hand, dinosaur organizations become extinct because they fail to adapt to their environment. Set goals for success that can be accomplished and seen to be deliverable. Perhaps going on a five-year mission is not the answer; a look round the corner may be all that is needed to guarantee success.

6 CHANGE IS A PERPETUAL PROCESS

How do we explain change that was successful? How do we explain change that never seemed to get going? How can we explain the change project that started off well but seemed to fade away after a couple of years? The answers seem to lie in the attention and resources devoted to managing change as a perpetual process.

We have cited throughout the concept of perpetual transition management. Change is about identifying triggers, seeking vision, recruiting converts to the vision, and maintaining and renewing the need for change on an ongoing basis. The effective management of change demands management action on all these fronts.

You have to be able to identify what is triggering change. This has to be expressed and clarified and communicated throughout the organization to gain understanding. There is also a need for some vision of how the triggers will affect the future of the organization. In this sense, there is a need to define what the future is, in terms of the challenges being faced and the future make-up of the organization. Having set a vision, there is a need to manage change through converting people to that vision. Most successful change programmes work on the basis of persuading people that this is the right way to go, by detailing the structure. Finally, watch the triggers. Change that fades away does so because circumstances alter: those involved at the start move on, and the triggers become unclear in the minds of those left to carry on. The systems intervention model deals with a dynamic change environment by incorporating, in the design, iterative processes where you can step back and reappraise your position in the light of environmental changes.

Perpetual change is what it says: you never get to the end, something else always comes along to impact the business in a new way.

7   EFFECTIVE CHANGE REQUIRES COMPETENT CHANGE AGENTS

The change management project has a certain number of needs that must be satisfied. One of these needs relates to the required skills, knowledge and position of change agents. Analysis of the change situation will determine the appropriate management team in terms of their attributes. It will not, however, ensure that the change agents have the necessary competencies to effectively contribute to the process of change. To be fully effective, the change agent must have certain capabilities, over and above their functional skills and knowledge.

The competencies of the change agent were examined in Chapter 9. These relate to being able to communicate with, on behalf of, and through people involved in the change situation. The change agent therefore needs to feel comfortable in dealing with interpersonal relationships, coping with conflict and ambiguity, and the 1001 different emotions that humans can display as a result of the change process itself. Change can upset people; they can also become overjoyed, be over-enthusiastic or indeed shy away from it. The change agent has to be able to facilitate those involved through this process by taking their feelings and emotions into account, getting them to address how these emotions relate to change itself, and steering the organization forward.

Many organizations have begun to address the management of change within their own organizations as a perpetual process. The competencies of the change agent are being directly dealt with by instigating training programmes to provide them with the necessary staff skilled in the techniques associated with organization development.

Technical skills, such as systems diagramming, network analysis and charting in general, can be readily taught and acquired.

However, people skills are the more important and often the more difficult competencies to acquire. If you are theory X, you are hardly likely to be able to develop good change management skills. You do not appreciate the enormity of the change. The basis of change management rests with the assumptions you make about people in organizations. Make the wrong assumptions and the management of change goes down the wrong path.

8   IN TERMS OF METHODOLOGY, THERE IS NO ONE BEST WAY

All we wish to say here is: do not take a singular approach. You must not be too blinkered about change management. In essence, there is no one best way. What works for one change situation may not be fully appropriate to another. For example, in takeover situations, the cultures of the organizations involved may be seemingly incompatible and may require adjustment. The obvious approach is to adopt an organization development methodology. However, such an approach will take time and will not bring about immediate improvements in performance. It may be better to start the ball rolling by adopting an intervention strategy in the short term. This could provide a quick-win example, whilst over the medium to long term an organization development cycle could be set in motion to accomplish the required objectives of change.

9   CHANGE IS ABOUT OWNERSHIP

We refer back here to people. What makes change happen? When it works beautifully, what causes this? The answers seem to rest with attaining ownership of the change process itself. In terms of the problem owner, the change agents, and those being affected by change, there is a need to feel ownership.

The management team must feel that they are responsible for the successful implementation of the change. This responsibility is best discharged through a desire to succeed rather than survive. What we are concerned with here is a movement from control to commitment. When people are being coerced or manoeuvred into change situations by threat or crisis, the result is at best indifference and at worst resistance. When people feel ownership of the change process, and feel that it offers opportunity, they are committed to its satisfactory accomplishment.

Get ownership by getting involvement; get involvement by openness and communication; get people to live the change.

10   CHANGE IS ABOUT FUN, CHALLENGE, AND OPPORTUNITY

When faced with a challenge, most individuals respond positively. The psychologists would argue that it brings out the best in people. On the other hand, when faced with a crisis people can go one of two ways. They can emerge as strong individuals to meet that crisis or they can become cowering wrecks under its enormity.

We have tried to make this book both interesting and easy to read. We work from the perspective that change management should be a challenging subject that offers the practitioner, the reader and those associated with change the opportunity to show their mettle. Change, as it implies, gives you the chance to move on. By providing opportunities you get to learn new and different things. Hopefully, you become a better person and contribute more to your organization. The challenges that you face through change management may be difficult or inspiring, and they may even make a better manager out of you. These challenges should be faced positively. Never shy away from the need for change. Sure, it's uncomfortable in some instances, but change can also be fun.

We use fun, in this instance, to denote an attitude of mind. Throughout the seriousness of it all – the drive for performance, the need to maintain a competitive edge, the desire for a better, more effective organization – there is also a need to show a human face. We teach change management because it fascinates us. The specific subject areas of systems and organization development are interesting, practical and challenging. However, if you have ever witnessed the way in which we teach them, you would also recognize that change management can be both gratifying and fun.

Make your management of the change project challenging. Provide those involved in it with the opportunity to develop themselves and the rest of the organization. At all points in time, remember, no one ever said that achieving effective change and gaining organizational performance cannot be fun!

References

Ackenhusen, M., Muzyka, D. and Churchill, N. (1996a) Restructuring 3M for an integrated Europe. Part one: initiating the change, *European Management Journal*, Vol. 14, No. 1, February.

Ackenhusen, M., Muzyka, D. and Churchill, N. (1996b) Restructuring 3M for an integrated Europe. Part two: initiating the change, *European Management Journal*, Vol. 14, No. 2, April.

Anderson, N. and West, M. (1996) The team climate inventory, *European Journal of Work and Organisational Psychology*, March.

Appelbaum, S.H. and Hughes, B. (1998) Ingratiation as a political tactic: effects within the organization, *Management Decision*, Vol. 36, No. 2, pp. 85–95.

Argyris, C. (1970) *Intervention Theory and Method*, Addison-Wesley, Reading, MA.

Argyris, C. and Schon, D. (1978) *Organizational Learning: A Theory of Action Perspective*, Addison-Wesley, Reading, MA.

Argyris, C. and Schon D. (1996) *Organizational Learning II*, Addison-Wesley, Reading, MA.

Beckhard, R. (1969) *Organization Development: Strategies and Models*, Addison-Wesley, Reading, MA.

Bedeian, A.G. (1980) *Organization Theory and Analysis*, Dryden Press, Chicago.

Beer, M. and Eisenstat, R.A. (1990) Why change projects don't produce change, *Harvard Business Review*, November.

Boddy, D. (1987) *The Technical Change Audit*, Manpower Services Commission, Sheffield.

Boddy, D. and Buchanan, D.A. (1986) *Managing New Technology*, Basil Blackwell, Oxford.

Boddy, D. and Buchanan, D.A. (1992) *Take the Lead: Interpersonal Skills for Project Managers*, Prentice-Hall, London.

Boddy, D. and Paton, R.A. (1998) *Management: An Introduction*, Prentice-Hall, London.

Brownlie, D.T., McCalman, J., Paton, R. A. and Southern, G. (1990) *The Glasgow Management Development Initiative: Selected Findings and Issues*, a commissioned research report for the Manpower Services Commission, University of Glasgow Business School.

Buchanan, D.A. and Badham, R. (1999a) *Power, Politics, and Organizational Change: Winning the Turf Game*, Sage, London.

Buchanan, D.A. and Badham, R. (1999b) Politics and organizational change: the lived experience, *Human Relations*.

Buchanan, D.A. and Boddy, D. (1992) *The Expertise of the Change Agent*, Prentice-Hall, London.

Buchanan, D.A., Claydon, T. and Doyle, M. (1997) *Organization Development and Change: The Legacy of the Nineties*, Leicester Business School Occasional Paper 43, De Montfort University.

Buchanan, D.A. and Huczynski, A.A. (1997) *Organizational Behaviour: An Introductory Text*, 3rd edn, Prentice-Hall, London.

Buchanan, D.A. and McCalman, J. (1989) *High Performance Work Systems: The Digital Experience*, Routledge, London.

Buckler, B. (1996) A learning process model to achieve continuous improvement and innovation, *The Learning Organisation*, Vol. 3, p. 31.

Burdett, J.D. (1998) Beyond values – exploring the twenty-first century organization, *Journal of Management Development*, Vol. 17, No. 1, pp. 28–9.

Burnes, B. (1996) *Managing Change: A Strategic Approach to Organisational Dynamics*, 2nd edn, Pitman, London.

Burns, T. and Stalker, G. (1961) *The Management of Innovation*, Tavistock, London.

Carr, A. (1997) The learning organization: new lessons/thinking for the management of change development?, *Journal of Management Development*, Vol. 6, No. 4, pp. 224–31.

Cotter, J.J. (1995) *The 20% Solution: Using Rapid Redesign to Create Tomorrow's Organization Today*, Wiley, Chichester.

Cyert, R.M. and March, J.G. (1963) *A Behavioural Theory of the Firm*, Prentice-Hall, Hemel Hempstead.

De Geus, A.P. (1988) Planning as learning, *Harvard Business Review*, March/April.

Drucker, P.F. (1997) The future that has already happened, *Harvard Business Review*, September–October, pp. 20–4.

Drucker, P.F. (1998) The coming of the new organization, *Harvard Business Review*, January–February.

Dunphy, D.C. and Stace, D.A. (1988) Transformational and coercive strategies for planned organizational change: beyond the OD model, *Organization Studies*, Vol. 9, No. 3, pp. 317–34.

Dunphy, D.C. and Stace, D.A. (1990) *Under New Management: Australian Organizations in Transition*, McGraw-Hill, Sydney.

Egan, G. (1994) *Working the Shadow Side: A Guide to Positive Behind-the-Scenes Management*, Jossey-Bass, San Francisco.

Firth, G. and Krut, R. (1991) Introducing a project management culture, *European Management Journal*, Vol. 9, No. 4, December.

French, W. L. (1969) Organization development: objectives, assumptions and strategies, *California Management Review*, Vol. 12, No. 2, pp. 23–34.

French, W.L. and Bell, C.H. Jr (1990) *Organization Development: Behavioural Science Interventions for Organization Improvement*, Prentice-Hall, Englewood Cliffs, NJ.

French, W.L., Bell, C.H. and Zawacki, R.A. (1994) *Organization Development and Transformation*, Irwin, Homewood, IL.

Frost, P.J. and Egri, C.P. (1991) The political process of innovation, in L.L. Cummings and B.M. Staw (eds), *Research in Organizational Behaviour*, JAI Press, Greenwich, CT, pp. 229–95.

Fulmer, R.M. (1996) A model for changing the way organisations learn, *Planning Review*, May/June, p. 20.

Galbraith, J.R. (1977) *Organization Design*, Addison-Wesley, Reading, MA.

Garratt, R. (1994) An old idea that has come of age, *People Management*, September, p. 25.

Garvin, D.A. (1993) Building a learning organization, *Harvard Business Review*, July/August.

Graetz, F. (1996) Leading strategic change at Ericsson, *Long Range Planning*, Vol. 29, No. 3.

Greiner, L.E. and Schein, V.E. (1988) *Power and Organization Development: Mobilizing Power to Implement Change*, Addison-Wesley, Reading, MA.

Gunn, L. (1994) *Public Management: Strathclyde MBA Open Learning Unit*, Strathclyde Graduate Business School, Glasgow.

Hackman, J.R. and Oldham, G.R. (1975) Development of the job diagnostic survey, *Journal of Applied Psychology*, Vol. 60, pp. 159–70.

Hackman, J.R. and Oldham, G.R. (1980) *Work Redesign*, Addison-Wesley, Reading, MA.

Handy, C. (1989) *The Age of Unreason*, Business Books, London.

Handy, C. (1990) *Inside Organisations*, BBC Publications, London.

Handy, C. (1997) The citizen corporation, *Harvard Business Review*, September/October, pp. 26–8.

Hardy, C. (1996) 'Understanding power: bringing about strategic change', *British Journal of Management*, Vol. 7, special issue, pp. 3–16.

Herzberg, F. (1966) *Work and the Nature of Man*, Staples, New York.

Hunt, J. (1979) *Managing People at Work*, McGraw-Hill, Maidenhead.

Huse, E.F. (1975) *Organizational Development and Change*, West, St Paul, MN.

Johnson, G. and Scholes, K. (1997) *Exploring Corporate Strategy*, 4th edn, Prentice-Hall, London.

Kanter, R.M. (1983) *The Change Masters: Corporate Entrepreneurs at Work*, Thomson, New York.

Kanter, R.M. (1989) *When Giants Learn to Dance: Mastering the Challenges of Strategy, Management and Careers in the 1990s*, Unwin Hyman, London.

Kanter, R.M., Stien, B.A. and Jick, T.D. (1992) *The Challenge of Organizational Change*, Free Press, New York.

Kilman, R. (1995) A holistic programme and critical success factors of corporate transformation, *European Management Journal*, Vol. 3, No. 2, June.

Klein, L. (1976) *A Social Scientist in Industry*, Allen and Unwin, London.

Kolb, D. (1976) *Learning Style Inventory: Technical Manual*, McBer, Boston.

Kotter, J.P. (1995) Why transformation efforts fail, *Harvard Business Review*, March/April.

Kotter, J.P. and Schlesinger, L.A. (1979) Choosing strategies for change, *Harvard Business Review*, March/April.

Lawler, E.E. III (1969) Job design and employee motivation, *Personnel Psychology*, Vol. 22, pp. 426–35.

Lawler, E.E. III (1986) *High Involvement Management: Participative Strategies for Improving Organizational Effectiveness*, Jossey-Bass, San Francisco.

Lawrence, P.R. and Lorsch, J.W. (1967) *Organization and Environment: Managing Differentiation and Integration*, Harvard Business School, Boston.

Lawrence, P.R. and Lorsch, J.W. (1969) *Developing Organizations: Diagnosis and Action*, Addison-Wesley, Reading, MA.

Leavitt, H.L. (1965) Applied organizational change in industry: structural, technological and humanistic approaches, in J.G. March (ed.), *Handbook of Organizations*, Rand McNally, Chicago.

Lee, R. and Lawrence, P. (1991) *Politics at Work*, Thornes, Cheltenham.

Lewin, K. (1958) Group decision and social change, in E.E. Maccoby, T.M.

Newcomb and E.L. Hartley (eds), *Readings in Social Psychology*, Holt, Rinehart and Winston, New York.

Likert, R. (1967) *The Human Organization: Its Management and Value*, McGraw-Hill, New York.

Lippit, R. (1959) Dimensions of the consultant's job, *Journal of Social Issues*, Vol. 15, No. 2, pp. 5–11.

Lippit, R. and Lippit, G. (1975) Consulting process in action, *Training and Development Journal*, Vol. 29, No. 5, pp. 48–54; No. 6, pp. 38–44.

Lippit, R., Watson, J. and Westley, B. (1958) *The Dynamics of Planned Change*, Harcourt, Brace and Jovanovich, New York.

Lockyer, K.G. (1991) *Critical Path Analysis and Other Project Network Techniques*, Pitman, London.

McCalman, J. (1988) *The Electronics Industry in Britain: Coping with Change*, Routledge, London.

McCalman, J. (1996) Technological innovation and work design, in R. Gill, J. McCalman and D. Pitt (eds), *Organization Structure and Behaviour 1*, Strathclyde Graduate Business School, University of Strathclyde.

McGregor, D. (1960) *The Human Side of Enterprise*, McGraw-Hill, New York.

March, J.G and Simon, H.A. (1958) *Organizations*, Wiley, New York.

Margerison, C.J. (1988) Consulting activities in organizational change, *Journal of Organizational Change Management*, Vol. 1, No. 1, pp. 60–7.

Margulies, N. and Raia, A. (1972) *Organizational Development: Values, Process and Technology*, McGraw-Hill, New York.

Margulies, N. and Raia, A. (1978) *Conceptual Foundations of Organizational Development*, McGraw-Hill, New York.

Margulies, N. and Raia, A. (1988) The significance of core values on the theory and practice of organizational development, *Journal of Organizational Change Management*, Vol. 1, No. 1, pp. 6–17.

Mason, R. (1998) Switch board, *People Management*, October, pp. 46–8.

Matsushita, K. (1984) *Not for Bread Alone: A Business Ethos, A Management Ethic*, PHP Institute, Tokyo.

Matsushita, K. (1988) The secret is shared, *Manufacturing Engineering*, March, pp. 78–84.

Megson, L.V.C. (1988) Building organizations for performance, Digital Equipment Corporation, unpublished article.

Moorcroft, D. (1996) Communicating effectively in a changing corporate culture, *Focus on Change Management*, June.

Morant, A.J. (1996) Video conferencing a tool for business re-engineering, *Management Accounting*, June.

Nonaka, I. and Takeuchi, H. (1991) The knowledge creating company, *Harvard Business Review*, November/December.

Pascale, R.T. (1994) Intentional breakdowns and conflict by design, *Planning Review*, Vol. 22, May/June.

Pascale, R.T., Milleman, M. and Gioja, L. (1997) Changing the way we change, *Harvard Business Review*, November/December.

Pasmore, W.A. (1994) *Creating Strategic Change: Designing the Flexible, High-Performing Organization*, Wiley, New York.

Paton, R.A. and Southern, G. (1990) *Total Project Management*, University of Glasgow Business School Working Paper Series.

Paton, R.A., Southern, G. and Houghton, M.G. (1989) European strategy formulation: an analysis technique, *European Management Journal*, Vol. 7, No. 3, September, pp. 305–9.

Pearn, M., Roderick, C. and Mulrooney, C. (1995) *Learning Organizations in Practice*, McGraw-Hill, Maidenhead.

Pedler, M., Burgoyne, J. and Boydell, T. (1991) *The Learning Company: A Strategy for Sustainable Development*, McGraw-Hill, Maidenhead.

Peters, T.J. (1987) *Thriving on Chaos*, Knopf, New York.

Peters, T.J. and Waterman, R.H. Jr (1982) *In Search of Excellence*, Harper and Row, New York.

Pettigrew, A.M. (1985) *The Awakening Giant: Continuity and Change in Imperial Chemical Industries*, Basil Blackwell, Oxford.

Pettigrew, A.M. (1987) Context and action in the transformation of the firm, *Journal of Management Studies*, Vol. 24, No. 6, pp. 649–70.

Pettigrew, A.M. (ed.) (1988) *The Management of Strategic Change*, Basil Blackwell, Oxford.

Pettigrew, A.M. and Whipp, R. (1993) *Managing Change for Corporate Success*, Basil Blackwell, London.

Pfeffer, J. (1994) *Managing with Power: Politics and Influence in Organization*, Harvard Business School Press, Boston, MA.

Piczak, M. and Hauser, R.Z. (1996) Self-directed work teams: a guide to implementation, *Quality Progress*, May.

Pritchard, W. (1984) What's new in organizational development?, *Personnel Management*, July, pp. 30–3.

Pugh, D.S. (1978) Understanding and managing organizational change, *London Business School Journal*, Vol. 3, No. 2, pp. 29–34.

Pugh, D.S. (1986) *Planning and Managing Change, Block 4: Organizational Development*, Open University Business School, Milton Keynes.

Pugh, D.S. and Hickson, D.J. (1989) *Writers on Organizations*, 4th edn, Penguin, London.

Richardson, P. and Denton, K. (1996) Communicating change, *Human Resource Management*, Summer.

Rickards, T. (1985) Making new things happen, *Technovation*, Vol. 3, pp. 119–31.

Roethlisberger, F.J. and Dickson, W.J. (1939) *Management and the Worker*, Harvard University Press, Cambridge, MA.

Schaffer, R.H. and Thomson, H.A. (1992) Successful change programs begin with results, *Harvard Business Review*, January/February.

Schein, E.H. (1988) *Process Consultation: Its Role in Organization Development*, Addison-Wesley, Reading, MA.

Senge, P. (1990a) The leader's new work: building learning organizations, *Sloan Management Review*, Autumn.

Senge, P. (1990b) *The Fifth Discipline: The Art and Practice of the Learning Organization*, Doubleday, New York.

Senge, P. (1995) *The Fifth Discipline Fieldbook: Strategies and Tools for Building a Learning Organization*, Brearley, London.

Sherwood, J.J. (1988) Creating work cultures with competitive advantage, *Organizational Dynamics*, Winter, American Management Association.

Simon, H.A. (1957) *Models of Man*, Wiley, New York.

Slater, S.F. and Narver, J.C. (1995) Market orientation and the learning organisation, *Journal of Marketing*, July.

Spector, B.A. (1989) From bogged down to fired up: inspiring organizational change, *Sloan Management Review*, Summer.

Standing, C. and Standing, S. (1998) The politics and ethics of career progression in IS: a systems perspective, *Logistics Information Management*, Vol. 11, No. 5, pp. 309–16.

Stata, R. (1989) Organizational learning – the key to management innovation, *Sloan Management Review*, Spring.

Stone, B. (1997) *Confronting Company Politics*, Macmillan, Basingstoke.

Thompson, P. and McHugh, D. (1995) *Work Organizations: A Critical Introduction*, Macmillan, Basingstoke.

Thorsurd, E. (1972) Job design in the wider context, in L.E. Davis and J.C. Taylor (eds), *Design of Jobs*, Penguin, Harmondsworth.

Ulrich, D. (1998) A new mandate for human resources, *Harvard Business Review*, January/February, pp. 124–34.

Van der Heijden, K. and Eden, C. (1994) Managerial cognition, organisational cognition and the practice of organisational learning, presented at the 2nd International Workshop on Managerial and Organisational Cognition.

Vennix, J.A.M. (1996) *Group Model Building: Facilitating Team Learning Using Systems Dynamics*, Wiley, Chichester.

Vroom, V.H. (1969) Industrial social psychology, in G. Lindsey and E. Aronson (eds), *The Handbook of Social Psychology*, Addison-Wesley, Reading, MA.

Warner Burke, W. (1994) *Organization Development: A Normative View*, 2nd edn, Addison-Wesley, Reading, MA.

Wright, M. and Rhodes, D. (1985) *Managing IT: Exploring Information Systems for Effective Management*, Pinter, London.

Yates, D.J. (1985) *The Politics of Management*, Jossey-Bass, San Francisco.

Index

Page numbers in *italics* refer to figures and tables.